WORKING WITH YOUNG CHILDREN

*encouraging their development
and
dealing with problems*

JENNIE LAISHLEY

*(now works and publishes
as Jennie Lindon)*

Second edition

Hodder & Stoughton

LONDON SYDNEY AUCKLAND TORONTO

Jennie Laishley took a B.A. and M. Phil. in social psychology at the University of Sussex. For six years she worked as a full-time researcher on a series of projects concerned with adolescents and young children. In 1979 she started to work as a free-lance applied psychologist, specialising in the under-five age group and the adults responsible for the children. She undertakes consultancy and in-service courses for a number of London boroughs, charities working for children, and colleges of further education, and she also works as a consultant to the National Nursery Examination Board. She continues to publish articles on her work (under her married name of Jennie Lindon), but this is her first book.

Jennie Laishley lives in South London with her husband, Lance Lindon, who works as an organisational psychologist. They have a son, Drew, and a daughter, Zoë.

© 1987 Jennie Laishley

First published in Great Britain 1983

Second edition 1987
  Fourth impression 1990

British Library Cataloguing in Publication Data

Laishley, Jennie
  Working with young children.—2nd ed.
  1. Child psychology
  I. Title
  155.4′23   BF721

ISBN 0-340-47908-6

Filmset in 10/11 pt Compugraphic English 49 by Colset Private Ltd, Singapore. Printed and bound in Great Britain for Edward Arnold, the educational, academic and medical publishing division of Hodder and Stoughton Limited, 41 Bedford Square, London WC1B 3DQ by Clays Ltd, St Ives plc

CONTENTS

To my parents, who, with their love and their pleasure in children, have taught me volumes.

To Drew and Zoë, who have taken such an active part in teaching me what it is to be a parent.

To Lance, without whom there would be no Drew or Zoë.

ACKNOWLEDGEMENTS

To the first edition

One of the pleasures of my work has been the opportunity to learn from other people. This makes it difficult to identify a small number of individuals whom I would particularly like to thank.

The staff of the many nurseries and playgroups with whom I have had contact have taught me a great deal — not least when they disagreed with my views! Of the individuals, I would particularly like to thank Helen Wilson, who introduced me to language development from the point of view of a speech therapist. The late Bernice Rothwell, whom sadly I can no longer thank personally, shared many practical ideas on helping children's language and behaviour. William Mitchell showed me the value of methods of behaviour modification. Tim Smithells made me aware of the practical applications of Adlerian psychology.

On the personal side, I would like to thank Angela Davison. It has been because of her loving and very competent care of my son, Drew, that I have been able to continue with my work and to write this book. My husband, Lance Lindon, has been supportive and encouraging to me throughout, and many of the ideas in the book have become clearer through discussions we have had together. The great pleasures, and the frustrations, of life with our son, Drew, have brought many of the issues of child care very alive for us. Lance also gave his time to take the photographs which appear in this book. The parents of the children featured kindly gave their permission for the photographs to be used. I would like to thank Patti Weait, who has patiently typed the final draft of this book. Lastly, I would like to thank Bob Davenport, of Edward Arnold (Publishers) Ltd, for his comments and suggestions on the various drafts of the book.

To the second edition

When I wrote the first edition of this book I was already working in the area of parent involvement. Since then, this aspect of my work has expanded and I am very pleased to have the opportunity to discuss this in a revised and extended edition. I have learned a great deal from the staff of under-fives centres when I have been involved in a teaching or consultancy capacity on 'working with parents'. I have learned just as much from conversations with fellow-parents and from reflection on my own experience as a working parent of two young children.

Some of my key ideas on parent involvement were sharpened as a result of my writing a paper (under the name Jennie Lindon) for the National Nursery Examination Board (*Parent involvement* —

developments in pre-schooling and the early school years). I am grateful to Michael Stanton, then Chief Executive of the NNEB, since our discussions about the paper helped to give shape to my views.

I would like to thank Cecily Guarerra, who, followed by Marion Preston, took such good care of Drew and Zoë while I was writing. I would also like to thank Patti Charlesworth, who again typed the manuscript.

My husband Lance and I together try to maintain a balance between work commitments and family. Other working women with children will particularly appreciate the import of my deep thanks to him for his support and encouragement.

INTRODUCTION

The overall aim of the book

This book is designed to provide a range of practical ideas and suggestions that can be used by adults responsible for young children. Some of the ideas are direct and simple, some are more time-consuming. Quite a number of the approaches imply some thinking by adults about how they are making sense of a situation with a child.

The assumption of the book is that readers will have some experience and knowledge of young children and wish to build on that. Some of the discussion is more appropriate to adults who are responsible for a group of children, for instance the staff of playgroups, day nurseries, or nursery schools. However, much of the material is equally relevant to adults who are responsible for a few children, for instance as parent, child-minder, or nanny. The book does assume some experience, but nevertheless I would hope that the ideas will also be useful to students training to be nursery teachers or nursery nurses — particularly to those students who have progressed beyond the early stages of their course.

Adults and children

The sources of the approaches and ideas in this book are many. I do not take the view that one particular theory of child development or one school of thought on dealing with problems posed by children has all or even most of the answers. For different situations and different types of problems, I have found that it pays to have a flexible approach. For me, the one consistent theme is the great significance of adults in the lives of children.

Adults' views on children vary. Some adults enjoy their company, some have unrealistically rosy views of children, some enjoy babies but resent the growing independence and self-will of the toddler and young child. Some adults seem to dislike any child and develop the convenient belief that they and their contemporaries never behaved in the terrible ways that children behave nowadays. Children, like adults, vary enormously — in their likes and dislikes, how they behave, how they face difficult or new situations, in their abilities and aptitudes, in how easy they find it to be honest, patient, tolerant — so it is no more reasonable to generalise about children as a whole than it is to group together all adults. Even adults who enjoy spending time or working with children do not, if they will admit it honestly, like all children equally. We all find some children easier to like or to handle and find our patience snapping more quickly with some children than with others.

For children, adults are among the best and the worst influences on their young lives. Adults who love and care for them, who gradually open out a child's world, and who make the space in their adult lives for the continual adjustments demanded by a child's presence will help to make that child's life happy and her development will progress. Adults who do not like children, who resent their presence, do not tolerate their different view of the world or their limited understanding, or who treat them with coldness or cruelty can contribute to problems for the child and for themselves which otherwise might not have developed.

Stressing the importance of adults' contribution to children's lives is not to underestimate how much children can mean to one another. They can enjoy one another's company and learn, as well as make each other miserable on occasion. However, I have noticed the major difference for children is when adults see themselves as active participants in a child's development, rather than as merely passive bystanders. The meaning of being an active participant is not to be an interfering and controlling adult: it is rather an attitude which sees adults in a child's world as individuals who need to be sensitive and prepared to adjust. Adults need to see themselves as people whose behaviour and attitudes can make a considerable difference to a child. This means that sometimes adults judge that they need to change rather than or more than the child. Sometimes it means standing on the sidelines, however hard that is, while the child makes a mistake. Sometimes it means stepping in to help. It certainly means seeing the child as an individual with personality and developing personal views and understanding. Overall it means thinking often about ourselves, rather than seeing the child as always the one who must change, learn, adapt. Adults who see themselves in this more flexible way can have a more enjoyable life with children. There are still frustrating and tiring times but, overall, life with children can feel much more positive.

The quality of this positive attitude emerged for me in a conversation I had with an experienced nursery nurse in a London day nursery. Kathy was describing a recent incident with a two-year-old boy in her group. He was very keen to be a 'big boy' and to stand up at the toilet in order to urinate. However, he clearly had not completely understood what to do. On this particular day he stood by the toilet, at the ready, but instead of urinating he had a bowel movement. Unaware that anything was amiss, he beamed and said 'Good boy'. Nobody enjoys cleaning up the results of such an accident, but Kathy did not mention this at all. She took the view that the incident was funny from an adult's point of view, that it was endearing, and that it was an insight into the stages that boys have to go through in learning about going to the toilet. There was no suggestion from her that the boy had been naughty or dirty. The accident was

There is pleasure for adults in just watching children enjoy life. ▶

evidence that he had not yet understood the full intricacies of this toilet business!

The contents of the book

This book attempts to cover four main areas.

The first part is concerned with observation of children's development and behaviour. The aim here is to show how such observation can contribute to adults' work with young children. The emphasis is on the practical uses of different ways of observing that adults can undertake as part of a regular involvement with children. The ideas in this part are relevant to gaining some perspective on the problems that are discussed in the second and third parts of the book. The final chapter in part 1 looks at sharing observations of children with parents. The practical suggestions made here are applicable not only to work on record-keeping but also to the broader issues raised in part 4 of the book.

The second part of the book concentrates on language development during the first five years of life. This includes discussion of the learning which takes place, common problems which can arise, practical suggestions for helping with problems, and looking at encouraging further learning when a child's development is already progressing well. The ideas in this part are not restricted to children's learning to talk, but also include the important areas of development associated with language, in particular the development of a child's ability to concentrate and the growth of all the abstract ideas in which are linked children's ability to look, listen, think, and talk.

The third part of the book considers children's behaviour. The emphasis in this part is both on what children do, including some of the common problems that adults face in their lives with children, and on ways in which adults can approach difficulties. The emphasis is on looking at the combination of child, adult, and situation to determine what could be the best way of tackling a problem.

Part 4 focuses on relationships between adults — particularly between parents and staff. There is a discussion of the development of 'parent involvement' and of what this can mean in practice. There are practical ideas on planning an expansion in staff's working with parents so that the work is effective, with an emphasis on the different perspectives of staff and parents and an exploration of the skills that adults need in working well together.

A practical point

Anyone writing a book of this type has to decide on whether the individual child in a discussion is referred to as 'he' or 'she'. Most books about children and child care use 'he' and I felt, as did Penelope Leach in her book *Baby and child*, that the relative usage of 'he' and 'she' could be more evenly balanced across the literature. Consequently, the single child in this book is a 'she'. If I am making a point specifically about boys or girls, this will be clear in the discussion.

PART 1
THE VALUE OF OBSERVATION AND PLANNING IN WORK WITH YOUNG CHILDREN

1
THE HABIT OF BEING OBSERVANT

The following chapters cover some aspects of the methods and practical uses of observation of young children. Such observation can range from informal watching without definite guide-lines through to structured observations which are planned in detail beforehand and which are undertaken with a definite objective in mind.

There seems to be an increasing interest in observation in all kinds of pre-school centres. In some cases, this has been stimulated by research projects. The Oxford Preschool Research Group, for example, worked with playgroup staff on a scheme for observing children's spontaneous play. A team from the National Children's Bureau worked with nursery schools and playgroups on their developmental guides for assessing children's progress. I have worked with a number of nurseries and play-groups where the impetus came from the wish of the staff themselves to be better informed about how children were progressing and to feel more able to pinpoint and deal with problems. In different situations there may be different objectives motivating the observation and so the same method is not always appropriate. The aim in this part of the book is not to make a partisan call for a particular method of observation! It is rather to look at how different methods of observing might fit different aims in working with young children.

Making the time to be observant

Adults who spend their days with young children have to be involved in a wide range of activities. The work itself — whether you are being paid for your skills or are caring for your own children — is physically demanding and can be mentally tiring. It is very possible even for aware and experienced adults to become so involved in the moment-to-moment handling of children that they forget to take the time to look closely at the children as individuals.

The skills of observation and the value of being observant are equally as important for adults who are experienced in their work as they are for students, who are still at the stage of learning skills and absorbing information about children. Students may be helped by particular observations to learn more about child development, to see it in action through an individual child. When they are qualified, these same adults still need the skills of observation to take a fresh look at their group, to remain alert to the progress the children are making and to develop a way

3

of noticing problems before these become too serious. Adults who feel they notice everything without making any special effort are misleading themselves.

Adults responsible for children tend to have a busy day which involves being physically active for much of the time. If adults come to believe that working hard with children is primarily about being active themselves — being on the move — they can fail to notice important changes in children. Some adults seem to feel that they are somehow being lazy unless they are continually involved in a definite task and moving around. This is a pity, since it loses sight of the value of the quieter but equally active involvement of watching children, listening to them properly, or making observations of what they can do.

Learning to be attentive — a general attitude

Unless adults learn to watch carefully, they do not notice some of the changes that can happen rapidly with young children. Unless adults learn to listen properly, they can miss something important which a child is saying or unintentionally ignore that child's approach altogether. It is important that adults learn to be attentive to children. This is not a passive and vague awareness that something is going on in the corner, or keeping an eye on children to make sure they are safe — active looking and listening means really paying attention to what children are doing and saying, what they are trying to do, what they are nearly managing, and what is still beyond their ability or understanding. An adult's active attention in conversations and children's play is crucially important for children. Children who are not given the respect of attention are unlikely to learn to attend well in return — there is no example for them to follow and no incentive to learn.

The tasks which surround a day with children can come to seem more important than the children themselves. This can be true at home — in some families, young children seem to be fitted in around the household routine, with playtime as an activity determined by adult convenience. When I have been playing with my children, other adults have sometimes said indulgently 'Children are such time-wasters, aren't they?' The curious implication seemed to be that my children were keeping me away from tasks more important than playtime and that playing with them was somehow time off from the real business of life.

This type of feeling can build up in pre-school centres, since there are always a number of routine, housework, or organisational tasks to be completed. Staff can feel — or be made to feel — that sitting down with the children to watch or listen is shirking the real work of tidying up, sorting out, organising the next activity, or completing paperwork. We are all plagued to a greater or lesser extent by conflicting demands on our time; however, I have been struck by the wide differences in how individuals deal with this.

When I was undertaking some research in day nurseries, I spent many hours observing different staff at work. Some staff seemed to be bustling around with routine housework or organising activities for much of the day. Others made a great deal of time to sit with the children — talking, watching, and taking part in activities. These staff members relegated the routine tasks to a swift clear-up or managed to involve the children in such tasks. In day nurseries, as in any other establishment, a certain amount of guidance as to what is judged really important comes from the person in charge. However, I have worked with nurseries whose head was committed to having staff spend as much time as possible with the children, but some of those staff still drifted towards the routine tasks far more than seemed necessary or desirable.

Even adults who say they value watching children do not always spend as much time on this as they believe. It is worthwhile monitoring yourself — checking that you do make the time. Philip Clift and his research team from the National Foundation for Educational Research (NFER) observed teachers and nursery nurses in nursery schools and classes. They found that, although many staff mentioned in interviews the importance of standing quietly and observing the children, the amount of time spent doing this was actually very limited.*

Relating knowledge to observation

Adults' watching of children is most effective when related to an interest in, and some knowledge of, child development. Such knowledge helps the adults to make sense of what they see, and the alertness to what a child is learning can make the time with children so much more interesting.

One instance of this is with very young babies. The routine tasks of physical care are many, and in the early weeks the baby may seem to be doing very little. People sometimes make comments like 'They're all much the same until they're three months' or 'They're not really interesting until they're six months.' In fact, babies show individual differences from birth and a great deal happens in the first few months. Knowledge that developments in muscle control, smiling, and alertness to light and shapes all happen during this time can give an adult something to watch for. It can make the caring for a young baby both more varied and stimulating.

*This research is reported in *The aims, role and deployment of staff in the nursery*, by Philip Clift, Shirley Cleave, and Marion Griffin, published by the NFER in 1980.

The watching and listening is also important in the context of a growing knowledge of individual children. A real interest in what children can do means that you notice what a child can nearly achieve and therefore might manage with some help. You can notice what the child is looking at or what causes her to stop and listen. All this gives insight into the world of that individual child and means that the adult's time can be best adjusted for that child's unique interests and abilities.

Close watching of a particular child can usefully shift your attention from one aspect of the child's behaviour to another. In a playgroup where I was working as an adviser, there was a three-year-old Asian boy, Gupta, who had very little English and an unknown amount of speech in the language the family spoke at home. We were finding it very hard to judge whether Gupta was seriously language-delayed. Then we changed to observing his spontaneous play, especially looking for examples of fantasy play, which can be a good indicator to language development. We found that his fantasy play was well developed, although he was not using any words we could understand. This gave some basis for work with the child, since the observations on play suggested that he was probably not seriously delayed in language development in his first language.

A sensitivity to children and a willingness to watch can make adults that much more effective with the children for whom they are responsible.

There are several possible ways of making organised observations. The most useful method depends on what you wish to learn from the observation in that particular situation. In chapters 2 to 4 some different methods of observing will be discussed in some detail. First, the approaches will be mentioned in outline.

Making child observations when a student

Developmental stages or abilities which seem just so many words to students in the lecture room can come alive through the behaviour of individual children. The aim of child observation as a student is for the observer to learn more about children in general by carefully watching one particular child at a time. The type of question being asked by the observer in this situation is 'What are children really like?'

Many of the points made in part 1 of this book are relevant to students. However, the best starting point may be to make an observation of one child. Some guide-lines to this type of observation are given in chapter 3. These particular suggestions should be useful both to student readers and to those who are supervising students.

Working in a planned way with children

Adults who are experienced would not be making a child observation as a student would, although they might want to observe an individual child. Adults who are working with children want their observations to generate information which will give practical help in their work with individuals or a group. To increase the chances that this will happen, observations need to be placed in a context of planning work with children. This is discussed in chapter 2.

Regular observation of all children in a group

It can be very useful to make regular observations of all the children in a group to see how they are progressing. This might be through the discipline of writing a regular report on each child; alternatively, the views of different members of staff can be discussed through group meetings, full staff meetings, or reviews. Such a bringing together of the available information and perceptions can be made more standard by the use of a developmental guide or chart. The aim of this activity would be to monitor whether children are progressing in the various areas of development and to pinpoint problems before they became too serious. The question which might be answered by this type of observation is 'What can the children do?', with the focus on each individual child in turn. This way of observing is discussed in chapter 3.

Observing children's behaviour

Regular observation of all children, using some type of developmental guide, can help to show what children can do in terms of skills. The way they actually spend their time may be very unevenly spread over the range of their abilities. The answer to the question 'What are the children doing?' may show that, although they are capable of dealing with a wide range of play activities, they actually spend most of their time on a narrow selection of games, unless specifically encouraged to try something else.

Observing children's spontaneous behaviour can help adults to keep fresh about what is actually happening in the group and whether their perceptions about how children are playing are accurate. The observation could be planned to move from one child to another in a deliberate way, so that an overview of the group is reached.

Children who are worrying the adults could be observed for how they behave in particular situations. Similarly, the adults could observe for the occurrence of a particular type of problem behaviour from the child. This observation of children's behaviour is discussed in chapter 4.

GENERAL POINTS ABOUT ANY OBSERVATION

Whichever method of observation seems most appropriate for your needs, there are some useful general points to bear in mind, as follows.

The need to decide what you will observe

When adults first consider observing young children, they can be at a loss as to what to watch. There is a bewildering range of possibilities — individual children or children in groups, particular play activities, certain types of behaviour, or themes which might run through children's play. Sometimes the reaction is to want to 'just watch', perhaps making the assumption that any kind of plan for observation will give the observer pre-conceived ideas of what is happening in the group.

Watching without any set plan can be a useful starting point, but only if it leads to decisions about organising observations in the future. As a long-term strategy, 'just watching' does not normally help an adult to learn very much about the children. Attention inevitably gets pulled from one child to another and from one area of the room to another and, by the end of a session, the result can be a rather confused set of memories of different children. Adults watching in this way can finish without any clear sense of whether what they saw was typical for the child. They may have no idea whether the child they noticed as upset early in the session was upset for much of the time throughout the day. It will be hard to judge whether the child who seemed to be, if anything, over-active in playing with the cars nevertheless stayed with that activity and concentrated better than the child who wandered from jigsaw to jigsaw. Observers tend to learn more if they plan the observation, to follow children or activities in a consistent way.

Preparation for making observations

The structure placed on the observation will, of course, depend on what you want to learn and hence which method of observing seems the most appropriate. This might be a descriptive developmental guide to monitor development, a plan of observation to judge how serious a child's problem behaviour is in the group, or observation to see how children use a new play area which you have recently set up. Whichever method you decide on for your observation, some ground rules always apply. The following suggestions can be useful reminders when you are experienced with children. If you are in a supervisory role with students, it can be worthwhile to explain the value of such preparations before students start to observe.

i) Allow yourself some thinking time for decisions about whom or what you are going to observe. The value of an observation comes from having a consistent and full record appropriate to what you want to learn and not an unplanned collection of observations of different people or activities with no common theme.

ii) Prepare yourself with paper and pens and something on which to rest the paper. It will save time later if you prepare your paper by dividing it up into appropriate sections and making any headings necessary. For instance, some observations may be made under different headings or at different set times of the day. Obviously, if you and your colleagues are using the same format for many observations, it is worthwhile preparing a master copy of the observation sheet and having a large number of copies made.

iii) If you are going to observe for set amounts of time, make sure you have a reliable watch with a second hand, a stop watch, or a calculator with a time read-out. It will be easier than glancing at a wall clock and, anyway, there will not always be a convenient clock. Always note down the time and/or the date when you are observing. For some observations you may only need the date.

iv) Explain to the other adults in the room that you are observing. If you are in your normal place of work, then you should have already discussed the question of observation between yourselves. If you are supervising students, then do explain to them that telling others that you are observing is not only a matter of courtesy, it is also practical. You can explain to the others that you would like them to carry on as normal, but that, when you are observing, you will not be intervening in the activities of the room, except in a crisis. If you are concentrating on an individual child, the other adults will know not to take her out of the room, unless it is really necessary.

v) A good rule for observation is never to write down a comment which you would be embarrassed for another adult to read. This does not mean that you never note down upsetting incidents or descriptions of activities which did not go as well as the adult concerned would have hoped. If you followed that avenue, then the observations would not be an accurate record of what was happening. It does mean that any observer should not write down offhand judgemental remarks and that observers should be prepared to support the opinions they have reached from what they have observed. This might be the difference between writing a description like 'Child calls to adult. Adult talking with second member of staff. Child fails to attract her attention', rather than a critical judgement such as 'Child calls to adult. Staff too busy chatting to bother.'

Some nurseries and playgroups like to discuss their observations with the children's parents. Many parents will be interested in what picture of the child's abilities or interests has emerged. If staff know that such observations are available for parents to see, then this is another reason for any comments to be supported by observations or descriptions of the child. This is as true of positive comments as of negative, although it is the negative comments which tend most to concern adults. Once again, this might be the difference between writing baldly 'This child's needs are not being met at home' instead of the expression of a personal opinion such as 'I feel that John might be less demanding if he had an uninterrupted playtime with his parents when he goes home.'

Final comment on preparation

The points listed above may seem like over-detailed preparation to some readers. However, some time spent on such decisions and anticipating practical problems can make the work of observation in the end easier and more satisfying. With preparation, the task is quicker in the long run. The points will not be repeated for each type of observation, although some specific suggestions may arise with some methods. The chapters which now follow will take some different approaches to observation of young children and consider what is involved in each method and how it may contribute to adults' understanding of the children for whom they are responsible.

2
TAKING A PLANNED
APPROACH TO WORKING
WITH CHILDREN

Several years ago I introduced the idea of regular observation of children to the staff of a group of day nurseries. The method we were using was a developmental guide, which was completed at three-monthly intervals, to show what individual children could manage in the various areas of their development. My expectation was that the value of this material would be self-evident; consequently, I applied all my time to introducing the forms and explaining the mechanics of using them — leaving the staff to decide how they wanted to apply the information they then gathered. When I talked with the staff as the project progressed, I realised that, without further discussion, the observation using the guides did not have any clear long-term aim. The guides were in danger of becoming just so much paperwork, because the information did not appear to lead anywhere.

These day-nursery staff taught me that discussion of why adults should bother to observe is as important as choosing a method of observing appropriate to what the adults want to learn. Chapters 3 and 4 consider some possible methods. This chapter looks at the question of 'Why bother?' and at the planning context in which observation needs to be placed. The many conversations I have had with pre-school staff since that day-nursery project have confirmed that this sort of discussion is necessary and useful.

Looking at the value of keeping a regular record of children

If you are responsible for children on a fairly long-term basis, it can be very useful to keep some written record of the changes in individual children so that it is possible to see if they are progressing and whether any problems are developing. The idea of a regular record is common for older children in schools but is less frequent in work with the younger age range. The concept behind keeping a record of younger children is not that of marking or grading the children: the work is more descriptive, with the aim of keeping a fresh picture of each individual child. It is not possible for anyone, however well trained or experienced, to keep clearly in mind the full range of abilities and interests of all the children in a reasonable-size group. Even adults who are responsible for one or two children can be surprised by what those children can or cannot do.

11

When you are focusing your attention on one child at a time, with the aim of judging her current abilities, it is feasible to look in detail at her skills and how she behaves. This can often help adults to become clearer about the child's strong and weak points and can give useful indications of what range of play might help the child to learn more readily. If some of the children in your care are delayed in their development, it can be doubly important to look closely at their progress from time to time, to check that their abilities are growing and, if there is little or no change, where most of the delay may lie. If a child is being affected by stress and difficulties at home, she may have been progressing well and then slow down dramatically or even regress in some abilities. It is possible to miss this, or the child who is developmentally delayed, especially if that child is easy to manage and 'no trouble' in the group.

If a child seems to be progressing well, then a check on her abilities can confirm this and probably point towards the skills that she is nearly achieving. If a child is not progressing well, this regular check can be the basis for planning some special time with the child to help in the areas where she is delayed.

There will be children for whom this regular record does not generate the type of information that adults judge they need. A child who is developmentally very delayed may be helped more effectively if adults take a more detailed look at particular areas of development. A child who behaves in a way that adults find hard to handle may be helped through an approach planned in the light of adult observation of that behaviour.

The discussion in this chapter does not depend on one particular method of observation. The point about any method is that it should lead to information that is then useful in work with the children.

Taking a planned approach to working with children

Making sense of the information from observation, and planning from this, is an area of skill which has to be learned like the skills of making observations. If adults are to work effectively with young children, it is helpful to have an overview of where their efforts are leading. The diagram on page 13 — 'Working with children in a planned way' — summarises the elements of this planning approach.

It is useful to place these elements in an overall structure. Without some guiding framework, even experienced staff can become lost — collecting observation data on children which do not seem to have the practical use that was anticipated. Similarly, they may work hard with an individual child but not realise the progress that has been made, because there is no earlier observation to provide a clear comparison. The approach to planned work with children summarised in the diagram is very much about doing an effective job with children and

Working with children in a planned way

The child arrives – background information of varying quality.

Settle the child into the group – adult skills in settling child and judging when she is settled into the group.

The first observation of the child – assess current stage of development and typical behaviour.

> **Identify areas of special need** – making sense of the first observations, judging delays or difficulties. In later months of work with the child, making further observations.

Judging the activity – check the child against observation of behaviour problem or developmental stage. Has the observation given the information wanted? Check the child's progress against goals set at the planning stage.

Planning the activity – plan a programme of special activities with the child, decide on further information or observation, on a strategy for dealing with any problem. In any of these, set concrete and realistic goals.

> **Carry out the activity** – carry out the planned work with the child; make further observations; be consistent in the approach to a behaviour problem.

being rather more confident that this has been achieved. For children, this can mean more thorough help: for adults it can mean more satisfaction in the job that they are doing.

Settling a child into a group

When a *child arrives* in a particular establishment, there is usually some background information about the child, although this may vary greatly in how useful or reliable it is. An initial note of how the child behaves in the early weeks of settling in can be valuable, since it is a reminder later of how this child adjusted to a new situation and new people. However, a reasonably reliable judgement of the typical behaviour and developmental stage of the child must wait until that child has *settled into the group*. Adults' skills and experience are important in determining when a child is settled. This may take as long as five or six weeks with some children, perhaps longer. When that point is reached, it is appropriate to make the first organised observation of the child. This will give a comparison point for later observations of the same child.

There are different ways of making observations that provide this first organised look at an individual child and which will provide a regular record of her as time passes. Chapter 3 discusses the value of the developmental guide or chart which offers a selection of items from the different areas of child development. Used at regular intervals, this material provides a way of checking whether a child is progressing or not.

Identifying areas for adult attention

The aim of the observation and written records is to *identify* areas in which special adult attention should be focused for this child. It is very tempting to try more of everything with children who are delayed or who are experienced as difficult to handle. However, with a non-handicapped child, there are usually some areas of development which are within the normal range for the child's age and special efforts are best concentrated on the areas which show the most delay. The observations of some children will show that their development is progressing well, with no problems. In this situation, adults' attention would best be focused on what the child can nearly manage — perhaps on making sure that play activities are available that encourage her to extend her abilities a little and provide a challenge.

Planning work for children

The next step is to *plan activities* for individual children. This might be planning a small programme of play activities for a child who will have special sessions with one adult. It might equally be planning a group activity with the intention of involving one or two individuals in particular.

Selection of the activities needs some thought, since they must give the best chance for the child's attention to be held. This means that the activities would be chosen, at least initially, from games or toys which are known to interest that child. They must also be appropriate to her existing abilities and span of attention. The most creative ideas from the adult's point of view will not help if the programme is pitched at too complex a level, requires a level of concentration which the child simply does not have at present, or will need an adult to spend energy coaxing the child into activities which that child does not like.

The planning of some special activities with a child is separate from the gathering of information on what she can manage at the present time. This is an important distinction to make. A developmental guide gives only a selection of the skills that a child learns; consequently, it would be inappropriate for any special programmes to be restricted to ensuring that a child would 'pass' particular items at the next observation. For example, observation of a child by means of a development guide or some other method of observation might show that she has great difficulty in using scissors whereas other children of her age are able to do this. Coping with scissors is not that important in itself, but it may be an indication that this child is experiencing difficulties with the finer physical coordinations. Consequently, a plan for some special adult attention for this child would draw on a range of play activities that could increase the child's physical ability and confidence. This might include building, pouring, or threading. Help in learning to cut with scissors could be one of the activities, but scissors would not be the moving force of the programme.

An adult's plans relevant to an individual child will not always be a programme of play activities. If there is an important gap in adults' working knowledge of a child, the first step could be to gather some more information. This might mean finding the answer to a particular question; for instance, does the child's family speak a language other than English at home? Sometimes, the first move must be to arrange for the child to be tested by a specialist — for example, if adults suspect the child has a hearing problem. At other times they might recognise the need to take a closer look at some particular aspect of a child's development or of that child's behaviour. Further observation of this kind can be important in giving a firmer basis to work with some individuals.

Making the effort to set clear goals

Part of the planning of either further observations or a play programme is the setting of specific and realistic *goals*. It is important that the goals are specific so that the adults have a clear idea of what they judge to be the problem for the child and are able to describe this accurately.

It is very easy to see a problem in too vague a way — the child seems 'slow', 'her speech is poor for her age', 'she does not concentrate well', 'she is aggressive'. If adults are to be effective in their work with children, they need to be able to pinpoint what it is about the child which makes her seem 'slow' — is she delayed in all areas of development; if so, to what extent? If her speech is 'poor', what is it that she does or does not manage which leads someone to come to this conclusion? For how long, approximately, does she concentrate, and are there some activities which seem to hold the child for longer than others? In terms of aggression, how does the child actually behave — what is it that she does that is judged to be aggressive?

Without some more definite description of the child, it is only possible to set vague goals. Furthermore, without some clear note of the problem as it appears initially, it can be very hard to judge whether the special efforts have had an effect in terms of changes in the child's behaviour.

The setting of goals is also the means to be concrete and positive about the skills or changes in behaviour that adults would like to see the child achieve after these special efforts. If adults are making further observations, then the goals would be expressed in terms of what they hope to learn from the observations. If the effort is in terms of special activities with a child, then the goal would be a concrete description, although brief, of what they would like the child to have learned or how they would like to see the child's behaviour change.

As well as being specific, it is important that the goals should also be realistic, in the sense that they could feasibly be achieved in a matter of weeks and not months. It is very disheartening for adults if they set too large a step, given the child's current stage, since there will seem to be little or no progress for a long time.

It can be well worthwhile keeping written notes on children, and this is particularly useful in the setting of goals and planning in general. One possibility is to note down plans briefly under three general headings. These are:

i) What is the problem, the area of concern? Try to be specific in your description.
ii) What would you like to achieve with this child within a few weeks? Be concrete and realistic in these plans.
iii) What activities would you like to undertake as special work with this child? If it is further observation, what do you want to find out? If you are ready for a programme of activities, select them as appropriate to the child's current interests and level of ability.

The way in which activities will be undertaken with children will vary. For some children it may be important that they have time alone with an adult in a quiet room. Other children may be successfully helped in a small group. The length of special sessions — individual or small group — needs to be tailored to the child's ability. For instance, work with a child whose ability to attend is very limited will be best organised initially in very short sessions — perhaps no more than a minute or so of encouragement to perform a simple task. The plan would be gradually to lengthen the sessions. On the other hand, an interested and motivated child who is learning English as a second language may benefit from sessions of up to half an hour. The keynote is flexibility.

Overall, it is preferable to plan shorter regular sessions which do happen, rather than hope to spend long sessions with children which require ideal adult – child ratios which are rarely met and so the sessions are often cancelled. From the child's point of view, the shorter but regular sessions will have a continuity and therefore build up learning more effectively than long sessions with lengthy gaps in between.

Carrying out plans

After the planning, adults need to *carry out* their activity. This is sometimes the point at which the whole planned approach to children breaks down. Perhaps the selection of goals, of activities or further observations, of a consistent strategy to deal with a behaviour problem has been discussed with care and the adult concerned is excited at the prospect of following what has been planned. Then, unforeseen difficulties start to upset the plans. Perhaps the child concerned is away ill, or the adult is absent and loses the impetus of the planned work. A strategy for dealing with a difficult child may not make the difference that was hoped as quickly as anticipated, or other adults' attitudes to the child may impede changes. It is often at the stage of carrying out the planned work with a child that adults need most support and encouragement from colleagues to persevere despite the difficulties, or at least to allow the plan a chance before giving up.

Judging whether goals have been reached

After the period of time agreed at the planning stage, adults have to *judge* whether they have reached the goals they set themselves. If further observations have been made, or an effort was made to find out some information about the child, does the information give the future guidelines that were needed? If a programme of activities was carried out, then it is necessary to check whether a child's skills or behaviour have changed in the direction hoped for when the goals were set.

For some children, a reasonable judgement may be that the problem area has been successfully tackled and the child will now benefit from general nursery or playgroup experience. The special sessions with the child may stop, although regular use of observation to monitor the child's progress will continue. With other children, the decision may be that the child has been helped to such a level that another problem area can now be faced. For instance, the child's ability to concentrate may have improved sufficiently that activities to help her delayed language development are now possible. Alternatively, new goals may be set in the original problem area.

If a child is very delayed in an area of development, then the long-term plan for her would have to include many smaller steps before she reached a level of development appropriate for her age. This is certainly the case when working with handicapped children, some of whose development will never reach a level comparable with that of non-handicapped children of their age. For a handicapped child, all the little steps in achieving a skill such as feeding herself are themselves successes, and adults who work with the child have to see her development in this way and plan accordingly.

So, for some children, the work of adults may circle again and again round the diagram showing planned involvement. Other children may not need adults' attention in so detailed a way, although a regular look at every child ensures that problems or delays do not become too serious before they are noticed. When children are progressing well, this regular look at individuals can be a great source of satisfaction to adults, as well as a reminder that the child is probably ready for new and different challenges through her play.

Some examples to illustrate planning

A few descriptions of particular children may help to show how the planning of work can develop. These examples are taken from real events in nurseries and playgroups. The names of children and staff, and sometimes other minor details, have been changed to maintain confidentiality. The examples are given to illustrate that a planned approach can be helpful, without assuming ideal conditions of working which rarely apply.

Yusif was attending Downview specialist playgroup, which had a high proportion of children with language difficulties. By nature of the referrals, it was also becoming a playgroup with many children learning English as a second language. Yusif was just over three years of age and came from a Pakistani family. He had been referred to the playgroup for help in learning English. After two months of his attending the playgroup, the staff decided that Yusif's social behaviour had to be tackled before his language.

The playgroup had a special group in which a small number of children were being helped with their language development. However, the staff felt that Yusif was not yet ready to join that group. He was described as a 'loner', who did not join in activities with other children. On the few occasions when he did approach a group, he was often aggressive towards the other children, pushing them or snatching their toys away.

Annie, the member of staff responsible for special work with Yusif, felt that a sensible first goal was to attempt to draw Yusif into a small group of children who were already busy on an activity under the control of an adult. She decided that she would make that attempt once every day, as a minimum, and that she would sit Yusif next to her. She had noticed that he would stay a little longer in a group if an adult was sitting next to him. The other advantage was that Annie was then on hand to stop the poking and prodding that tended to follow on Yusif's joining a group. Furthermore, she had noticed that Yusif needed help on what to do with common play materials, since these seemed to be unfamiliar to him. For example, he would simply hit play dough, rather than attempt to make anything with it.

Annie's goal was that, in two to three weeks, Yusif would have gained the confidence to join a group of children without having to be coaxed and would stay at least a few minutes without any adult pressure. As far as she could judge from the developmental guide that the playgroup used, Yusif had very few English words. However, it seemed more sensible to leave any help with language until Yusif could take part in group activities and could play more happily with other children.

Unfortunately, Yusif was not regular in his attendance at the playgroup over the next couple of months. The absences made observation of his behaviour difficult, and attempts by Annie to draw him into group activities were divided by long intervals. This was very disheartening for her. However, other staff noticed that Yusif was beginning to join groups of children of his own accord and were able to reassure Annie that some changes were happening. There was also the general feeling that adults were not having to intervene so often to stop Yusif's aggression. After about ten weeks of irregular attendance at the playgroup, his behaviour also showed that he was attending to simple suggestions from staff about his play. It was still difficult, however, to judge how much he understood of the words spoken and how much he was depending on gesture. He also used a small number of English words himself. At this point, Annie decided that Yusif was ready to join the special language group.

Comments It is not unusual for some children to attend irregularly at their nursery or playgroup. Readers might like to consider whether they are dealing with children like this. Are you waiting for a regular pattern of attendance which is unlikely to come? Sometimes it is possible to build a good relationship with the child's parents, so that they can understand how irregular attendance can reduce the benefit of playgroup or nursery to the child. What might you say in such a conversation with parents? However, sometimes there will be no easy way through to the parents. How might you have to adjust your plans to take account of the situation? Do you get support from other staff when you are feeling disheartened?

Susan was nearly four years old and was attending Boundary Road nursery centre for half-day sessions. Her development, as judged by the developmental guide used by staff, seemed to be average for her age. However, the staff were concerned about her behaviour. They found themselves irritated by Susan, who seemed to delight in being uncooperative when asked to do something, preferring to do the opposite and be cheeky. After discussion, staff came to the conclusion that perhaps Susan was competing for attention in the only way she knew. Her family ran a local shop and seemed to be busy much of the time when Susan was around. Her play experience was very limited, and she seemed to see adults as being unpredictable in terms of the attention they were prepared to give her.

Marion was the member of staff responsible for special activities with Susan. She felt that there were two goals she wanted to achieve within a couple of weeks. The first goal was to discourage Susan from trying for attention through uncooperative and cheeky behaviour. Marion decided, as far as possible, to ignore Susan on these occasions and to make herself available for Susan when the child was being cooperative and trying to play. The second goal was to interest her in some play activities appropriate to her age. Drawing was chosen for this purpose, as something in which Susan had shown some interest. The aim was to help the play and to encourage her to see adults as useful resources.

Susan regularly attended this nursery centre and reacted very well to the structured attention from Marion. Within two weeks there was an improvement in Susan's behaviour which all the staff noticed. Susan was more cooperative and her cheekiness seemed now to be more in fun than from a desire to create a dramatic situation. She had enjoyed the special drawing sessions and was clearly proud of what she had produced. She showed signs of wanting to have a conversation, and would listen to the adults as well as making her own comments. Marion heard from Susan's mother that the nursery experience had generalised to her home — Susan had wanted to talk about what she had done at nursery and to have her parents involved in similar play at home. Her parents had enjoyed this and seemed relieved that Susan was asking for attention in a less irritating way. They made an effort to play with her more and to give her little jobs to do when they were serving in the shop, so that her afternoons were more interesting.

Marion felt that Susan did not need further special attention, since the problems were much improved. Her aim was to continue to interest Susan in different play activities and to meet her reasonable need for attention through play and conversation.

Comments   It is very easy to see a problem with a child totally in terms of her behaviour. Are you dealing with children similar to Susan? What sense do you think these children are making of the situation? Is there a basis for looking at what you do and at your feelings as well as at the children themselves?

Julie was the only child of a teenage mother. She had been in several different day nurseries and nursery schools and had spent some time in residential care. When she was four-and-a-half, the day nursery she was attending was closed and she was moved to Edward Road day nursery. At the previous nursery, Julie had tended to have bouts of sulkiness and could be spiteful to other children when she could not have her own way. Within a few weeks of joining Edward Road nursery, Julie had become a severe problem to staff because of her frequent and violent temper tantrums.

Staff noticed that Julie lost her temper over almost anything which frustrated her. This included not being able to have staff's attention when she wanted it, sharing toys with another child, being thwarted over forbidden activities (for example, climbing the fence), having to rest on her bed after lunch — in other words, any potential confrontation.

When she went into a tantrum, Julie would cry and scream, attack adults or children, throw toys or other objects, and be very hard to control or comfort. It came to the point where she was having at least one tantrum (minor or major) each day, and some of the other children were becoming wary or even frightened of Julie.

The two staff responsible for this group — Mary and Barbara — were very concerned about Julie and were prepared to try almost anything to deal with the problem. They had initially made allowances for her, feeling that, since she had experienced so many changes, their main aim should be to give her affection and support. Unfortunately, Julie seemed to exploit this by pushing staff's patience to the absolute limits. There was an additional problem in that internal conflict in this nursery had produced a very poor working atmosphere. Julie seemed to sense the stresses and, again, exploit any weaknesses.

Mary and Barbara agreed that their goal was to attempt to reduce the number of tantrums Julie was having each day. In order to achieve this, they felt they had to set clear limits on what Julie was and was not allowed to do. However, they wanted to manage this without placing restrictions on her that they would not normally place on four-year-olds in nursery life. This was a brave decision, since allowing Julie to join staff on short local trips or to help out around the nursery sometimes led to worrying situations, such as Julie dashing off down the road without warning.

Mary and Barbara tried several related approaches to the problem. Whenever possible, they tried to distract Julie out of a potentially conflictful situation and to provide some encouragement for cooperative behaviour, such as promises for her to help with bringing in lunch. This helped sometimes, but there were other times when they could see a trouble-spot developing but neither of them could intervene in time. They held to consistent limits and, if Julie lost her temper, they put her in a corner of the room or outside the door until she cooled down. However, this approach was made much less effective since some of the other staff would sometimes remove Julie from outside the door and take her away with them. In Julie's view, this meant that her 'bad' behaviour had led to positive attention from other adults.

A continuing difficulty arose because of the poor working atmosphere in Edward Road nursery. Other staff seemed poorly motivated to hold to Mary and Barbara's limits on what Julie was allowed to do, and so there was much inconsistency in the point at which adults stepped in to stop Julie and in how they dealt with her temper outbursts.

Julie seemed happiest if she had the attention of one adult who was playing and talking with her. She needed the challenge of adult conversation and of more difficult play activities than many of those available in the group rooms. Arrangements were made for some special play sessions with a visiting educational psychologist. Julie enjoyed these sessions very much, and Mary and Barbara continued the work with her on her projects. However, they had to face serious tantrums from Julie almost every time the weekly special session came to an end and Julie had to return to her group.

The problems this day nursery faced with Julie were not solved before she left for school, although there was some improvement. When consistent limits on what was allowed were set and kept, Julie's tantrums were more containable and she would allow herself to be comforted rather more quickly by the two staff whom she knew best and seemed to have come to trust. The special play sessions broadened her interests and prepared her for school to some extent. However, a further improvement in the situation was frustrated by the relatively short time before Julie started school and by the poor working atmosphere in the nursery.

Comments   Julie was a child who would have been difficult for anyone to handle. Have you any ideas about how you would have approached her? Inconsistency between adults in dealing with a child is likely to worsen the situation. Have you faced this sort of frustration in your work? Have you ideas about how to tackle the working relationships between adults which can seriously affect children?

Concluding remarks

These three examples give some idea of a planned approach to dealing with children in a realistic setting, where plans do not always work out ideally. In the case of Yusif, his irregular attendance made Annie's plans difficult to undertake and the encouragement of her colleagues was important in stopping her feeling that she was making no progress at all. The staff in Downview specialist playgroup worked closely together, and this proved useful since they discussed their individual observations of children. On several occasions a child happened to show what she had learnt from special activities to a member of staff who had not been the one to carry out the special sessions. Good communication between the staff was important, since the adult primarily responsible for that child was sometimes becoming disheartened because the child did not seem to be learning.

In the case of Susan, what could have become a serious problem in the nursery centre was forestalled because staff were prepared to see the child's behaviour as other than just 'naughty' and to make some plans which involved changes in their behaviour to Susan as well as looking towards changes in her.

The situation with Julie had very swiftly become difficult to handle. Although the staff who were mainly responsible for her could see some improvement in line with their goals, lack of time and the poor atmosphere in the nursery placed restrictions on how much change was actually likely.

When discussing the idea of a planned approach in working with children, it is important to realise that plans do not always go smoothly. An approach that seemed right in discussion does not always work in practice. Adults become disheartened when unforeseen obstacles upset what are basically sensible and practical plans. All these hiccups in the procedure have to be seen as part of a planned approach — they are part of working with children. If adults are willing to persevere, the planning approach will benefit the children and will make the work more satisfying to adults.

3
OBSERVATION TO JUDGE DEVELOPMENTAL STAGE AND PROGRESS

The discussion in chapter 2 stressed the value of keeping a regular record of children which can be a basis for identifying problems or for reassurance that a child is progressing at a normal rate. This chapter considers the use of developmental guides as a way of making this regular check. Towards the end of the chapter, some suggestions are given which are more appropriate to students learning about child development.

Open or more structured reports

It is possible to look at children every few months in an open-ended way — perhaps through keeping a diary-type record or writing an impressionistic report. There is a disadvantage to this type of method. Unless there is a definite structure to the observation which is common each time, adults may find that rather different aspects of an individual child have caught their interest on different occasions. Without a clear framework, adults can sometimes be undecided as to what is worth writing down, and so each report covers rather different areas. At a later date, they might become concerned about, for instance, the very limited fantasy play of an individual child and look back over their reports, only to find that some other aspect of the child's development had caught their eye earlier. There might be very little information on play to give them the perspective they now wanted.

Instead of writing open-ended reports, it is possible to use the structure of a developmental guide or, as they are sometimes called, assessment charts, forms, or check lists. The point of such a guide is to build up an accurate picture of an individual child at one point in time. Then, by repeating the observation every few months, it is possible to judge whether a child is progressing in her development.

Such a guide does not, of course, include all the possible skills and changes that happen in child development. However, the selection should provide enough of a range for adults to be able to judge a child's current abilities and her progress or lack of it.

The contents of a developmental guide

The different guides which are available use slightly different labels or ways of organising the various areas of child development. However, most cover the following areas:

a) *Physical development* — both the larger movements, such as walking or climbing, and the finer coordinations of eye and hand involved in drawing or building.

b) *Communication and language development* — both expressive language (speech) and understanding. Included in this area tends to be the learning of concepts such as of size, colour, or number.

c) *Social development and play* — including a child's relationships with adults and children, how she plays, her interests, and perhaps also her ability to concentrate.

d) *Self-help and independence* — a child's learning to cope without adult help in areas such as feeding, toilet-training, and dressing, and her ability to help adults and take part in group activities and routine tasks.

e) *Behaviour* — sometimes this would be placed under social development or self-help. It may, however, be a separate section in which to note any problems or difficulties that the child seems to be having.

Using a developmental guide

The layout of a developmental guide is usually a list of items for each area of development. These items are in approximately the order that children will manage them. The guide is completed by ticking those items which a child can definitely do, and perhaps putting a question mark against items on which there is some doubt. There is no score at the end. Such a guide is not a test of any kind, nor is it providing the type of formal assessment that a speech therapist or psychologist might complete. It is a way of taking a 'snapshot' of a child at one point in her development, for planning on the basis of what emerges about that child, and a comparison point for future 'snapshots' of the same child.

The layout of such guides varies, but a section might look something like the example on page 26.

There is normally space for the same items to be assessed on several different occasions. In the example shown, a section on large physical movements has been completed on a baby at three-monthly intervals. It is possible to see that the baby is making progress in this area of development. The format is that of ticks, which makes the completion simple and quick. However, an adult may sometimes wish to add a brief note as shown. There comes a point when some of the 'younger' items are no longer applicable. In the example above, by the time the child is ten months old, the 'roll from back to stomach' is no longer relevant,

Example: part of a developmental guide completed for a young child

Large physical movements

Date:	6/4/86	7/7/86	1/10/86	31/12/86
Child's age:	4 mths	7 mths	10 mths	13 mths
Can the child				
Roll from back to stomach	√	√	—	—
Sit without support for short periods		√(long time)	√	—
Throw objects		√	√	√
Crawl on all fours		(trying)	√	√
Pull self up by furniture			√	√
Stand without support				√
Squat down from standing				√
Walk with help			√	√
Walk alone				√

because the child has progressed to more mature ways of moving from one place to another. Adults have to use their common sense as to where to start in a guide. A possible way around the problem of the wide range of skills learned by under-fives is to have two types of guide: one for use with younger children up to about two or two-and-a-half years of age and the other for older children. This avoids the problem of having many items which are too simple for the older child, or too difficult for the younger.

Some areas of interest cannot really be noted by ticking single items. Making a note of children's play and aspects of behaviour can often be done simply by ticking which alternative out of several most closely describes a child's behaviour. The example on page 27 looks at the behaviour of a child who is three years of age at the last observation.

The child in this example has been gaining in the ability to concentrate over the period covered by the three observations using the guide. However, there has been no change in her general relationship to other children in play and she may be something of a 'loner', perhaps even nervous of the others. Clearly an adult would make sense of the information in the light of further knowledge of the individual child.

Example: part of a developmental guide on a child's behaviour

Social development and play

	5/2/86	25/5/86	20/8/86
Date:			
Child's age:	2:6	2:9	3:0
How does the child react to something that is difficult for her/him?			
Gives up quickly			
Tries for a short while	√	√	
Tries persistently			√
How does the child react to a quiet activity that requires some thought?			
Fidgety from start	√		
Concentrates for a minute or two		√	
Concentrates for five minutes or more			√
In play with other children, does the child			
Usually play with other children, joins in			
Usually play alone, but near other children			
Usually keep away from other children	√	√	√

The first time a guide is completed on a child can be quite time-consuming. However, on subsequent occasions it is quicker, since adults only have to look for the additional skills a child has learned and whether her play and general behaviour have changed.

Creating the chance to observe

When a guide is being completed, there may be some items which you have seen the child do in the course of an ordinary day. However, some areas of interest may not emerge through the child's spontaneous play.

In that case, it may be necessary to find out if the child can manage a certain skill by organising a particular play activity.

An example of this might be that you want to see if a child can hop on one leg. You may not have seen this in her play, but, of course, because she has not chosen to do this does not mean that she cannot. In this instance, you can show a child what hopping means by demonstration and then invite her to try it. If you want to see if a child can pour water from a large to a smaller container, you can arrange some water play or a tea party. You would then see if the child can pour without help. In this play activity, if the child has difficulty in pouring, then it would be a natural move on the part of the adult to help the child. However, that item would not be ticked as something the child could do. A clear distinction needs to be kept between observing what the child can do unaided and the process of helping her to achieve a new skill. Observing children at regular intervals does not mean that you stop helping and showing; however, it does mean that the inclination to teach and demonstrate has to be resisted when you are trying to judge what children can do by themselves.

The way in which adults should introduce a particular skill is often included in the description of items in the guide. Different ways of exploring an item can make the skill more or less difficult. For example, if you are finding out if a child can build a simple bridge with three bricks, it is an easier task for the child if you leave your demonstration model standing as a comparison. Some children may be at the stage of managing this task but are not able to build the bridge if you take yours apart and leave them with single bricks. Similarly, exploring a child's knowledge and understanding of colours is quite different if you ask a question based on matching colours rather than identifying them. It is a simpler problem for a child to be given one red brick and told 'This is a red brick, give me another red one' rather than being given the same single brick and asked 'What colour is this?' For this reason, it is important to be consistent over the wording of questions and the introduction of a skill each time a developmental guide is used.

The aim of using a developmental guide is to reach a picture of a child which can be compared easily with another picture of that same child at later dates. For this reason, it is wise not to spend too long completing the guide each time. If the completion is spread over weeks, then the picture is more accurately of that child at the end of the period in terms of skills and at an unknown point in that period in terms of behaviour. Ideally, items should be completed within a few days, or at most a week. If this is not proving possible because the child seems unwell or very uncooperative, it is better to stop and leave the observation until she is better or to deal with the problem of lack of cooperation. Problems which can affect completion of a guide, such as uncooperativeness or very poor attention from a child, are discussed in later chapters.

Sometimes you want to see what a child can manage without help.

The child does not have to perform all the tasks during the few days in which the guide is being completed. For instance, if you saw a child draw a circle last week, this can be ticked — there is no need to take the child through that skill again just because the guide is being completed this week. Clearly adults have to use their common sense on this. In a development like toilet-training, if a child was dry all last week but has wetted once this week, then the note in that section of the guide might indicate that she is nearly toilet-trained but has the occasional accident.

Making sense of the information

It has been stressed that a developmental guide is not a test. It does not have a score and is not a pass/fail procedure. The pictures which emerge of children of the same age may, of course, differ. A child may appear to be progressing well for her age, or she may be delayed in one or more areas of her development. Her development may be normal but she may be posing some problems or worries in her behaviour. Clearly, adults have to make sense of the information through their knowledge of child development. This same knowledge will indicate that children learn many skills which are not included in the particular guide being used. So the point about delay is that the child may need some special help in a particular area of her development, not that she specifically needs to master the items in the guide. The aim would not be to teach a child to ride a tricycle because that is the next item: if a child seemed to be delayed in her physical development, you would look at a range of physical activities that seemed to be nearly within the child's grasp and would try to help and encourage her in those. If the child's problem seemed to be that of low confidence in her own physical ability, adults would look for ways gradually to increase that confidence.

The use of developmental norms

There are two basic ways of making sense of information from developmental guides. It is possible to compare a child's present abilities and behaviour against the yardstick of the average for her age. Psychologists and speech therapists use tests of language, intelligence, and other areas of development which have norms — an average range of scores which can be expected from children of particular ages. This means that a child's score can be compared with what most children of her age can achieve. Norms for the different tests are built up by a programme of testing many children, so that it becomes possible to say what the different ages can, on average, manage in this selection of items. Comparison of the test score against the norms will indicate whether, in this particular area, a child is delayed, about average, or advanced for her age. A different way of interpreting information on the child's development is to compare the child against the yardstick of herself at a younger age. The developmental guides for use by pre-school staff tend to compare a child against her earlier performances rather than against developmental norms.

These two ways of comparison are not, of course, mutually exclusive. Speech therapists assessing a child's language would look both at the child's changing abilities and at how she compares with norms for her age. Users of developmental guides have their knowledge of child development as a context for judging individual children. However, research teams who have produced such guides tend not to provide specific suggestions as to average ages when children might have mastered particular items. It is possible to understand the concern that material should not be used as a test for labelling children — the developmental guides are designed to encourage adults to see children as individuals as much as possible and to view their progress in an individual context. Equally important, a detailed testing programme is needed to give accurate norms for all developmental items. Even after such a programme, norms can only be given in the form of 'Most children of three years of age will have learned to do item 6.' This means that some children will have achieved the skill at a younger age and some will still not be managing it at three years.

Despite the difficulties, there is a need for users of developmental guides to relate their observations to some averages in child development. Using the yardstick of a child's previous performance, she may be gaining in skills each time she is assessed. However, the overall picture is very different if she was advanced in her development initially rather than if she was over six months delayed at the outset. In the latter case, her skills will still be more typical of a younger child, despite the progress she has made.

Since it is difficult to hold information on child development fresh all the time, some material for reference is invaluable. One useful booklet is Mary Sheridan's *Children's developmental progress* (third edition published by the NFER in 1975). This gives a range of developmental skills in a way which makes for easy reference. Not all the items in every developmental guide are covered, but there are sufficient for adults to gain some 'anchor points' within the guide that they are using.

Adults who work with children need to build some understanding of the balance between using developmental norms and the child's own previous performance to judge how well the child is progressing. It is important to keep in mind a clear idea of the range of skills children usually show at different ages. This enables the child to be judged against reasonable expectations for her age. However, if a three-year-old is functioning more like a two-year-old, then she has to be helped to develop from that two-year-old level of ability. While working with the child, the adult needs to bear in mind the progress the child is making, given the initial delay. This can sometimes be a difficult balancing act.

It is easy to lose developmental 'anchor points' in either direction. If adults work with many children who are delayed in their language development, then it can be easy to forget that most children are using many recognisable words and some simple word combinations by two years of age. In several nurseries where I worked some years ago, there were many children with delayed language development. After some time, I realised that both the staff and I had shifted our expectations in line with the children whom we saw day by day. We were beginning to feel that it was not unusual to have non-talking two-year-olds, and were therefore not worrying about language until the children were older! The shifting of expectations can, of course, be in the opposite direction. If staff have a group of three-year-olds who are adept at recognising colours, it is wise to recall that this group is progressing well for their age, especially if they can identify as well as match colours. It is not unusual for some four-year-olds to be confused in this area of learning.

Choosing a developmental guide

The National Children's Bureau has published a set of developmental guides for children from birth to five years old. These are thorough and cover the major areas of child development and behaviour. Some of the staff with whom I have worked have found these guides too long to complete regularly and we have produced slightly shorter ones. Some balance has to be found between having a form which staff will actually complete, in the time they feel is available to them, and having sufficient items in the guide for a reasonably full picture of the child to emerge. If there are too few items, there may not be enough to show the progress of the older children, or there may be too wide a gap between items in terms of the age at which children will attain the different skills. In the latter case, the children may seem to be making little progress.

The National Children's Bureau guides were developed for use with non-handicapped children. When working with children who have definite mental or physical handicaps, it is important to remember that their rate of progress will be slower. Items which represent finer steps in development will then give a more useful picture of the children. In some cases, handicapped children go through the stages in a similar order to non-handicapped, but this depends on the nature of the handicap. Specific guides for use with handicapped children are usually necessary. A child with a visual handicap — either with some visual impairment or total blindness — will not be able to respond to many of the items in, for example, a section on language development in the usual guides. The phrasing of items in this section of guides often depends on sight.

A team at the Hester Adrian Centre at the University of Manchester developed charts specifically for use with handicapped children. These resulted from the Parental Involvement Project, designed to help the parents of handicapped children, and were published by Hodder and Stoughton Educational in 1976 as *PIP developmental charts* by Dorothy M. Jeffree and Roy McConkey. Parts of the charts are also reproduced in the very practical books *Let me speak*, by Dorothy M. Jeffree and Roy McConkey, and *Let me play* by Roy McConkey and Penny Price (published by Souvenir Press in 1976 and 1986.) The charts give the intermediate steps that children go through before reaching different skills. These would not always be noticed as separate stages with a non-handicapped child, but are important successes in a handicapped child's development.

There are other developmental guides available — for example, the Progress Assessment Charts (PAC) for use with handicapped children and the Keele Pre-school Assessment Guide. If you are trying to choose a guide, it would be worth obtaining the survey by Margaret Bate, Marjorie Smith, and Jeannette James ('*Review of tests and assessments in early education, 3—5 years*, published by NFER—Nelson, 1981). This gives some information on guides and how to obtain them, and there are also descriptions of other common assessments for three- to five-year-olds that it may be useful to know about, even if you are unlikely to administer them yourself.

The important point about choosing a developmental guide is not to keep looking for the *perfect* format for your own needs — it is unlikely that the existing material will be completely suitable. It is better to choose the one which most closely fits what you want. It is always possible to make brief notes on a form to cover a particular child or to make minor changes so that there is space to cover a particular aspect that is of relevance to your group. The exact items in a developmental guide are less important than the fact that, as a whole, it is providing you with a clear picture of the child which will help you work more effectively.

OBSERVATION FOR STUDENTS TO LEARN ABOUT CHILD DEVELOPMENT

Students may have a practical placement in a nursery or playgroup where a developmental guide is used. If this is the case, the student can be introduced to observational skills through use of the guide. The same material will be a way of illustrating child development through individual children. However, the following discussion does not depend on the use of a developmental guide. The ideas which follow are offered both for students themselves and for those readers who are responsible for supervising students.

The aim of this type of observation is to build a full picture of one child so that, for that age group in particular, the observer is encouraged to think about what the child might be able to do, what she can nearly do, and so on. The exercise also introduces students to the skills of observation. For one child, at least, the student has had the discipline of looking at all the areas of development.

Guide-lines for a student

Students, even those training for the same qualification but at different colleges, do not always have the same brief for the observation component in their training, so these guide-lines are kept at a general level. They assume that the student will observe one child over a period of weeks or months, rather than days, with the view of writing a report on that child at the end of the observation time. Basically, students need to develop a clear picture of what the child is like at the beginning of the observation period, what new abilities she has learned, how she has changed as time passed, and so to what she is like at the end of the period.

Students have to decide on which baby or child they would like to observe. They need to find out the child's name and date of birth (so that they have an accurate note of the child's age at the time of observation) and make sure that they are right about the child's sex. This last point is worth mentioning, since it is not always obvious from children's appearance or names whether they are boys or girls. Since the observation will take some time, it is sensible to make sure that the child selected is not going to leave the nursery, playgroup, etc. in the near future or is not absent a great deal. Since students will be watching on different days, they should always date their observations — when they look back on them in later months, it will be very difficult to remember what happened and in what order. If they are observing over a period of months, they will also need the date in order to determine the child's age.

Students need to understand the principle of confidentiality when they are making observations of children or of the working of a group as a whole. This may have practical implications, such as not using a child's real name when discussing the observations outside the nursery or play-group. This issue of confidentiality obviously has wider ramifications for how students talk about children, parents, or the staff of establishments where they are on placement — the hard-to-define business of 'professional' behaviour.

The value of making a child observation is that students can see the changes and learning in children over the weeks or months. Since children are learning continually, it is wise to place some time limit on gathering observations of what the child is like at the start. A possibility is to decide to gather material on the child's current abilities over a one- or two-week period. A few changes may happen in this length of time, but not so many that the initial picture of the child will be too confused. After the first set of observations, the student would be noting down changes in the child's behaviour and new skills that she had learned. At the end of the whole period of observation it is then possible to look back at the first set of observations for a clear contrast on how the child has changed.

For a full observation of the child, students will have to watch for the child's abilities in the various areas of child development. These areas are covered thoroughly in the various books on child development, so they are only mentioned in outline here. When making an observation, students may need to be reminded of the range of abilities it is reasonable to expect from the age of child they are observing. This is just a reminder, since they may find that the child has mastered more, or less, than the average for her age group. The child observation can reasonably cover the following areas.

Different aspects to child development — questions students might ask themselves

What are the child's abilities in the area of *physical development*? What can she manage in terms of the large movements? Depending on age, it might be appropriate to ask if the child can crawl, walk, climb, jump, or hop. Does the child seem confident in her body movements or is she nervous? Is she generally very active, rushing about the place, or is she quieter or slower in her movements? What can the child manage in terms of the finer movements — the physical movements which need good coordination of eye and hand? Again it would depend on the age of the child, but this could include grasping, picking up and exploring objects, building, pouring, cutting, and any other activities which need coordination of eye and hand.

What are the child's abilities in the area of *communication*? How does she try to communicate with others? If she is too young for words, does she make a range of sounds to express emotions — has she grasped that sounds and pointing can communicate that she wants something? If the child has a small number of words, it will be feasible to make a list of these. However, it soon becomes a mammoth task to note down a child's total vocabulary. With an older talking child, students can note down examples of the phrases and sentences the child uses. They can look for whether she uses her speech confidently. Does she ask questions? Can she take part in a simple conversation? Is her speech understandable to strangers?

Other than speech, a major part of language development is understanding — what the child can comprehend and follow of what others say. The child may show through her behaviour that she understands simple commands or the names of familiar objects or people, or can identify objects by use. An older child may show that she understands more complex instructions such as questions about objects and pictures, or has grasped some abstract ideas.

The abilities that can be observed for language development are often also relevant to *intellectual development*, since language, thinking, and learning are intertwined. Depending on the child's age, it might be appropriate to look at understanding of colour, size, number, shape, or ideas of time or of relative speed. Students could also try to watch for whether the child seems interested in learning new skills. For example, will she persevere with new toys which are not easy for her to handle? Will she try a different approach if her first attempts fail, and does she see adults as people who can help her?

In terms of the child's *social development*, students could express an opinion based on the child's behaviour that they have observed. The questions they might look to answer could include the following. How does the child seem to get along with other children or with adults? How does she react to new situations or new people? Does she seem to have settled into the nursery or playgroup? An observation of social development can also include the child's self-help skills in terms of feeding, going to the toilet, washing, dressing, and similar areas of learning.

Observation of the child's *play* also has to take account of her age and abilities. Allowing for these differences, a student might observe which toys or activities a child enjoys and can manage; whether she is curious about new toys; whether she plays with other children; whether she has definite preferences for particular types of toys; whether she shows any fantasy play. Related to these questions can be observation to see how long the child tends to stay with one activity; whether she is easily distracted; whether she remembers where her toys are in order to return to them.

Finally, students might gather together their ideas on the child's *behaviour*. These would be opinions based on what they have observed of the child and might include some of the following ideas. Is the child generally on the quiet side, or does she tend to be noisy and active? Does she enjoy being a leader in games, or does she tend to be a follower? Does the child have any fears, for instance of spiders or dogs? Is she ever aggressive towards other children? Does she concentrate well, considering her age? Does she have tantrums? Does she have any problems in feeding or sleeping?

Creating an opportunity for a particular observation

Students may be fortunate since on the days when they are observing a particular child all the areas in which they are interested arise naturally through the child's play. It is very possible, however, that students will be interested in some abilities which do not arise through the child's spontaneous play. In this case, they may wish to set up a situation which enables them to see if the child can manage a certain activity or can understand a particular idea.

For instance, a student may be interested in whether the child can build a tower with bricks, but on the days when the observations have taken place the child has not played with bricks at all. The student could therefore make sure of a playtime with the child when she is encouraged to play with the bricks. The student would build a tower and show it to the child, with an invitation of 'Can you build one like this?' With a younger child, the gesture of handing over a brick and pointing towards the ready-made tower can also communicate the same message.

When students are exploring what a child can do by being involved in her play, they can become confused as to what the child has managed herself and what they, as adults, have really done for her. Even experienced adults can be unaware of the unintentional hints they have given a child when they were actually attempting to judge what the child could do with no help at all. For inexperienced adults, the difference between what a child has achieved solely from her own abilities and what was dependent on the help that came from adults or older children can be a hard distinction to see. Understanding this difference is a part of the learning process for students.

Sometimes you can see a helping hand is needed. ▶

Learning from the child observation

A completed child observation of this kind could include descriptions of the wide range of skills which the child had at the beginning of the observation period, the new skills which she learned as time passed, and the abilities which are nearly within her grasp at the end of the observation time. The child's interests and preferences can emerge as well as her typical behaviour in the setting in which she was watched, including any problems which were observed. Opinions about any problems or difficulties should be supported by descriptions of the child's behaviour as seen by the student — for instance, what it was about the child that gave the impression that she lacked confidence or that her concentration was poor.

For students to gain the most from a child observation, what they see has to be placed in the context of what it would be reasonable to expect from a child of the age that they observed. Relating the progress and behaviour of one child to a more general view of child development is something which students are learning through their training. However, it is a context which qualified staff also have to keep fresh in their minds, since they too are making sense of their observations and aiming to learn from what they have seen. For this reason, supervising observations by students can stimulate the ideas of experienced adults.

4

OBSERVING HOW
CHILDREN BEHAVE

A developmental guide is a way of looking at what a child can do. However this way of observing does not show how a child actually spends her time in the course of an ordinary day. One reason why completing a developmental guide can bring some surprises is that, although a child can do certain things, perhaps build very competently with bricks, she may not actually have bothered to do this.

Researchers interested in children's play have spent time observing the spontaneous play of children of different ages and social backgrounds and in different pre-school settings. Pre-school staff such as teachers, nursery nurses, or playgroup workers will not have the same amount of time for observing as researchers; however, the methods used by the latter can offer a way of finding out what children are doing in the course of an ordinary day.

An equally important incentive to observing children's behaviour is adult concern about behaviour problems. In this case, the aim of the observation is to gain some perspective on the difficulty. When adults are experiencing a child as difficult, it can seem as if that child is being a problem most of the day. Making planned observations of the child can help adults towards a more realistic judgement of the seriousness of the problem. Observation may also show whether there are particular situations or events which make matters worse or whether there are days when the problem is less serious. Sections on general behaviour in developmental guides usually provide space for indicating if there are any problems. Since not all children present behaviour difficulties, it would not be appropriate to make more detailed observations for all children. However, if a child is found to be difficult to handle by some adults, then observation can provide a perspective, sometimes some ideas, and usually a basis for comparison at a later date.

OBSERVING CHILDREN'S SPONTANEOUS PLAY

Although adults may want to observe several children in total, they will probably have to focus on one child at a time. A team from the Oxford Preschool Research Group (OPRG)* called this the 'target-child'

*The OPRG project is described in *Childwatching at playgroup and nursery school*, by Kathy Sylva, Carolyn Roy, and Marjorie Painter. This book was approach. This is certainly more practical than attempting to watch a group of children, especially if you are interested in the details of what individuals are doing.

There could, however, be times when you would want to watch a group, perhaps in terms of their use of a particular activity or a play corner. Realistically, it would then be possible only to note down more general aspects to the play. This might include numbers of children involved, the coming and going of individuals, a judgement of whether they were playing together or alongside, how long the play lasted, and perhaps whether a leader emerged. So much happens within a group of children that it is not possible to write down details such as what individuals said and did, unless you video-tape the episode and play and replay the scene at a later date.

If you are watching an individual child, it is still necessary to make decisions about how and what you will watch — it simply is not possible to watch continuously and write down everything. A method called 'time sampling' enables an observer to watch for set regular periods of time that allow for watching, writing down, and pausing for rests. Different schemes of observation involve different ways of dividing up time, and decisions about this depend on how skilled the observers are, how fast (and legibly) they can write, and whether there is a system of shorthand they can use for different behaviours of the children.

One possible approach might be to decide to watch an individual child for a total of thirty minutes and to observe in half-minute bursts, with a break of half a minute between the observations. There is not one ideal pattern of dividing up the time. The length of each burst of observation has to be long enough so that some sense emerges as to what the child is doing, but not so long that it is impossible for observers to remember what they have seen. Some noting down can take place while watching, but often observers will be finishing the notes during the brief pauses.

The complexity of the note-taking will depend on how busy the child is. If a child is silently watching another activity for half a minute, the observation task is obviously much easier than if she is painting a picture, talking to another child, and looking around the room at the same time.

Another way of observing children's spontaneous play (equally applicable to watching adults' behaviour) is the 'trail observation'. You need to prepare a sheet of paper with a map-type layout of the room. Noting the time you start, you then draw lines in for the movements made

---

published in 1980 by Grant McIntyre, and the research team also produced several pamphlets for pre-school staff.

Observation of spontaneous play can show how children choose to spend their time. ▶

by one individual child (or adult), adding brief notes including the length of stay at each part of the room. Depending on the aim of your observation, you might also want to note, for example, how many other children are present at each stopping point. You would need to continue the observation for at least 15 to 20 minutes, since you need a reasonable sample. The results can show the pattern of a child's or adult's movements and stopping-off points. You can then compare different children or the same child on different days and so on.

Making sense of the observations

When researchers are observing children's behaviour, they develop a system of different codes or categories to cover all the different things a child may be doing or saying. Such systems are more detailed than is practicable for pre-school staff.*

The Oxford Preschool Research Group suggested a possible system of categorising children's behaviour in play.† This can be followed up by readers who would like to approach this type of observation in more detail. A source of ideas on categorising children's language, in particular, can be found in Joan Tough's book *Listening to children talking* (published by Ward Lock Educational in 1976). This is also discussed in chapter 9 of this book. It is possible, however, for adults to make sense of observations of children's play by asking themselves some pertinent questions about an individual child or group. An example will illustrate this.

An example of observing one child's play

An adult has observed Stephen for half an hour on each morning of one week. The section of the observation given as an example on page 43 is for only part of one morning. The adult was observing for half a minute, then taking a half-minute break. The example therefore covers five minutes in total.

Looking back over a week's observation of Stephen, an adult might ask questions like:

— What activities has Stephen spent time on — does he seem to have favourites or activities he rarely, if ever, joins in?

*Readers might like to look at two articles on children's play which show some of the distinctions that can be made. These are by Barbara Tizard, Janet Philps, and Ian Plewis. 'Play in pre-school centres' appears in two parts in the *Journal of child psychology and psychiatry*, October 1976, volume 17(4).

†This work is described in *Childwatching at playgroup and nursery school* by Kathy Sylva, Carolyn Roy, and Marjorie Painter, published in 1980 by Grant McIntyre.

- Does he approach adults readily or wait until they approach him?
- Does he join in groups of children easily?
- Does he talk more readily with other children or with adults?
- Does he spend a lot of time looking on?

Example: observation of a child's play

Child's name: Stephen   *Age*: 3½ years old

Tuesday 7 September

Note: S=Stephen, K=Katherine, J=Jackie

10.00 a.m.
Standing at water tray.
Looking on at other children (three round water).
Tries to get into space. K pushes S away.

10.01 a.m.
(Mrs T made children give S space.)
Pouring water from jug. Looks over at what J is doing.
Picks up funnel, uses like J is.
Smiles to self.

10.02 a.m.
Pouring from arm's length into tray. J is as well. Both laughing loudly.
Splashes self. Squeaks. (Water is splashing on to the floor.)
Mrs T calls to stop. S looks up. Listens. Brings arm down.
J still pouring from height of her extended arm. S says
'She said don't. She said stop.'

10.03 a.m.
K tries to take funnel from S.
S holds on. 'No. No, it's mine.'
K succeeds. S leaves tray.
Walks across room to jigsaw table (Mrs T sitting at this table).

10.04 a.m.
Sitting next to Mrs T looking at jigsaw of farmyard.
Listens to Mrs T. Mrs T asks 'What can you see in the picture?'
'Dogs. Some dogs and a man. A man on a . . . riding a. . . .' Hesitates.
Mrs T answers 'A tractor'.
'Riding a tractor. Lambs, little lambs. They go "baa". I saw lambs at the
farm. When we went to the farm.'

— Approximately how long does he spend on each activity before he moves on?

If the rest of the observation was at all similar to the incidents in this example, it would be appropriate to ask such questions as

— Does Stephen usually need an adult's help to break into a group?
— Is he bullied or cowed by more strong-willed children?
— Does he seem concerned about pleasing adults?
— Does he give up easily in a conflict with other children?

The aim of making a series of observations of a child's spontaneous behaviour is to reach some understanding of how the child usually behaves in the setting where you are observing. However consistent the picture of the child which emerges from this observation, adults cannot assume that this is also the way the child behaves elsewhere, or that this observation is necessarily reflecting the child's top potential. The method is, however, a sound way of looking for pointers which can help in adults' involvement with this child in this setting. There may be useful indications as to where the child needs encouragement to persevere or to what extent she needs an incentive to be more self-sufficient.

Watching a child's play over a period of time can provide ideas on which activities interest the child, approximately how long she stays with each activity, and whether she plays in cooperation with other children. Pre-school staff sometimes have opinions about what are more or less valuable activities. This may lead them to judge that a child who shows an interest in jigsaws, books, or matching shapes is playing 'better' than a child who is very absorbed in trains or cars. However, observation of these different children may show that the first child flits from book to book or never completes a jigsaw. The second child perhaps perseveres in building tunnels for her trains and has vivid imaginative play and plenty of conversation built around the play with cars.

OBSERVATION TO GIVE SOME PERSPECTIVE ON BEHAVIOUR PROBLEMS

Part 3 of this book looks in some detail at ways in which adults might approach different behaviour problems. In this chapter, the discussion is on the use of observation in gaining a perspective on problems. Such observation can help decisions about how adults could best deal with particular children.

Describing the behaviour which poses a problem

There is a difference between labelling a problem behaviour and describing it. Several adults may agree on a critical label for a particular child, such as 'defiant', 'spiteful', or 'aggressive'. However, each adult will have a slightly different, or very different, view on what actual behaviour from the child is judged to be 'defiant'. If these different adults observe the child to judge how often this problem occurs, a different picture is likely to emerge from each adult. As a result, some adults might conclude that the child was a more serious problem than was felt by others.

Almost inevitably, we tend to talk in 'shorthand' when expressing frustrations about children. However, this 'shorthand' must be filled out if an observation, and a broader perspective on the problem, is to be achieved.

An example of describing a problem behaviour

Sally, Bill, and Margaret are the three adults responsible for one group in an all-day children's centre. Nancy is a four-year-old girl in their group. All three staff are agreed that Nancy is 'uncooperative'. To help their discussion about what to do, they separately write a short description of what Nancy does that leads each of them to judge her as 'uncooperative'. These are their comments:

SALLY: Nancy is an uncooperative child. Particularly at meal-times — she will not finish her dinner, however hard I coax her. She just stares and looks sulky. At other times she just looks through you if you ask her to do something.

BILL: Nancy is not at all cooperative in the group. She takes no notice of adults unless you talk directly to her, so you end up having to say everything once to the whole group and two or three times to Nancy. Even then, she sometimes just stands and you have to guide her along.

MARGARET: Nancy is sullen and uncooperative. She does not join in and takes little notice of what we ask her to do. It looks sometimes as if she is setting out to annoy, that she likes the drama of us flapping about her.

The three adults are describing the same child, but a slightly different emphasis emerges from each brief description. Sally has focused more on Nancy's behaviour at mealtimes and on confrontations between an adult and the child at these times. Bill and Margaret have focused more on Nancy as a child who is neither part of the group nor acting like the other children. Particularly in Margaret's description, there is an element of taking Nancy's behaviour as a personal affront. The annoyance that each of these adults feels towards Nancy would need to be discussed, otherwise there would be a risk of their viewing any observation as a way to obtain 'proof' that Nancy was a difficult and irritating child.

One possible approach to observing Nancy might be to avoid the label of 'uncooperative' altogether and to concentrate on discovering under what circumstances Nancy does follow a request and, from the adults' viewpoint, how many instructions they are giving her. Such an observation might show that adults are giving Nancy many more instructions than are given to the other children. It might also show that, however many times the instruction is repeated, Nancy usually has to be guided physically or shown what is being requested. Repeated instructions to Nancy to eat up her dinner might rarely have an effect. The child might seldom, if ever, respond as an individual to an instruction given to the whole group. Such findings would suggest that some changes in adult behaviour could help — reducing the number of instructions, accepting the inevitable over dinnertime conflicts, and not expecting Nancy to respond to group instructions at present.

Ways of observing behaviour problems

Once a problem has been clearly described in terms of the child's actual behaviour, it is possible to observe the child and reach a judgement on the seriousness of the problem. There are three main aspects which can be assessed fairly simply through observation. These are

  i) *Frequency* — how often does the problem occur?
 ii) *Duration* — for how long does the difficult behaviour last on each occasion — or — for how much of the day does this behaviour seem typical?
iii) *Severity* — is it possible to decide whether this is a mild, fairly serious, or very serious instance of the problem behaviour?

Not all of these are relevant questions for all problems. It would not be appropriate with a passive withdrawn child to ask 'How often does the problem occur?' unless particular circumstances seem to lead the child to withdraw into herself. If withdrawal is a state which seems to be characteristic of the child, it would be more appropriate to observe in order to answer a question like 'How much of the day does she seem to spend withdrawn into herself?'

Frequency — observing for 'How many times?'

It is possible to observe a child over a period of days and simply to count up the number of times the problem behaviour occurs. This is called a frequency count. It would be important to observe in this way for more than just one or two days — the aim is to see how much the problem

Example: observation of a child by frequency count

Child's name: James   *Age*: 3½ years old

Description of problem
Aggressive — James attacks other children, usually smaller than himself. His attacks are usually because he wants something like a toy or because he is cross. He isn't very patient if other children provoke him, but we are more worried about the unprovoked aggression.

Observations of unprovoked attacks

Day	Total attacks	Comments
Tuesday 2 June	4	(1) Janet had the new bike and James wanted it. He tried to pull the bike away and slapped at Janet's hands. (2) James cornered Janet again five minutes later. He tried to get control of the bike and pushed Janet so hard that she fell off. (3) Tried to get through the door at the same time as Matthew. James kicked out at Matthew and Matthew promptly kicked him back. James let Matthew through. (4) James was told to stop slamming the door. He rushed off and knocked into a smaller child (Andy) — it looked deliberate.
Wednesday 3 June	1	(1) James seemed rather under the weather today. He kicked Andy when they were both in the book corner — Andy did not seem to have started anything.
Thursday 4 June	0	He hit Katie but she had been very provoking — poking and tickling him when James was trying to paint.
Friday 5 June	2	(1) Generally pushing and hitting in the queue for the outdoor slide. (2) Couple of minutes later — James was taken away from the slide for pushing. He rushed over to one of the toddlers and pushed her over really fiercely.
Monday 8 June	About 6	We lost count. James was really aggressive first thing this morning — biting, hitting, pushing. He became very upset by mid-morning and cried. For a change, he was prepared for one of us to comfort him. We actually persuaded him to say 'Sorry' to David, who was badly scratched.

varies from day to day and not risk assuming that a couple of days are typical.

The example on page 47 shows what might emerge from a frequency count. In this instance, a boy — James — has been watched whom adults judge to be aggressive. The behaviour that concerns the adults includes physical attacks on other children — often on children smaller than himself.

Several points emerge through this set of observations. James seems to be worse after the weekend, and this may mean that adults will have to be especially vigilant with him on a Monday. He seems to have little patience with other children, taking his frustrations out on them. Adults will need to help James to express his frustrations in ways other than hitting out. His ability to express himself in words might be important here.

Another approach could be through specifically encouraging any attempts James makes to be more patient with other children and more tolerant of them in his play. Another way of using the frequency-count observation can help here — it is possible to observe for examples of positive, rather than negative, behaviour by a child who is seen as difficult. In James' case, adults might look out for times when he is patient for even a short while or allows himself to be distracted from using hitting as a way of expressing frustrations. The value of the observation for positive behaviour is that it can help adults to shift their attention towards opportunities for encouraging a child rather than seeing that child almost completely in terms of the problem behaviour. To adults' surprise, there may be times when a difficult child is cooperative or tolerant of other children.

The frequency count of problem behaviour may also bring unexpected results. Adults can have the impression that a child is being 'naughty' for much of the day. After observation, it may emerge that there are long stretches of a day — or whole days — when the child is not difficult at all. However, when the problem does occur, it is very disruptive or particularly irritating to adults. The impression is then that the child is a continual problem. However, what is really continuous is the adults' worry about the problem.

Duration — observing for 'How much of the day?'

There are some problems which are not easily observed through the frequency count. A child who is very withdrawn or who seems to be a loner, rarely mixing with other children, may be more usefully observed through watching at regular intervals throughout the day. This uses the method of 'time sampling' described earlier in the chapter. Adults will have to decide on what they feel is a realistic schedule of observing, given their other responsibilities.

Example: observation of a child's behaviour at regular intervals

Child's name: Mark   *Age*: 4 years old

Description of the problem
Withdrawn — Mark seems to sit on his own a great deal. He rocks to and fro or sucks his thumb. He doesn't seem to play with other children or even take much notice of them. He doesn't seem to relate to any of the staff here.

Observations

Monday morning, 5 July
10.00   Mark is sitting in an armchair, rocking to and fro. Doesn't seem to be looking at anyone in particular.
10.30   Out in the garden, looking over at children in the sandpit. Janie (staff) holds out her hand to him. Mark ignores her.
11.00   Crying on his own. No obvious reason why he is upset.
11.30   Wandering about the garden. He doesn't seem to be interested in anything.

Tuesday morning, 6 July
10.00   Sitting alone in book corner, sucking his thumb. Andrew (staff) sits down with Mark and points to things in a book. Mark looking at A. Hard to tell if he is listening.
10.30   Crying by the door to the room. Andrew has just gone to fetch our coffee. Mark did not start crying until Andrew had left the room.
11.00   Watching another child painting. Janie says 'Would you like to do a painting?' Mark does not answer but lets Janie guide him to the easel.
11.30   Crying — pushed over accidentally by Daniel. Allows Andrew to comfort him. (Comment — Mark does not cuddle up like so many of the other children would.)

Wednesday afternoon, 7 July
1.30   Standing in the doorway, watching other children in the garden.
2.00   Sitting in the armchair, rocking to and fro.
2.30   Sitting with a rag doll in his lap. Mark is patting the doll but not looking at it.
3.00   Crying. Janie trying to comfort him. Mark will not say what the matter is. Turns away from Janie. Goes across to the rag doll.

Thursday afternoon, 8 July
1.30   Sitting on large wooden truck but not moving it. Looking at children building with bricks.
2.00   Watching Andrew fix up paintings. A lifts Mark up to help with this. Mark touches A's glasses. Looks closely at his face.
2.30   Sitting on truck and seems to be trying to move it.
3.00   Wandering in the garden. Does not seem to have any particular purpose.

The example of Mark, on page 49, shows an observation under-taken because of concern about apparently very withdrawn behaviour. The adults responsible for this boy wanted to see whether their impression of him was typical of most of his day. They decided that someone would be made responsible for noting down what Mark was doing at half-hourly points during the morning and afternoon play sessions. The example gives the observations from two mornings and two afternoons.

The picture of Mark that emerges is of a child who seems to be on his own quite a bit. He is often upset and comforts himself by rocking and thumb-sucking, rather than seeking comfort from adults or a favourite toy. He seemed to be a little more responsive to Andrew, and it might be that Andrew would be the best person to draw Mark out of his shell. Mark showed some interest in the rag doll and the truck. He may be interested in the activities he watches, but he clearly needs coaxing to join in.

In this case, observation of the child has confirmed the impressions of adults and their worries. Sometimes observations will show that the child's behaviour is not as worrying as it at first seemed. Mark, for instance, might have emerged as a quiet child who did not speak to adults but who played in an absorbed way on his own and spoke with other children when the situation was not too noisy. This would be a very different picture and would suggest rather different behaviour from adults.

In Mark's case, the aim was to gain an impression of how typical his withdrawn behaviour was throughout the day. With some problems, it is possible to look at how long each particular incident lasts, given that any difficulty is handled in the usual way by adults. It can be useful to know approximately how long a child's temper tantrum lasts, or for how long she will persist in irritating attention-seeking ploys. The length of time is, of course, a judgement on the part of the adults, since opinions will vary as to when a particular incident is over. This aspect of duration appears in the next example.

Severity — observing for 'How serious is each incident?'

The example of Jane, on pages 51—2, shows an observation of a child which included a frequency count, an estimate of how long each incident lasted, and a judgement of the seriousness of each tantrum.

Jane is not having more than one serious tantrum each day; however, on these occasions she is hard for adults to control. An important point which emerges is that the person doing the observation and her col-league, Letty, do not seem to be consistent in their approach to Jane. This is likely to aggravate the problem. Although Jane has some severe tantrums, the observation suggests that she can sometimes be diverted.

Example: observation of a child including frequency, duration, and severity

Child's name: Jane   *Age*: 4 years old
Description of problem
Temper tantrums — Jane screams and cries loudly when she cannot have her own way. She is very hard to bring round. If she is particularly angry, she will hold her breath for what seems like a very long time.

Observations

Day	Total of tantrums	Duration	Comments on seriousness
Monday 14 Feb.	1	About 20 minutes	Very serious. Jane wanted to go on a shopping trip with Letty (staff), but it wasn't her turn to go. She screamed, swore, and kicked me. I left her in the corner. Several times she became quieter and I glanced across to see if she was ready to join the group. She then started shouting again and drumming her feet.
Tuesday 15 Feb.	2	A few minutes each time	Mild. The two incidents were close together and seemed to be because she could not fit together the new construction toys. I helped her.
Wednesday 16 Feb.	0	—	Jane almost had a tantrum over who was to have the new book first. She took in a breath and held it. I said 'All right, you get on with it' and walked away. She followed me almost immediately and we tidied up the dressing-up clothes together.
Thursday 17 Feb.	1	A few minutes and then at least	I feel the problem here was that Letty tried to punish Jane after I had already

Observations (continued)

Day	Total of tantrums	Duration	Comments on seriousness
		10 minutes	sorted out the problem. (Jane was quarrelling with Martha and Derek about who was to have the tea-set.)
Friday 18 Feb.	1	About 15 minutes	I came back from coffee break to find Jane screaming and Letty shouting. It seemed that Letty had said 'No' to something that I let Jane do. Letty and I must talk!

The results give some suggestions as to where the adults' energies might best be directed.

Concluding remarks on observation of children's behaviour

There is no doubt that observing children's behaviour takes time — however, this is time well spent. The observation of children's spontaneous play can be a very useful source of information, complementing the picture which has emerged from using a developmental guide. Observation of play or of problem behaviour will sometimes confirm adults' initial impressions and will sometimes provide a new insight which implies a readjustment by the adults.

A general advantage of making this sort of observation, at least a few times, is that the experience can sharpen an adult's powers of observation. Once adults have seen what can be learned from carefully watching a child or group, they often become more alert when not making any particular observations. The discipline of observation seems to remind adults of just how much is happening during an ordinary day. Observing a child who is experienced by adults as a problem often provides a jolt to adults' belief that they know all about this child's behaviour. This type of observation can also help adults to feel more in control of the situation, since the information provides some basis for planning what to do with the child. Parts 2 and 3 of this book include many practical suggestions which can be part of plans for working with children such as those in the examples in this chapter.

5
SHARING RECORDS AND OBSERVATIONS WITH PARENTS

Who should see your written records?

So far, in looking at the practicalities of how you might go about making observations and keeping records on children, the discussion has focused on the person who is completing the observation. There is, of course, the question of who else — if anyone — should see the written material.

Records, such as developmental guides or the observations made of children's behaviour, are written reports about individual children and need to be taken seriously. They have a 'life' of their own, partly independent of the person who has completed them. Staff may agree that records of this kind should be regarded as confidential material — but confidential to whom?

In any establishment or centre, you need to think about, discuss, and come to a policy decision to address the following two questions:

i) What is the 'active life' of records on individual children? At what point should the records be destroyed? Does written material such as developmental guides have a different 'active life' to other material?
ii) Who should be able to look at the written material on individual children in the nursery?

- All the staff in the nursery?
- Other professionals supporting the work of the nursery?
- Professionals from other establishments that the child attends after leaving the nursery?
- Students on placement at the nursery?
- The parents of the individual child?

Both these questions deserve thorough discussion, leading to a clear-cut policy understood by all staff. However, arguably the most critical question — which stirs up very strong feelings — is whether parents should be able to see observations and other kinds of written material on their own children. 'Parents' was placed at the end of the above list deliberately. Until recently, it seemed that parents were the 'last' group in the minds of many pre-school and school staff. Children come equipped with parents, yet it is only relatively recently that the justification for holding records that are closed to parents has been seriously questioned. Whether written material on children should be easily accessible to their parents is now being asked for two reasons. Firstly, there has been a tremendous development in talk and action in the area of parent involvement (part 4 covers this in detail), and parents' involvement in assessments or observations of their children is one of the topics that arise. However, the question of access has also been put forcibly because of a more general concern for people's rights of access to information about them. As parents are responsible for their own children, it is they, rather than their children, who are having (or do not have) this right of access.

'Do I have to share my records with parents?'

The simple answer to this is that it depends on where you work. It is something you have to find out. In the three broad areas of employment — education, social services, and medical services — at the time of writing (early 1987) there is no across-the-board directive in any of these areas that says that you must, or you must not, make records on children available to parents. However, there are developments of which you need to be aware.

The Education Act 1981 gave to parents of children with special needs the right to contribute to formal assessments and to see reports provided as part of the assessment. Sheila Wolfendale* points out that, in practice, this works very differently in different local education authorities.

There is no equivalent legislation affecting children in schools as a whole. Individual local education authorities can adopt a policy of open access, but only some half-dozen UK LEAs have done this. In facilities run by social services departments, policy is again set at local level and sometimes at the level of individual establishments. The DHSS sent out guidance on access to records to local authorities in a 1983 Circular (14/83), but this was *not* a directive. Medical records are by tradition closed to 'patients' and, currently, any variations from this are rare local initiatives (see, for example, Aiden McFarlane's report of his work in Oxfordshire, in *Concern*, number 58, Spring 1986). If you are working for organisations that do not fall neatly into mainstream education, social, or medical services, you will need to check not only whether there is any overall policy on access but also how this is put into practice.

Whatever the exact practice, one feature is consistent in access to records: you can choose to make accessible to parents only the material that you have produced in your own establishment (or service). Other information ('third-party' information) cannot be placed in an open file

*Sheila Wolfendale, *Parental participation in children's development and education*, published in 1983 by Gordon & Breach Science Publishers.

without checking with the other 'parties' who originally produced it, and they have the right to keep their records out of your open file if they so choose.

'If we don't have to share our records, why should we?'

There are several arguments in favour of written records on children being both open and easily accessible to the parents of those children. These are:

a) Parents have long-term responsibility for the well-being of their children. They have a right to share in the perspectives and opinions of other adults who *temporarily* share that responsibility.

b) The vast majority of parents are very interested in their own children. It is very likely they will be interested in observations. Apart from interest, there may be information that will be helpful to them in handling their child or making decisions about their child.

c) It is possible that records may have factual errors that parents could correct. For example, it is not unknown for a mistake to be made in writing down a child's date of birth.

d) When records are open to parents, it increases the possibilities of exchange of information, views, and ideas between the adults responsible for the same child. People can learn from each other.

e) While files are closed to parents, there is an opportunity for others to write down unsupported opinions and offhand remarks as if they are facts.

f) The very existence of closed files makes parents suspicious that something uncomplimentary has been written about themselves or their child. The same is true if parents have to give warning before they are allowed to look at their child's file — this raises the suspicion that material will be removed from the file. Hopefully, in most cases, there is nothing offensive in these written records, but. . . .

The reasons given for keeping files closed to parents tend to cluster around the anxieties of staff and their expectations of likely negative reactions from parents. Staff worry that parents may be annoyed by what they read in records, will disagree, or will not understand what has been written. Staff seem to expect difficulties more often than the opportunity of positive gain from sharing with parents. In my experience, this is an unrealistically gloomy view. I have worked with a number of under-fives centres that have moved to open access. It has been rare for any parent to get angry: it has been more usual that parents are interested and are relieved that they now have access. Open access shows respect for parents, and it can be an encouragement to work with under-fives staff rather than feeling excluded. Parents can be involved in the completion of developmental guides or other observations. In my experience, this can lead to useful conversations about the different pictures emerging of a child at nursery or playgroup and at home. In short, I have found that the benefits of open access far outweigh any disadvantages.

'If parents can read my records, won't that change how I write them?'

The straight answer to this is 'Yes, it probably will.' However, it will not be helpful if you feel obliged to be tactful to the point of not saying anything of substance. I have found that knowing that a parent can read your observations or reports does make you think hard about *how* you write your comments about a child. However, the end result can be an improved report, not a censored statement of just the 'nice' things. What follows are some practical suggestions that I think should guide any report-writing, whether parents are likely to read the material or not!

GUIDE-LINES FOR COMPLETING REPORTS ON CHILDREN

Putting opinions in their rightful place

Some people say that opinions should not be written in reports. I do not agree. The opinions of an adult spending time responsible for a child are valuable, because they should be rooted in knowledge of that individual child. However, they need to be presented as opinions and not as universally agreed facts. This means writing (or saying) 'I think that . . .', 'I feel that . . .', 'I am worried about . . .', 'I am pleased about. . .'. It means being prepared to sign what you write (and date it, since this will be useful information later, to see whether a child has changed). The key point is: if you are not prepared to take personal responsibility for your opinions about a child, expecting that the child's parents will read your comments, have you any business writing them down in the first place?

Give reasons for your opinions

You need to explain how you have reached a particular opinion. You will have reasons — based in your day-by-day experience of an individual child and your broader knowledge of an age range of children. It is not a question of building up a defence case: it is a sharing of your observing and thinking. If you are yourself uncertain, if you have a 'gut feeling' about a child, it is your responsibility to identify the sources of this feeling so that you can explain it to another adult — parent or staff colleague. If parents can understand how you have reached your opinion, then a discussion is possible. Since parents' experience of their own child will be different in some ways from your experience, they have an opportunity to express a different opinion. There does not have to be an argument.

If you take responsibility for your opinions and support them by describing what leads you to hold those opinions, you are unlikely to write bald unhelpful judgements. If you are expecting that the child's parents will read what you have written, you are unlikely to write unsupported negative comments about the child or parents which could be seen as biased or unfair. However, neither are bald positive judgements necessarily helpful. It may seem pleasant for a parent to read 'I think that Carol is a bright child'; however, without the supporting reasons — how you come to this view — nobody will know if your opinion is a reasonable description of Carol or not.

Stick to what you have observed — don't generalise beyond this

This means remaining specific to what you have experienced of a child and not generalising — either in a positive or in a negative way. You can observe and comment on a child's behaviour when she is with you, but this does not give you a basis to generalise to that child's personality (this point is taken up also in chapter 11), nor can you assume that the child necessarily behaves in the same way in other settings. So, it is better to write (or say) 'Jamie seems to be much shorter on patience in the mornings' than to generalise to 'Jamie is a short-tempered child.' It is better to write (or say) 'Debbie really seems to enjoy helping me with the baby and that makes it enjoyable for me too . . .' rather than 'Debbie is always such a helpful child'. Debbie may be very different in other settings — children who are quick to offer help in nursery sometimes give their parents a very hard time at home. The more descriptive detail you can share with parents, the more they will be able to understand under what circumstances their child behaves in a particular way.

Present your observations as descriptions — don't seek to lay blame

You may have opinions about what is making matters worse or better for a child. You may have reached some conclusions about cause and effect. However, this is guesswork. Where you judge there is a problem, you may be tempted to find fault with the parent. However, if you express this in a blaming way, it will not encourage the parent to do much other than to blame you back. You will have much more chance of a discussion if you comment (in a descriptive way) 'Damian seems to settle better on those days when his mum is able to stay with him for a few minutes' rather than 'He's upset because his mum won't stay to settle him' (which is blaming his mother).

Be provisional — yours is one opinion among many

This means expressing an opinion (for reasons) which leaves space for other people's opinions. You are not a 100% expert; you could be wrong. There will always be aspects of a child's life about which you are ignorant. It is better to write (or say) 'Perhaps Sandy needs more . . .' or 'I think that maybe . . .', rather than 'Nicholas should have . . .' or 'If only Winston had. . .'.

See yourself as equal with parents rather than expert over them

Both you and the child's parents will bring different packages of knowledge and expertise to your discussion about the child. You need to respect, although not necessarily agree with, each others' views. This means writing (or saying) 'In the nursery, Abigail often gets upset when I suggest she tries something in a different way. I wonder if she is like this with you at home.' In a similar vein, you might comment 'I have found that if I stick to what I've told Andy to do, he stops arguing fairly soon. What do you find works best at home?'

Focus on what is going on rather than why

Reasons (the 'why's) may well emerge through discussion about an individual child. However, as a starting point, 'Why doesn't Michelle pay attention?' is likely to put parents on the defensive. A starter like 'What do you find best to get Michelle to pay attention?' focuses on the behaviour and asks for the expertise of parents. Other good starters include 'What do you think is going on in his mind?', 'What sense do you make of it when he. . .'. These ask for description, step aside from any issues of blame, and acknowledge that parents can have ideas to contribute.

To sum up . . .

These points do *not* mean saying essentially the same thing as before open access but in flowery language. From the same starting point of your knowledge of an individual child, you can give a more or less constructive message depending on how you make your comments. There is no magic solution that will ensure that no parent is ever upset or confused by what you write (or say). These practical guide-lines will, however, increase the chances of your making comments about an individual child that are likely to be helpful feedback to parents and, as a result, encourage a discussion rather than an argument. The ideas are adapted from the area of communication skills known as *feedback*, which is the sensitive sharing of information by taking account of the reaction of the person on the receiving end.

A key principle of constructive feedback is that *feedback should be helpful to the person on the receiving end.*

This is true of any kind of information given as feedback, not just information to parents about their own child. All the suggestions made so far add up to three major points to bear in mind if you want to give parents useful feedback. *For feedback to be helpful to parents, the information must be given in such a way that*

- parents can understand the information,
- parents are able to accept the information,
- parents are able to do something about the information.

This means applying these suggestions to what you write or say. It means taking a cool look at the language that you use in conversation or in written reports. Most professions have a shared professional language, and some words and phrases are used so often that people forget that the rest of the adult world does not talk like that. If you create a more conversational atmosphere with parents, they will feel more comfortable to ask sometimes 'What do you mean by that?' (The need to become aware of your own professional language is discussed in the context of communication skills in chapter 15.)

As far as I can gather, parents whose young children are in some type of pre-school provision are more likely *not* to have access to records on their children than to be given access. Parents of children with special needs have a right of access, but often a system exists which makes that access difficult. I hope that readers who are part of an open-access system, or developing access, will find the suggestions of this chapter helpful. Readers who work for establishments or local authorities where files are closed can effectively use the suggestions to develop more constructive conversations with parents — this can be a very positive move in developing friendly and mutually beneficial relations. Because it is such an important area, feedback is also discussed in part 4, on working together as the adults in children's lives.

PART 2
LANGUAGE DEVELOPMENT – CHILDREN LEARNING AND ADULTS HELPING

6
STAGES IN LANGUAGE DEVELOPMENT DURING THE FIRST FIVE YEARS

So often when people discuss language development, the emphasis is almost exclusively on the spoken word. Likewise when adults are looking at the toddler age group, the question is so often 'Does she talk yet?' The first words are a significant milestone in the same way as the first smile and those first tottering steps of a baby learning to walk. However, in the same way that much learning goes on before the first smile or the first steps, so a great deal happens — and can be seen to happen — before those first recognisable words. It is for this reason that language development is more usefully seen within the general context of communication, in terms of both children's learning and the extent to which adults are helping this learning.

An essential basis of adults' helping is an awareness of the stages through which children usually pass in their language development. Of course, not all children will pass through the stages at the same age — there will be variation in language development as in other areas of development — however, even experienced adults need to remind themselves of what are reasonable expectations of children of different ages. This becomes especially important when working with a group of children who are very delayed or particularly advanced — the adults' expectations can become subtly shifted until the group with whom they spend most of their time becomes the comparison point for children in general.

This chapter looks at some of the major changes that happen in the development of children's language. Firstly, however, it is valuable to look at some basic distinctions in describing the growth of language.

The difference between speech and understanding of speech

The growing ability to understand the speech of others is as important as learning to speak. Young children with few or no words of their own, or very shy children who cannot bring themselves to talk, can still show that they understand information or instructions through their behaviour. When testing children's language, it is possible to look at their understanding separately from their ability to use words. This understanding is sometimes called comprehension or *receptive language*.

The words children produce themselves constitute their speech or *expressive language*.
The clarity of children's speech — how they speak — is called *articulation*. A child may therefore be said to have clear articulation, or poor articulation, or problems in articulating certain sounds.

The sounds before the words

Before children produce recognisable words, they will produce sounds which become steadily more varied and deliberate. When babies have progressed to making repetitive and really rather tuneful strings of sounds, this is referred to as *babbling*. Many children, before speaking recognisable words, pass through a stage of producing *jargon*. The sounds they are making are varied and have a conversational tone, but there are very few, if any, words in the stream of sound. This is the stage at which adults may feel sure that a child has said words but they cannot work out what those words were. A child's sound-making moves steadily towards real words because adults, and perhaps older children, take the baby's sound-making seriously and respond.

SOME IMPORTANT EVENTS IN LANGUAGE DEVELOPMENT OF THE UNDER-FIVES

The aim in this chapter is not to give a lengthy account of the stages of language development — it is assumed that readers will have knowledge in this area and some favourite books to which they can turn for a reminder of detailed information. The aim is rather to point to some of the major events for which adults are watching, as a companion to the discussion of common problems that follows in chapter 8.

Babies in their first year of life

Some babies will produce a real word before their first birthday, some will produce a sound which fortunately is similar to 'mama' or 'dada', and many will produce little that can be genuinely claimed as a word. The first year of life is the time to watch out for and encourage the building blocks which will form the basis of the child's language. It is a time when important developments are unfolding which are of a 'pre-language' nature.

With very young babies, their immediate state of alertness or sleepiness, hunger, or discomfort influences strongly how they react. Individual differences in overall responsiveness can also be seen. Nevertheless, by about three months of age babies are usually responsive to voices and curious about the source of voices and sounds. When a three-month-old is alert and content, she will be producing a variety of happy sounds if — and this is an important 'if' — her early attempts at smiling and sound-making have met with positive responses from adults or older children. Babies do not make a range of sounds other than crying unless people in their surroundings have been encouraging — have given the babies time, looked at them and talked with them. Three-month-old babies who have had this sort of attention can usually manage a range of sounds and trills of linked sounds which they clearly enjoy making. They will vocalise — make sounds — in response to adults or other children, and it is sometimes possible to see the beginnings of attempts to imitate the sounds and mouth movements made by adults. The exchanges between a baby and one other person at a time have the quality of conversations, if the baby is given time to reply. The baby will often stare intently at the face of the adult, enjoying these exchanges of sounds. Babies who have discovered enjoyment in sounds often vocalise when they are alone or may develop a favourite toy to whom they 'talk'.

In the months leading up to their first birthday, babies learn many skills which will build the basis for their language. They learn to listen to the extent that they can distinguish familiar from unfamiliar voices. They show through their behaviour that they understand some of the different emotional overtones to what is said to them, such as playful chatter or a warning not to do something. With encouragement, the sounds that babies themselves make become more varied and more expressive. By about nine months of age, there are usually clear signs that babies have grasped that making sounds can bring about some action from others. This important understanding about the usefulness of making sounds can be seen in the deliberate way in which a nine-month-old baby will pause after her chatter to see if the attention, the reply, or the object she wanted will result.

By about one year old, or slightly afterwards, children will often show through their behaviour that they understand a few familiar words in context, or can follow very simple requests, supported by adult gestures. Children will be responding to and learning from all the non-verbal hints which are part of adults' language behaviour. At this point, some adults start to claim 'She understands everything you say to her.' However, at this age, and for some time to come, a more accurate view would be that she understands a growing amount of what you say and a considerable amount of what you do.

The second year of life

Between one and two years of age, most children make noticeable strides in the skills of speech and understanding. They show a steadily broadening understanding of single words and of simple instructions. Usually this level of understanding outstrips the number of words they themselves use. Children of this age often understand a few key words rather than every word in sentences spoken to them. Their making sense of more complex speech is supported by the non-verbal clues and their memory of routine events — where their shoes are usually kept, for example — or by what is the usual relationship between two objects, such as toys being replaced in the toy-box and not underneath it. By such means, children of this age fill in the gaps between the parts they understand.

Children's own sound-making becomes very varied and, at some point, sounds appear which are clear attempts to produce words and these are used reliably for the same object, person, or need. These first words are often hard for a stranger to understand and may be part of a stream of jargon. However, what should be accompanying the growth of words is the belief by the child that other children and adults ought to understand her. The words and jargon are pronounced with growing confidence, supported with gestures and expressive changes in her face. These say clearly to the other person 'Don't you agree?' or, with growing frustration, 'I've told you what I want — why don't you do something about it?'

Children during this period will be showing the beginnings of spoken exchanges with adults, in that they will listen to words spoken directly to them and will attempt to reply with words and jargon of their own. It is not unusual for them to repeat, in an echoing way, the last or most prominent word in the sentence they have just heard. Perhaps the child is practising words or giving herself a breathing space before replying. Such echoing is not a problem at this age unless adults make it into one.

By two years of age, children should have grasped that words for familiar objects in their lives are also used for the same object when it appears in a picture or as a small doll's-house-size object. This is obvious to adults, who have lived with the knowledge for a long time, but children have to learn that the picture of a banana is called by that name, although this banana is flat and cannot be eaten. Likewise, the doll's-house-size chair is also called by that name, although the child herself cannot sit on it.

The age at which a child's first words and then first word combinations appear varies a great deal. However, adults should be looking for clear signs that some language development is happening by two years of age. By this time, many children will have a large number of recognisable words, although not necessarily pronounced clearly in the adult way. They will also be combining two words in a simple and often ungrammatical fashion. This might be a combination of the child's own name

The words will soon follow for ideas learned through play. ▶

with her possessions or the word for something she wants. It may be a combination of a key word such as 'more' or 'gone' with other words. The child will probably also have a stock way of asking for more information — 'What's that?' or 'What's this?'

Children of two years, and slightly older, often ask the names of the same objects or people again and again. This may be partly because they forget the answer, but often the next repeat of the child's question is coming almost before the adult's answer is completed. It looks more as if the child is enjoying having the adult's attention and is also enjoying the skill of being able to ask a question. By adulthood, we tend to see language as our means to a specific end, such as getting a reply to our question, expressing emotions, or enjoying a good conversation. However, young children seem to enjoy the sheer use and practice of what they are able to say. Just as they delight in leaping and running about without seeming to go anywhere in particular, so they seem to enjoy the flexing of their language muscles without this always getting them somewhere from an adult's viewpoint.

From two to three years old

In this year of life, children's speech and understanding should be clearly advancing. As they move from two to two-and-a-half years old, a lack of development in language would be a cause for concern, however well the child was progressing in other areas of development.

The number of words a child learns during this period should make it a time-consuming task to compile a full list. Her words should be appearing in short phrases and simple sentences. However, there will be many grammatical mistakes in comparison with adult speech. The flow of the child's speech, although improving, is likely to be of a stop—start nature, as the child searches for the words and ways of explaining what she wants to express. A child's wish to communicate can outstrip her available speech and sometimes lead to a form of stuttering. Like the echoing of words, which is still not unusual at this age, this falling over words in eagerness and the stopping and starting of children's speech will usually improve over time, unless adults, or perhaps scornful older children, turn it into a problem.

Children's ability to understand the speech of others should also be improving, although there will still be many gaps. Their understanding of instructions or comments to do with danger, with sharing, or with past and future time is still very limited. They are likely to be confused by two-part instructions of the 'Do this and then do that' variety or promises and explanations based on 'If . . . then' relationships ('If you eat your cabbage, then you can have a biscuit').

If adults have made storytime and singing enjoyable activities, children will be showing an increasing interest and ability to join in, and a willingness sometimes to perform themselves. Like any of the other developments, this type of interest does not appear out of the blue. The enjoyment will develop because in the preceeding months someone — most probably an adult — has made books or songs a pleasurable activity and one in which the younger child has had the full attention of that adult.

During this period, a child's play — particularly her developing make-believe play — will both reflect her growing language ability and be a spur to her trying hard to express what she wants. The conversations she has with herself in play should gradually become more intelligible to the listening adult. If her previous experience has encouraged this belief, the child of this age should be seeing adults as people who will answer her questions, will listen to her comments, and will help her out when her language does not stretch to the ideas and experiences she wants to relate.

From three to four years old

Three-year-olds will normally be expressing themselves through speech that varies in loudness and pitch, so giving an expressiveness that is closer to the speech of older children and adults. They should have a large vocabulary — in excess of 200 words. Their speech should be largely understandable to a stranger who is a local adult — one who speaks with a similar accent to the child. Three-year-olds should be capable of carrying on simple conversations, although they are likely to make mistakes in comparison with adult grammar and still to have some difficulties in pronouncing some sounds. Their conversation is also likely to have more of a stop—start quality than the conversation of older children or adults. Much of the conversation will be about the present, since three-year-olds' understanding of past and future is limited.

Three-year-olds' understanding of others' language should be clearly advancing. They may well be able to follow a simple double instruction — remembering the first part while listening to the second. With the encouragement of adults, a more abstract level of understanding will be developing. The three-year-old should have advanced beyond recognising the names of objects to being able to identify familiar objects by use ('Which one do we drink from?') to relating two or more objects together in simple relationships (putting one object 'in', 'on', or 'under' a second) and, as they approach four years of age, to being able to use words to describe a familiar object or event which is not present at the time ('What's an apple?' or perhaps 'What does shopping mean?').

Three-year-olds will be at various stages in understanding the abstract concepts that combine thinking, looking, and use of words. They may be able to count up to ten, but there will probably be little understanding of number beyond two or three — the child has learned the list of numbers much as she learned the words of rhymes. There may be some under-standing of colour and some confident use of colour labels. However, although some three-year-olds may be reliably identifying colours, others will still be tentatively linking colour names with differences they can distinguish by visual matching.

From four to five years old

The speech of four-year-olds should be largely correct when compared with the grammar of the adults from whom they have learned. Some problems in pronouncing certain sounds are not unusual at this age. Four-year-olds should have developed the ability to use their speech to many different ends, if adults have encouraged this by their attention. Children of this age should be able to give a reasonably connected description of recent events and to talk about the past and future, although not necessarily with the same time perspective as adults. They should be able to use words to recount stories, although again the distinction they draw between fact and fantasy is not necessarily that of adults. A sense of humour based on words has often developed. Children will have found certain events, actions, or pictures funny for a long time — however, four-year-olds have usually developed the ability to follow and tell simple jokes and plays on words, where the amusement depends on what is said or how it is said.

The questions of a four-year-old can become very challenging to adults who try to give a reasonable answer, rather than brush off the child's curiosity. Adults have to think hard to answer questions like 'Why does wood float?' or 'What makes car wheels go round?' Some children will also be asking the meaning of words that are new to them. They should be able to give some answer to abstract questions such as 'What is a ball?' or 'What does "cold" mean?' The progress in memory and think-ing, linked with speech, should enable four-year-olds definitely to talk about objects or events which are not immediately in front of them. This should show through their conversation.

As children approach five years of age, their understanding of abstract concepts of number, colour, size, speed, or time is progressing but will still show many gaps when compared with the understanding of an older child or an adult. Adults will remain important as the ones to identify the point at which the child's understanding breaks down.

In terms of a child's speech, several general developments can be seen in the late pre-school and early school years. For instance, by four to five years of age, children's conversations to themselves in play are becoming internalised — the conversation or experimenting with ideas is taking place inside the child's head and she does not have always to speak out loud. However, much of the enjoyment in imaginative play comes from speaking the fantasy roles. Furthermore, a child will probably still talk herself through a difficult or new task, just as adults sometimes mutter out loud when they are grappling with something challenging.

Children who have a broad experience of language also have a growing vocabulary — both of everyday words and of less usual words which arise from their special interests. As well as knowing and being able to use a large number of words, the older child should show confidence in using speech in many different ways. This aspect to language development is discussed in chapter 9.

By the time the child starts infant school, the ability to communicate through spoken language has advanced incredibly compared with the abilities of the young baby. Children's understanding is sophisticated, although they will not understand all the concepts that an adult or an older child will manage. If development has not gone normally, the child's language may be delayed in comparison to the average, or may have problems which need some specific help. However, if all has progressed well, five-year-olds should see language as a method of communication and as a source of enjoyment in its own right, and as the way to make contact with adults and children. They may also take pleasure in teaching the young baby who is at the very beginnings of the same process that they passed through not so very long ago.

7
LOOKING AT HOW CHILDREN LEARN

Chapters 8 and 9 include many suggestions for practical approaches to problems in language development and to encouraging further development in a child who is already progressing well for her age. Important to many of these ideas and general approaches are common themes to what appears to make learning for children (or for adults) easier and more enjoyable. These general themes are not relevant only to language development: they are applicable to all of the ways in which children learn the many skills they are attempting to master in their first five years and beyond. Several major themes are summarised in this chapter.

Help from adults

Children undoubtedly learn a great deal from each other. However, other children do not substitute for adults in the help needed in learning. This is especially true when children are delayed in their development or are having to tackle a major task, such as learning English as a second language. It is unrealistic to expect that placing such children with others who are speaking well will lead to some rub-off effect, without additional adult help.

There are several reasons for this. Children do not usually have the patience or the ability to repeat something in a different or simpler way for a child who is experiencing difficulty in understanding. They are often too close in age and level of development to be able to grasp what it is that the other child does not understand — this can be difficult for an adult, and adults can usually stand back rather more than a child is able to. Although children enjoy helping each other on occasion, this teaching tends to end when either party has become bored, rather than when the child being taught has actually grasped something new. Adults are more likely to have the patience to continue. It is the role of adults to persevere when a child is having difficulties, to provide some continuity in how the learning takes place, and to strike the difficult balance between providing a child with the answer and encouraging her to find it herself. Adults can make a great deal of difference to a child's language development by being aware of the language they are using themselves and the quality of attention they are giving the child.

Verbal and non-verbal communication

As adults, we send many messages which are not spoken. Our bodies — especially our faces — express a great deal about our feelings. The way we say something often communicates as much as the words themselves. Sometimes the message which is given by the words is not the same as that which is communicated by gesture, body posture, or facial expression. Young children are not particularly skilled at hiding their own unspoken messages. However, they do become sensitive to the unspoken messages from adults — the words that say 'Leave that alone!' and the tone of voice and tired face that say just as loudly 'I really haven't got the energy to keep stopping you.' Adults need to be aware of how much the child learns through facial expression, gestures, or the direction in which the eyes are looking. For instance, adults look and behave very differently when they say 'No' as a command meaning 'Stop, or else!' and when they are pretending to be overwhelmed by a child who is tickling them and are saying 'No, no, stop it' in mock fear. This non-verbal communication is an important source of information to children. A request such as 'Put the paper in the rubbish bin' is usually supported by the adult pointing or gesturing so that a younger child is helped to understand. When trying to judge how much a child is understanding of the words alone, then it is important to reduce all the non-verbal clues to a minimum. However, in the normal course of events, these clues are a major part of a child's learning from adults.

Attention and language

Communication is an exchange between two or more individuals. For the communication to take place, these individuals have to pay attention. A person who is talking needs to watch the people listening, in order to judge their reactions. The listeners need to attend to the words and the unspoken messages. The reason why communication is often so poor between adults is that this attention — the listening and the looking — is so variable. Perhaps it is not surprising that some adults do not attend well to children.

Some adults expect children to attend to them — this is seen in terms of 'good' behaviour — but are poor at giving those same children their own adult attention when a child wants to talk. A child who has not had the respect of an adult's attention is less likely to learn to attend well in her turn.

Attention is an *active* awareness of what is happening. It involves listening and looking. Both of these are important in a child's learning. Sometimes children who are having difficulties in language development have not learned to attend well. They are then losing a lot of information, as well as probably irritating the adults around them. Often the best way to help such children is to work directly on their ability to attend. This is discussed in chapter 8.

Learning is active

Learning is an active process and it is done by the learner. This is as true of adults as it is of children. You cannot *make* a child learn any more than you can *make* an adult learn. You can only provide the best situation possible and what seems to be the most appropriate encouragement. You can teach a child but you cannot learn a child — the child does the learning. This does not mean that it is necessarily the child's fault if she does not learn — people or circumstances may be blocking her most determined efforts.

Praise, rewards, and encouragement

As a culture, we are often unthinkingly miserly about making the effort to say to other people that they have done well. This is as true between adults as between adults and children. Most adults have thought at some time 'Why is it that I get nagged when things go wrong, but nobody says "Well done" or "Thank you" when everything has gone really smoothly?' An honest look at ourselves can help to identify whether this imbalance can be seen in our relationships with children.

Many people use 'praise' and 'encouragement' as interchangeable words. However, they are different and looking at the differences gives a further perspective on how adults can help children to learn. The emphasis on encouragement, as opposed to praise, comes from developments of the school of psychology started by Alfred Adler. There are books which discuss these ideas in more detail than will be covered here.* The importance of encouragement is also discussed in chapters 11 and 12, in the context of the behaviour of young children.

Encouragement for children is concerned both with what the adults do or say and also with their attitude towards children. It is possible to be overall encouraging or discouraging, and spoken praise along the lines of 'Good boy' or 'That's clever' will not offset a discouraging atmosphere created by adults. The positives in adults' behaviour with children are usually a mixture of praise, rewards, and encouragements.

---

*Two books which describe these ideas are D. Dinkmeyer and R. Dreikurs, *Encouraging children to learn: the encouragement process* — published in 1963 by Prentice-Hall Inc., New Jersey — and R. Dreikurs and V. Soltz, *Happy children*, published in 1970 by Souvenir Press and in 1972 as a Fontana paperback.

Rewards involve some definite event or something tangible given to the child. This may be allowing the child to do some favourite activity, planning a special outing, or giving the child a gift of some kind. Rewards can be used as incentives. This means that the promise of a reward is offered 'if' the child does something in particular now. Rewards, and rewards as incentives, have their place in dealing with children, especially if they are not built up to be such significant events that the child is resentful on days when no rewards are forthcoming. Children who are learning new skills are often provided with that additional bit of motivation by something extra which an adult sensitively builds into the learning situation. Children who are slow in learning to walk may try to totter a few more steps to an adult who greets the child with an excited hug and a swing around. Children struggling to learn to unscrew a jar may be motivated to try harder in order to reach an attractive toy inside.

The advantages to using encouragement

Praise and encouragement are the two positives that are sometimes hard to distinguish. In describing the differences, I am indebted to some unpublished material by Tim Smithells, a child psychologist trained in the Adlerian tradition.

Generally speaking, spoken praise — rather like using rewards — emphasises the child. Encouragement tends to emphasise what the child is doing. An encouraging remark on a child's activity would be 'Well done!', whereas praise would be 'What a clever boy!' Such praise tends to be for actual achievement, for the finished performance.

Children tend to be praised after they have completed something, after they have pleased an adult or 'been good'. Encouragement tends to stress enjoyment and effort or qualities like the helpfulness, patience, or considerateness of an action. Encouragement is used to help a child try out new activities and to persevere when she is finding something difficult, or when she is beginning to fail. So children may be praised with 'That's a lovely drawing', whereas encouragement would be used when efforts were flagging — 'You've done really well so far. I'm sure you can manage this. Let's try it this way.'

There are times for praise, especially when it is genuine and used sparingly. The risks of praise are that, as it is a spoken reward, the child's view of herself can vary with how much praise she receives. In this way the child learns to feel that her value goes up and down, depending on whether she is praised or not — today she had four 'good girl's but yesterday she did not have any, so the implication is that yesterday she was not as 'good' as today. In fact, the child needs to learn that her value is unchanging — she is always liked or always loved. Being encouraging by saying 'Thank you for your help. That made a real difference to me' is giving appreciation for a particular happening. Saying 'You're such a helpful girl' or 'What a tidy little girl' carries the implication for the child that she may be less valued when she is not helpful or not tidy.

Because praise emphasises the end product — the successful completion of something — children can come to feel that there is no point in trying something unless they can do it 'properly'. Depending on praise alone to help children to learn runs the risk of their not trying when they doubt their chances of success. It can also increase the chances of children not enjoying the activity, only trying to finish it to reach the end product which receives the praise. Adults need to realise, with older children as well as with under-fives, that genuine encouragement and recognition of effort have to be given for children eventually to hazard themselves in something new and achieve within their own limitations. Insincere and faint encouragement of the kind 'I can see you've tried, but . . .' is truly discouraging.

It is well worthwhile looking at how to replace some of the remarks which are praise with encouraging remarks. This also implies looking for opportunities to encourage in the normal course of events. Praise such as 'Good boy' or 'Clever girl' can be replaced with 'Well done', which can be said enthusiastically during or after an activity and recognises effort, not necessarily followed by success. Often, instead of 'Well done', remarks like 'That's the way' or 'That's fine' are equally encouraging. Remarks that comment on effort can help to signal to a child that you recognise how hard she tried, whether or not she succeeded — 'I can see the hard work you put into that.' During an activity, remarks like 'Keep trying — I'm sure you can do it' can help a child to try again, especially if supported by a friendly adult presence and specific help or suggestions if needed. Adults can point out improvements to the child with remarks like 'That's much better' or 'That's coming on really well.'

Punishment and learning

Punishment is a very inefficient way to help anyone to learn. This is true of both physical punishment and spoken — by criticism, nagging, or harping on a child's or adult's failings. Children who are punished for not learning do sometimes still learn, but the process is being made more difficult and much less enjoyable than if they are encouraged in their trying and given credit for their achievements.

A little bit of thinking about your own experience during childhood or adulthood may highlight this. Anyone who is nagged about mistakes often becomes so anxious about the whole business that the anxiety blocks any chance of learning. The fear of failure becomes stronger than any wish to master the new skill. If the situation becomes really stressful, the child or adult is almost paralysed with the worry and can appear stupid, uncooperative, or inattentive to the adult who has actually caused these feelings. For example, if someone teaching you to play the piano is impatient, harps on your mistakes, and shouts at you, it can become almost impossible to play even the music that you have mastered.

Learning through play

The phrase 'learning through play' occurs regularly in the language of adults who work with young children. Because so many of us use this phrase, it can be easy to assume that everybody believes that play is a workable route to learning. This is not the case — some parents, for example, are doubtful that children are learning identifiable skills through the play the parents see in nurseries or playgroups. This may be because staff are not explaining clearly to parents the changes they hope to encourage in individual children, but the parents' doubts may sometimes be well-founded. I have worked with some staff groups whose way of putting into practice the 'learning-through-play' philosophy ignored many of this chapter's key points about the process of learning. An effective use of learning through play will certainly not allow adults to sit back uninvolved.

Appropriate play materials for learning

A child needs play materials that involve activities which are sufficiently challenging to stretch her but not so difficult that the leap from her present abilities to the new skill is too great. Children, like adults, learn both by practising something familiar and by trying something different or slightly difficult.

Variety in play materials is helpful but is not an end in itself. There are times when what a child needs to have available is precisely the equipment she had yesterday. A variety in play materials appropriate to a particular skill or concept is important if a child is having difficulty in learning this. She may become bored and frustrated with the same toys, especially since she links them in her mind with *not* being able to do something.

Choice of appropriate play materials may be different with children with special needs. Children who have a specific handicap which restricts their development may have even more need of an adult who provides variety through different play materials geared to the same learning task. These children may spend much time at each stage of development and will get bored with the same old play activities. This need can stretch the creativity of the adults. The Human Horizons series of books (published by Souvenir Press) provides a source of play ideas to add to a repertoire which may be creaking under the strain. *Let me play* by Roy McConkey and Penny Price (1986) and *Let me speak* by Dorothy M. Jeffree and Roy McConkey (1976) are from this series.

The phrase 'children with special needs' also covers children whose development is very advanced compared with norms for their age — so-called 'gifted' or 'exceptional' children. Finding appropriate play materials for these children can be equally challenging. Adults will need to familiarise themselves with materials usually associated with much older children. They may also need to accept that if a 'gifted' child is developing a special interest or aptitude then the usual roles may well be reversed and the adult will be the learner.

Children's learning is helped if the materials available — toys, outdoor environment, everyday objects — are appropriate to their interest as well as to their ability level. Children's attention will be held longer by activities which interest them. A child who is absorbed by toy cars and lorries may not want to draw paintings on an easel. She may, however, be very interested to mark out a town and a system of roads for her cars. Recognising this requires observation and sensitivity on the part of an adult. It does not mean that a child with a very narrow range of interests should be left with that narrowness. It does mean that it is common sense to *build* on the interests a child already has.

When under-fives workers have become committed to a philosophy of 'learning through play', there is a risk of this becoming as exclusive an outlook as the philosophy that is voiced as 'The children can't possibly be learning, they're just playing.' The child-oriented environment of the nursery or playgroup may effectively limit appropriate resources for learning by removing children from many domestic activities. An exchange between me and my six-year-old son highlighted children's wish to be a part of significant adult concerns. I was offering him a range of table-top play activities to occupy him while I cooked. 'No', he told me firmly, 'I don't want to do playdough or painting. I want to help you make the dinner. That's fun.'

A child's level of understanding

What is obvious to an adult is new and possibly confusing to a child — she has just learned what we have known for some time. As adults, we often forget what it was like not to know something. Perhaps we never realised the small stages of knowing and learning that we passed through. To be useful to a learning child, adults often have to work hard to see the world as the child sees it and to try to understand her perspective — to understand what it is that she does not understand. A bonus for adults is that this effort made to help a child can recapture the excitement and newness of learning for the adults.

Some adults — even those who have been trained in working with children — are quick to assume that children are being naughty or uncooperative rather than that they have failed to understand. Some children may be being difficult, but often they have not grasped the basics of something which the adult is trying to help them learn. It can take effort on an adult's part to work towards finding at what point a child's understanding has broken down and then to start to help the child from that stage. It is no use taking the approach 'She's four years old, she ought to know her colours' — if she does not, then a genuine effort at helping the child has to start where her understanding stops at the moment.

Encouraging children to feel competent

One possible source of difficulties for adults in helping children to learn is that adults sometimes have a limited view of learning — limited to 'Does she know this?' or 'Can she do that?' However, an important role for adults is to encourage children in ways of approaching new challenges that will help the children in future attempts to learn. What is needed is behaviour from adults that helps children to feel competent and to feel confident of their abilities to face something that initially they cannot do. Adults can encourage this by working with children — individually and in small groups — to plan together how to tackle something new, to follow through together decisions that have been made, and (again together) to reflect on how plans have turned out.

A vital ingredient of this approach of helping children to feel competent about their ability to learn is the way in which adults handle mistakes. Many adults say blithely 'We learn by our mistakes', but few follow this through in their behaviour. For children, the experience of mistakes is all too often an experience of adults showing disappointment or frustration, of unconstructive feedback that says bluntly 'That's wrong', or a lesson that most attention comes if you get things right. Adults need to communicate through their behaviour to children that mistakes really are useful information about how far a child's learning has reached and are clues to misunderstandings that child and adult can unravel. The child can then become convinced that mistakes are a step on the way, not a failure.

In fact, children's mistakes are very often a source of information to adults who are trying to help. Many researchers have argued that young children are illogical, but this does not seem to be the case. Children are much more often logical, given their limited information and frame of reference — their mistakes are often logical steps from what they have learned so far.*

*See, for example, the discussion in *Young children learning — talking and thinking at home and at school* by Barbara Tizard and Martin Hughes, published by Fontana in 1984, or Margaret Donaldson's *Children's minds*, published by Fontana in 1978.

Learning in development

The points made in this chapter are relevant to all the areas of child development and the role of adults in the gradual expansion of the child's world. Learning is not always enjoyable to children. It is not pleasant to learn that climbing along rotten tree branches can lead to painful falls. Nor is it necessarily enjoyable to learn that adults will not allow you to express your frustrations by kicking your younger brother. However, much of learning should be enjoyable, and the reason that children do not enjoy learning or are failing to learn can at least sometimes be seen as the responsibility of the adults in the situation.

8
COMMON PROBLEMS IN LANGUAGE DEVELOPMENT AND SOME SUGGESTIONS FOR HELPING

Chapter 6 considered some of the major points in the progress of children's language development when everything is unfolding normally. Part of normal development is that many children wrestle at some stage with difficulties with particular sounds, or pass through a phase of echoing, or have problems with the ease of expressing what they want to communicate. This chapter looks at ways of helping children through what might be called normal problems and also considers how some special attention from adults can help with other minor, or more serious, difficulties in language development.

What is a problem?

It is sometimes difficult for adults to decide to what extent a child needs some special attention. A difficulty for adults may sometimes come from their having lost sight of realistic expectations for children at different ages — they may be expecting too little or too much. It can be difficult to judge how much a child genuinely cannot manage and how far she is choosing not to use her language abilities. Some careful observation and the opinion of someone coming fresh to the situation, such as a speech therapist, can help.

Although the aid of a speech therapist or a psychologist may be essential in the assessment and helping of some children, this chapter concentrates on those areas of problems where a sensitive adult, without specialist language training, can make a great difference to a child.

The range of reasons underlying language difficulties

There are, of course, many reasons which can underlie problems in language development, and it is not always possible to say what has led to a particular difficulty or delay. In some cases there may be an identifiable physical problem. Partial or total loss of hearing will affect how a child is able to learn, understand, and produce speech. Conditions such as cleft lip or cleft palate can be linked with physical difficulties which affect language. However, not all handicaps place physical barriers to language. Children with Down's syndrome, for instance, may pass through the same stages in language development as non-handicapped children, but at a noticeably slower rate of progress.

Language difficulties can be influenced by a child's emotional life. This includes the child's own feelings, how she relates to other people and her surroundings, her reaction to events in her life, and the behaviour of adults and other children. The impact of emotional factors is obviously very varied, and generalising about 'good' and 'bad' experiences is risky since different children respond in very individual ways to what would appear to be similar situations.

If there is very limited conversation from an adult to a baby or young non-talking child, then that child may be failing to experience enough speech for her own learning. The failure would be in terms of not hearing sufficient words and also in not learning that exchanges between adult and child are enjoyable. An older talking child may be inhibited if she has very limited conversation with adults, and if the adults' main use of speech is prohibitions, such as 'Don't!' and 'Shut up!' The importance of adults in a child's language development also emerges through adults' understanding of what is normal or through their judgements about what is 'proper' speech. Adults can make temporary phases of echoing words or minor stuttering into more serious issues if they react by making the child feel silly or treating her as naughty. Adults who have unreasonably high expectations for a child's language may discourage her efforts by always highlighting her mistakes.

In some cases a child can be inhibited by another child. This other child may have learned to feel better herself by making fun of the first child's minor difficulties. Sometimes that second child restricts the first child's opportunities to learn by assigning her the role of 'baby' and answering for her. The 'baby' is not always the younger child. In a few instances, twins have become a self-sufficient unit of two who have even developed a language of their own, which excludes other children and adults.

Sometimes children's reactions to major changes in their life or to continuing unhappy circumstances may be reflected in their language development. This is something to look out for, although of course not all children react in a similar way. Often, there may be no clear-cut reason why a child is experiencing problems in language or is very delayed in her development. It is not worthwhile searching endlessly for reasons — adults can help by making a start on some practical work with the child.

The problems which are discussed in the following pages all benefit from the thinking and planning activities which are discussed in part 1. Use of the various techniques of observation can also provide a firm basis of information on which to plan work with a child. Even if the decision is that someone like a speech therapist needs to work with the child as the first step, the information gathered from a developmental guide or other observation will provide useful background for the specialist.

The discussion of problems which can occur in language development of young children is divided into three parts. Firstly, there is discussion of the onset of children's speech and possible problems in how they produce their speech. Secondly, the chapter looks at problems of attention and the development of children's learning to listen and to look. Finally, discussion concentrates on some common problems that can arise as children learn abstract concepts such as colour or number, and how adults can smooth the way in this area. Practical suggestions are given alongside a description of the ways in which such problems may show themselves.

PROBLEMS IN CHILDREN'S SPEECH AND IN HOW THEY SPEAK

Children who are late in starting to talk

Some children produce a recognisable word before they are a year old. Most start to use words at some point in their second year. By the time a child is two years old, there should be some signs of speech. Children who are close to reaching two-and-a-half and are showing no signs of trying to talk are a definite worry.

A non-handicapped child who is approaching two years of age but is not showing signs of talking needs to be watched during her typical day. Adults would do well to gain some idea of whether the child tries to communicate with adults through sounds or gestures of any kind. If she will not approach adults, perhaps she does try to make contact with other children. If the child is attempting to communicate in some way, the words may follow in the months to come. If a child of eighteen months to two years is progressing very well in other areas of her development, her energy may be going there rather than on language. However, as a child fast approaches two-and-a-half, the lack of speech would be a concern, however advanced the rest of her development or however expressive her communication without words. A child may show through her behaviour that she understands a certain amount of what is said to her. This may be a sign that she is definitely learning language from others and is listening. However, as the months pass after her second birthday, it would still be important to look for speech from the child herself.

The starting point with each child would depend on her previous experience. Planning of special time with some children might well start with some selected play activities. Other children might need to learn, before or alongside these special sessions, that the adults they are now with behave differently from those they have previously experienced. A child who has known adult speech as largely nagging will have to learn that some adults talk *with* children, not at them, and are willing to listen to what children say. A child who has experienced a lot of pressure to speak 'properly' may have withdrawn from the unequal struggle: her fear of failure may have become stronger than any chance of success and excitement in learning. She will need plenty of encouragement, no criticism, and — initially — some play with simple activities at which she can easily succeed.

If a child who is not learning to talk is also unresponsive generally, or reacts only to certain levels of sound, it is important to have her hearing checked. It can be very difficult to assess the hearing of the under-threes, since their ability to pay attention is limited. The problem can be to decide whether they actually cannot hear or are rather choosing not to listen. However, despite the difficulties, it is necessary to press for a hearing test if partial or total hearing loss seems a possibility. The earlier this is diagnosed, the more quickly adults' time with this child can be made appropriate to the world as she hears it and the child can be fitted with a hearing aid.

Some ideas for encouraging children to start to talk

Some special time in play activities with an adult can encourage a child to learn single words. The activities which are used to introduce the words should be enjoyable, and there should be enough chance of success for the experience to be encouraging to the child. At this basic stage, the play will be most useful to the child if she is learning the names of objects that are fairly common in her environment. She will then have a chance to practise.

A good basic kit to use with children who are either not talking or who are at the early stages of learning to talk is a collection of half-a-dozen familiar objects and pictures of the same objects. These might include a doll, cup, spoon, toy car, book, comb, or other objects which the child is likely to encounter day by day. An easy way of collecting suitable pictures to match to these objects is to cut out the separate pages of one of the basic Ladybird books, which provide one clear picture on each page. These single sheets have a longer life if they are stuck on card and covered in plastic film. There are many different ways of using such a collection of objects and pictures. Some children may be ready to enjoy a simple question-and-answer routine. The questions can be asked in different ways so that the extent of a child's speech or understanding will be highlighted. If a child is shown an object or picture and asked 'What is this?' or 'What is this called?', then the questioner wants the child to give the correct name. However, a child can show she recognises the name for an object without speaking. If she is asked 'Where's the teddy?' or 'Show me the cup', the child can point to or pick up an object or picture. If adults suspect the child's problem may be extreme shyness, then it is wise to phrase questions so that the child can choose whether to point out or to talk.

If adults sense that a child has been pressurised in the past, it may be best to avoid asking direct questions. However, this does not mean that adults have to be silent — they can chat about the play activities and demonstrate, through what they do, the game that they are encouraging the child to try. Children who have limited language can understand what is wanted after several repeat demonstrations by an adult, for example, of simple matching or sorting games.

Another way to approach learning single words is through matching familiar objects to a picture of the same object. This can be made very simple by restricting the number of possible pictures to two or three. The word for each object plus picture is introduced through the adult's simple conversation. Another simple game is to have the child sort out a collection of toys, so that all the cars go in one box, all the spoons in another, and so on. Pictures can be cut in half to make a very basic jigsaw, and several pictures can be mixed up together. The child has to match up tops and bottoms and the adult will be providing the names, looking for opportunities to have the child say the word herself when she is ready. In any of these examples, the conversation of the adult would be simple and would be a way of repeating the key words without putting undue pressure on the child — 'Now, we're looking for the cup', 'Well done, you've found the teddy', 'There's the spoon.'

A further use of pictures requires two sets of identical pictures — one set stuck to a master board and another loose in the manner of picture lotto. Matching the loose card to the identical picture on the board can be demonstrated by an adult — the child does not have to understand the words necessary to explain the rules. A child learning single words would use one board at a time and be helped by an adult; she would be unlikely to manage a game of picture lotto with other children.

The key to these types of game is initially to keep them simple. As a child gains interest and confidence, an adult will be able to draw on other play materials and on simple question-and-answer exchanges to extend the child's knowledge of words.

Children who choose not to talk

Some children choose not to talk, although they are able to, and this 'elective mutism', as it is called, can be specific to certain people or situations. If an adult (parent or not) has been very repressive and authoritarian with a child, then that child sometimes reacts by ceasing to talk. Some children refuse to talk in nursery or playgroup, although they talk happily at home. Many shy children who start off silently, gradually gain confidence in using words, but for some children there seems to be more to the problem than shyness. It can be very hard to fathom the reason behind the silence of such a child, and adults can find themselves feeling hurt and angry. Adults have to be honest with themselves about these feelings, so that the emotions do not sour their contact with the child.

A first step is to attempt to discover whether a silent child is talking or communicating with anyone. Some day-nursery staff with whom I was working at one time were very concerned about an apparently silent three-year-old boy who seemed to take little notice of nursery life and could not be coaxed to join in activities. Their concern was lessened when one afternoon someone heard him — alone in the bathroom — singing the song that he had refused to join in that morning. Conversations with his mother revealed that he talked about nursery activities at home and was clearly learning.

A few children do choose not to talk at all in nursery or playgroup but are content to talk at home and, for some reason, talk when they go to infant school. It is not possible to force a child to talk — it is only feasible to be available and encouraging. If the child is clearly learning, you need to reassure yourself and try not to let your feelings of frustration build into a negative attitude towards her. It is worthwhile giving the child the regular opportunity to speak. However, there is little value in refusing to give her toys, second helpings of dinner, or whatever because she will not speak. This often does nothing to encourage the child to speak up and only creates a feeling of power struggle between adult and child.

A child who chooses not to talk but who will cooperate to the extent of pointing or picking up toys can show complex levels of understanding of language. As long as a child will listen and point, it is possible to check her understanding of requests from the simple 'Where's the doll?' to the considerably more complex 'Please put all the yellow pencils under the box and hand me the ruler.' A speech therapist can help by testing a cooperative, although silent, child on the Comprehension scale of the Reynell Developmental Language Scales.

The task for children of learning more than one language

Some children face language difficulties that are not developmental problems. There are now many children whose first language — the language of their home — is not the language spoken in their pre-school group or school. Children under five can and do become successfully bilingual. Adults need to assist this by helping children to grasp that there are two language systems. This is harder if adults switch without warning from one language to another or if, as used to be the case, parents are bullied into speaking an unfamiliar language to their children rather than their fluent home language.

There is no space here to do justice to a discussion of methods in helping young children to learn a second language, nor to discuss appropriate situations for 'mother-tongue teaching'. Readers who are particularly involved in this area might like to read *Supporting children's bilingualism*, by D. Houlton and R. Willey, published by Longman in 1983, or *Language in school and community*, edited by Neil Mercer and published by Edward Arnold in 1981.

CHILDREN WHO ARE HARD FOR OTHERS TO UNDERSTAND

Children who are in the early stages of learning to talk produce some very idiosyncratic sound-and-word combinations that only familiar adults and children will understand. As a child's speech develops, it should become easier for strangers to understand. It is very easy for familiar adults to get into the habit of filling in the gaps in the speech of a child they know well. The risk then is that they will not realise the extent to which they are doing this with an older child whose speech should be clearer. The experience of visitors, who are unfamiliar with the child, can be a very useful source of information in this case. There will be times when the familiar adults must be honest about how many unhelpful allowances they are making for an older child and then look for ways to help the child towards clearer speech.

Such children need a model of clear and simple speech from adults and play activities that will help them to focus on a few clear words at a time. A place to start is to attempt to slow the child's speech to discover how many real words are hidden in the incomprehensible stream of sounds. Some children who have had speech difficulties have gained the habit of not saying the beginnings or ends of words. If this is combined with a cluttered delivery of speech, sudden stops and starts, and some expressive jargon, a child can be largely incomprehensible.

It is possible to discover whether the child has some real words by asking her to identify single pictures or objects. She may have a number of single words which she can say clearly but the same words in a sentence are run into other words, so that they cannot be heard clearly. If the words are there, some simple and structured play activities may help. Many of the more basic activities suggested in this chapter are appropriate to encourage the child to slow down and produce short clear phrases. If the child enjoys songs and chants, these can help since the steady rhythm may help her to produce her speech with a more even delivery. If the child is still incomprehensible when producing single words and short phrases, the advice of someone like a speech therapist is necessary and a hearing test for the child would probably be advisable. It is certainly unwise to leave this type of problem or to pretend to understand an older talking child. It is unfair on the child — she will either be deluded into believing her speech is clear to others or will become very frustrated since others clearly do not understand her.

Problems in articulation of sounds

It is not unusual for children of nearly school age to have difficulty with some sounds. If it is only a few sounds and the child is not made to feel stupid, then some sensitive adult help can improve the situation. Speech therapists will be able to offer help and advice on how serious the problem is and what would be a sensible approach. The following are just a few ideas for helping children through play.

It is worthwhile listening carefully to a child who seems to be having difficulty with sounds. Some children are able to produce a particular sound but they produce it in the wrong place. For example, they may be able to make the hard 'c' sound that comes in 'car' but they actually say 'tar' and not 'car'. They may not be able to hear the mistake they are making, but will probably be able to focus on the deliberate mistake of an adult. Other children may not be able to produce the sound at all. Children may cope with the difficulties by replacing the sound with another ('wun' for 'run' or 'fing' for 'thing'), or they may drop the sound altogether ('poon' for 'spoon').

Sometimes, children may get into worse difficulties when they are trying to hold a conversation, especially if they are trying to speak quickly. For this reason, a valuable way to listen carefully to a child can be with a very simple picture book or collection of objects, asking the child to name objects one at a time. If the selection is made so that it includes some names which have the difficult sound, then it can be possible to hear clearly how the child copes. Then adults can make a list of the sounds which are difficult for that child by writing down examples of words and how the child pronounces them. Adults who have been trained in phonetics can list the appropriate symbols; however, examples of actual words to show the child's mistakes provide a very practical way of listing information on the problem.

If a child is having difficulty with many sounds, this can seriously distort her speech and make her very hard to understand. Even a few difficulties may frustrate a child and are worth some sensitive help. The keynote to helping is to provide the child with a clear example of the sound and a chance to practise without feeling that the spotlight is on her. Pictures, toys, songs, and sound-making games are all sources of ideas. An adult can also make use of the 'deliberate mistake' method described by Joan Tough.*

If a child tends to substitute 't' for 'c', then some pictures or objects can be picked which include names starting with 'c'. The adult can pick up a car or point to a picture. Using a wrong sound but not the mistake that the child makes, the adult asks 'Is it a par?' — with a smile and a slight shake of the head to help the child to understand the game. Then the child may be given the usual mistake — 'Is it a tar?' Finally, she would be asked 'Is it a car?', and the nods and smiles should show her that this is the correct sound. Once the child sees the idea of the game, you would not give any clues and would be looking for her to identify the correct sound. For instance, 'Is this a nup? No? Is it a pup? No? Is this a tup? No? Is it a cup?' — wait for the 'Yes' and emphasise 'Yes, it's a cup.'

Another approach is to have the child repeat the problem sounds in a sound-making game. If she has difficulties at first, it is not a failure to produce a word and so she may be more confident to keep trying. With some imagination on the part of adults, different sounds may be practised by playing at being animals or vehicles and through chanting. An 's' sound can be practised by playing at being hissing snakes, 'w' and 'f' sounds come from the 'woof' of barking dogs, 'grrr' from growling bears, and so on.

Once the child can manage the sounds in games, she may be willing to try jingles with nonsense words or funny phrases. Joan Tough suggests that simple phrases like 'Peas in the pan go pop, pop, pop' are much better than adult tongue-twisters. As the child's confidence builds by using the problem sounds, she will gradually be able and willing to repeat phrases and try songs and nursery rhymes which would have been too difficult earlier on.

One final comment — if a particular sound substitution is common in the child's community (for example, using a 't' for 'th' as in 'ting' in Irish and some West Indian speech) then this is not a problem: it is correct in terms of the child's adult models — she is learning from what she hears. As she gets older, the child will realise that other people pronounce words differently and it will be her choice whether she tries to develop a different accent.

Problems of fluency

Quite a number of young children hesitate or repeat themselves as they search for words to express what they want to say. If adults give a child time and attention, her speech gradually becomes more fluent. A child is

---

*This approach is described in Joan Tough's book, *Listening to children talking*, published in 1976 by Ward Lock Educational.

not likely to improve if she is made to feel silly — it is best to show the child that you are prepared to wait patiently for what she has to say. There is no point in getting cross with such a child; this will only make things worse. It is better to reassure the child that you are listening, and wait for the words to come.

Some children clutter up their words because of simply trying to say too much too fast. Such children may stop and start and pause at odd places. Again, it is very important that adults show a child that they have the time to listen. Adults can ask simple questions about what the child is saying and ask, if necessary, 'Tell me that bit again — slowly.'

Children who often stammer or clutter up their words can be helped by repeating rhymes or jingles in a deliberate way to set up a regular rhythm. This helps a child to pace herself. Tapping out a rhythm for songs or playing games with sounds may help. Adults can talk about events such as children climbing higher and higher (with the voice rising) to the top of a slide and coming down (with the voice deepening) to the bottom.

The onset of stammering may be linked with emotional difficulties, although not always. If there do seem to be upsetting events or upheavals in the child's life, then adults may have to be sensitive to these, as well as patient with the stammering. The child may need an opportunity to talk or to express her concerns in some other way, for example through fantasy play. Most children who stammer grow out of the problem with the help of adult patience and encouragement. However, some specialist advice should certainly be sought if there is a family history of stammering.

Children who stammer may be more relaxed in some situations than in others and therefore less likely to stammer. Observation of this is useful information for the adult. However, if the child is very often tense and anxious, if the stammer can be seen to be linked with the worrying or if the stammer itself is obviously making the child anxious, then the help of a speech therapist should be sought. Another cause for concern is if other aspects of the child's behaviour are becoming affected by the stammering problem, such that stereotyped patterns of twitching, eye-closing, or stamping are accompanying the stammering.

Helping children with their physical coordination

It is a characteristic of some seriously language-delayed or language-disordered children that they are also poorly coordinated. The clumsiness may show in difficulty with finer coordinations such as building or drawing or in a general tendency to bump into objects, drop things, and be generally ham-fisted. If any readers are dealing with a number of children with both language problems and problems of coordination, they may like to look at an article by Helen Haig on dealing with 'clumsy' children.* Speech therapists will be able to offer advice on this problem as well as an assessment of the child. Many common play activities for young children help their learning in the area of physical development. A child with poor coordination will benefit from some planned play activities which focus on the physical side. Use of pencils, scissors, chalk, and other materials which help the fine coordinations may be too frustrating and difficult initially. Games which encourage the larger physical movements are better. These would include games with large balls — rolling, simple throwing and catching, and kicking. Clapping or marching to music can help a sense of physical rhythm. A game of 'Simon says' with simple instructions may help the child — she has the adult model to copy, and this can be part of an enjoyable game involving other children as well. An adult helping such a child would need to be sensitive to how much the child can do. Fantasy play involving large physical movements, such as being trains, the finer coordinations of pouring water, or fun with shape boxes, peg boards, or 'feely' bags can be introduced as and when the child can really manage them.

PROBLEMS IN ATTENTION CONTROL

Sometimes children whose language is delayed, or who are experienced as difficult by adults, have limited ability to concentrate. This usually means that the child is neither listening nor looking as carefully as most children of her age. This will limit her learning.

Part of deciding how to help a child with poor attention is gaining some idea of the level of attention control she has reached so far. Jean Cooper, Molly Moodley, and Joan Reynell† suggest that there are six stages through which children pass as their attention control improves. As with any set of stages, children pass gradually from one to another, so that individuals may show features of more than one stage. The stages are approximately linked to the years of life — so that children in the first year of life are normally in stage one of attention control. The problems arise when older children are still behaving in a way typical of the early stages.

*'Integrated speech and occupational therapy programmes in paediatrics', which appeared in *Early childhood* in March 1982, vol. II, number 6. Recommended in that article was a book, *Helping clumsy children*, edited by Neil Gordon and Ian McKinlay, published by Churchill Livingstone in 1980.
†*Helping language development*, by Jean Cooper, Molly Moodley, and Joan Reynell, published in 1978 by Edward Arnold.

The stages of development of children's attention control

Stage one — very distractable

This stage is normal in the first year of life. A baby's attention is held momentarily by whatever is the major source of interest in her surroundings. She is easily distracted by any new sight or sound. Adults tend to expect this with babies and allow the baby's interest to determine play. However, some children much older than a year are still in this stage. They are distracted by noises, other toys, and the activities of other children. This very limited attention control may show itself in very active behaviour — the child who physically moves from one activity to another and will never sit still. However, a child may be equally distractable but not move away physically — the rather lethargic child whose look becomes glassy as her attention drifts away. Less usual is the child who is distracted by the fantasies or worries which are inside her own head — this child may well be emotionally disturbed.

The keynote to helping a distractable child is to arrange that special time with one adult happens in a quiet room with very few distractions. It is very unlikely that an older child with very limited attention control will improve in a group situation — she will need the full attention of an adult just on her. Initially, this special time will not last long — the attention of a very distractable child may only be held for a minute or two. This will gradually improve if the adult perseveres over the days and weeks.

Toys or activities should be chosen which are likely to interest the child. If a very active child is only interested in footballs, then imaginative adults can plan some simple games with a ball — not aimless kicking about, but perhaps rolling the ball at skittles, kicking it into a goal, or bouncing it through a hoop. Very distractable children will need adults to catch their attention with 'Angela, look at me' or 'John, listen now.' Touching the child lightly can provide emphasis.

When you are helping an older child in this stage, the aim is to have as little to distract her as possible. If the child will not look at you, you can play games to help this. Games of hiding; playing peek-a-boo; blowing 'raspberries' at each other; clapping hands; looking in mirrors; holding a toy, which you know the child likes, close to your face — all these can improve eye contact. You can turn the child's head towards a toy, or place her hand or finger on the toy you want her to look at. You can sit the child on your lap or sit behind her holding her gently to reduce the fidgeting and increase the chances that she will look and listen.

Initially, it is unrealistic to expect the child to spend long on one activity. The game should be short and successful for the child; for instance, a very distractable child may post only one brick in a posting box. Adults should be encouraging about this success and, as the days go by, increase the number of bricks the child posts before she can rush off again or drift into her own thoughts. If the child will tolerate a sequence of more than one activity, adults can have the next toy out of sight (behind you, in a bag, under the table) and only bring that out when the first activity has been tidied away.

Stage two — fixed attention

A child in the second year of life can usually concentrate on a task of her own choice. However, this concentration tends to be fairly rigid, and the child may not tolerate suggestions from adults or the intervention of other children who want to do things differently. At this stage, children are sometimes described as 'obstinate'. However, it is not a deliberate refusal to cooperate. Children in this stage cannot cope with listening to conversation and continuing with an absorbing activity at the same time.

Some older children have not progressed beyond this stage. They may not be noticed as a problem, since they can appear to be absorbed in play. However, observation of an older child with attention control at the stage-two level will show that she is limited in her choice of play activities and probably treats the toys in a rather repetitive way. She might, for instance, always go to the sandpit and use the same bucket and spade to make pies. The first task in helping such a child to progress is for an adult to ease the child away from the rigid pattern. A first step could be to sit beside the child and hold her hand or gently turn her head. An encouraging smile from the adult will then help to gain the child's attention. The adult can then introduce some slight variation into the child's game to extend her play.

Whatever the play activity undertaken with a child with rather rigid attention control, adults must be ready to give plenty of gentle reminders to gain the child's attention. It is useful to gain the habit of saying the child's name at the beginning of any instruction — 'Sally, listen now' or 'David — look. There are your shoes.' Play activities undertaken with the child need to have built-in rewards or interest and to be fairly obvious in terms of how to use the play materials. Shape boards are a good choice, since it is immediately obvious whether the shape fits the hole. Jigsaws with single pieces set within a scene will be better than those where the picture is not obvious until several pieces have been fitted together. A child may take apart nesting barrels to find out what little object is making a noise inside. She may build a tower of bricks if she is allowed to knock it down straightaway, or place shapes over a pillar in the type of toy where a lever can be pressed to shoot the shapes up into the air.

Stage three — more flexible 'single-channelled' attention

This stage normally develops sometime between two to three years of age. At this level of attention control, a child's attention is 'single-channelled' but is becoming more flexible. The child is beginning to manage a shift from her activity in response to directions and back to the activity again. However, the adult is still very important in focusing the child's attention, as the child cannot fully manage this herself. Before any directions are given, adults must still make sure that the child is both listening and looking. In a group, the child may not be aware that an adult is speaking to her, especially if that adult is not close by. Children at this stage often do not attend to general instructions given to a whole group, and adults have to be patient in repeating the request directly to individuals. When adults are making a suggestion to a child about her play, they will often need to encourage the child to apply this suggestion or simply help the child to focus once more on her activity.

Once a child is clearly progressing from stage three, there are unlikely to be problems. The adult can help by encouraging the child's progress, being a good model by paying attention to the child, and being understanding about how much the child still has to learn.

Stage four — established 'single-channelled' attention

Between three to four years of age, children become far more able to shift their attention from one interest (people, toys, spoken words) to another. The child's attention is still 'single-channelled' — she can only concentrate on one thing at a time — but she is far more able to stop what she is doing, look up or listen, and then return to her activity. Of course, this does not happen perfectly all the time. There will be occasions when the child is so absorbed in her play that she does not realise that someone is speaking to her or she may choose not to listen.

Stage five — the beginnings of 'two-channelled' attention

Between four to five years of age, children are becoming able to sustain 'two-channelled' attention for short periods of time. This means that a child will be able to talk and point at the same time, or listen to spoken instructions without stopping what she is doing. If the task or the instructions are particularly difficult, she may have to attend to just one at a time.

By this stage, children are far more able to cope with learning in a group and understand that instructions given to a whole group of children apply to each individual equally.

A four-year-old can really concentrate well on an activity. ▶

Stage six — established 'two-channelled' attention

By about five years of age, children can sustain the 'two-channelled' attention for longer. They can cope with learning in a group situation, as in infant school, and attend well unless they are tired, unwell, or very distracted.

The further suggestions in this part of the chapter do not assume a particular stage of attention control: they are a source of ideas for helping any child whose listening, looking, and remembering could be improved. Many of the ideas are play activities which are equally enjoyable for children who have no problems at all in this area.

Games to help listening and discrimination between sounds

If you have a number of children who seem to be poor listeners, a first step is to take an honest look at the children's environment and the adults in it. If children are in a room (home, nursery, or playgroup) where there is a continuously high level of noise from adults calling, radios playing, or televisions blaring, then children may well filter out all noise. They will not necessarily pay attention just because one particular item of noise is addressed to them. Adults can help children listen by making sure that there is not continuous background noise. There will be noisy boisterous playtimes, but there should also be quieter episodes.

Adults can also help by stopping the bad habit of shouting at children from a distance. There will be times, when a child is about to do something dangerous to herself or very harmful to someone else, when adults have to call out. These should be exceptions, because if shouting becomes the rule then children, not surprisingly, learn to shout too and to ignore as much as they can of the shouting around them. As far as possible, adults should make sure they are close to the child with whom they want to speak and that they move towards a child who wants to speak with them. It is important that adults create a situation in which children can become confident of getting adults' attention. This does not mean that children should be allowed to interrupt at will — there are going to be occasions when adults will have to ask them to 'Wait a minute.'

If you have taken an honest look at a child's immediate environment and the adults' role in it and feel that the child still has a listening problem, then it is worth playing some basic sound games with her. At the simplest level of sound game, you can have two identical tins or cartons and place a small toy or bell in one of them. The tins are then moved and shaken. The child has to indicate which tin contains the toy. It is possible to vary this by having different containers, toys which will make different sounds, and toys which are quieter or louder. Another approach is to have two toys which normally make a sound (bells, squeaky toys, trumpets), but to have one of these toys silent. The child has to identify which bell is ringing, which toy is squeaking, and so on.

Playing games with sound can be made more complicated if the child cannot see the object being shaken. An adult can have two different toys — for instance, a bell and a brick rattling in a wooden box — and shake one of these behind a screen or under a table. When the objects are brought into view again, the child has to say which one made the noise. Another way of helping a child to discriminate between sounds is to make up a game in which noises come from adults standing in different parts of the room. The child has to identify which adult is making the noise. Obviously, any of these games has to be played in a quiet atmosphere.

Helping children to look carefully

Simple enjoyable games can help a child to look more carefully and eventually to attend to quite small details. Outdoor activities can be as helpful as indoor and will be the best place to start if the child prefers outdoor physical play. Playing 'Simon says' or 'What's the time, Mr Wolf?' requires close looking as well as other, physical abilities. Games of hide-and-seek and sardines may also encourage a child to look, as long as an adult is prepared to help her to the point at which she understands the game. Children who are at an age when they cannot grasp games with rules can play simple games of 'peep-bo' and hunting hidden objects which are spread over a very small area.

Indoor activities such as picture lotto or a simplified version of pairs can help children to look. Odd-one-out games can also be made very simple. A child may be shown a line of chairs with one facing in the opposite direction, or a row of cups with one upside down. An adult can demonstrate finding the odd one out or ask a child to 'Make them all the same.' Imaginative adults can present many variations on a simple odd-one-out theme, games of simple pictures with obvious mistakes, or deliberate mistakes made by an adult in play or simple domestic routines. Through play or helping with adult tasks, a child can be encouraged to look carefully — to find the car hidden in the box of bricks, or the spoon in the plate compartment. Odd-one-out and other looking games can become more challenging and enjoyable for children with no problems in looking. However, activities need to be selected which are simple, if a child is experiencing difficulties.

Helping a child with poor memory

Children with poor attention are sometimes also poor at remembering. It would seem that they either forget quickly or, probably, are not listening properly in the first place. Asking children to go on simple errands of fetching within the same room may be one way of helping. Conversations about very recent past events — for example, what happened in the morning — encourage a child to make an effort because of your interest. There are also a number of games which require a child to remember for very short periods of time.

Once a child can distinguish simple sounds, you can try a game of copying a short sequence with different objects which she can hear. An example might be to shake a bell and then hit a drum. The child copies this with her own set of instruments. If she enjoys this, the sequence of sounds may develop into simple tunes. A child could also be encouraged to remember a short sequence of small toys posted into a cardboard tube. An adult posts a sequence of car—brick—marble into one tube and the child then has to do the same with her tube. If the child has real difficulty remembering, the game can be started by having adult and child post simultaneously and then the child can be held back with a 'Watch me . . . now you do it.' Games can be developed which require a child to remember for very short periods of time. These might involve simple instructions or demonstrations — for example, to touch parts of the body; hiding objects; or simple hop, skip, and jump sequences. Since it is very likely that poor memory will be linked with poor attention control, adults need to be prepared to ensure that they have the child's attention at the start of each sequence.

Once again, memory games can be made steadily more complicated. An older child may enjoy very simple versions of the party game of remembering objects on a tray or playing 'I went to the zoo and I saw. . . .' However, once she is playing these with confidence, it is unlikely that she has any memory problem.

DIFFICULTIES IN LEARNING ABSTRACT CONCEPTS

When children are clearly having difficulty in talking, adults seem rather more inclined to look for ways of communicating that do not depend on words, so the adults may use gesture and demonstration. However, when talking children are having problems in understanding abstract concepts such as number or colour, the learning activities which are attempted often depend on spoken explanations. There is, however, a great deal of sense in returning with a confused child to a pre-language stage in particular areas of learning — to visual recognition; to simple sorting and matching activities; and, for the present, away from the words that are only confusing the issue.

Many of the concepts which children learn require subtle visual discriminations between objects. Learning about colour, for instance, requires children to ignore many other features of the different objects that we tell them are 'blue'. They have learned so far that a particular collection of objects includes a jumper, a brick, a toy car, and a bike and now an adult is stressing that all these different objects are called 'blue'. Additionally, one is also 'soft', another is 'hard', another one goes 'fast', and another is 'big'. Children learn to apply these abstract ideas (concepts) by hearing the information consistently from adults. This dovetails with their experience and play with objects which have different qualities. All children show some level of confusion before the various concepts become clear. The confusion for some children lasts a long time. If a child has also become rather anxious about a particular area of learning, there is even more reason to build some special time around very simple activities. This may provide an opportunity for the adult to say, 'Well done. This is really easy for you, isn't it? I bet you could manage something a bit more difficult.'

Learning about colours

It is important for adults to bear in mind the major difference between matching and identifying colours. Matching different colours requires a child to pay attention to the colour differences she can see and basically to judge whether the colour of one object is the same as or different from the colour of another object. There is a direct comparison which the child can see in front of her. This is a simpler task than identifying colours, which requires a child to produce the right colour word for one object or to find one particular colour without any comparison point.

If a child is learning colours without too much confusion, then the gradual move from matching to identifying may not be very noticeable. The child is learning through conversation and play activities in which sometimes colour and sometimes other concepts feature. Adults' comments such as 'Shall we get out your red trousers today?', 'Do you want some more green paint?', or 'Is it the yellow blanket you're looking for?' gradually build up the information. Sorting and matching games link words with what the child can see. A younger child will enjoy such games, and a confused older child will need their simplicity.

The simplest level of colour-matching is to have two large containers, such as plastic bowls, which are different colours — perhaps red and blue — and a collection of smaller objects which are identical (all cars, all bricks, etc.) except that some are red and some are blue. The adult would then demonstrate the game to the child by placing one or two of the smaller objects in the same-colour bowl, perhaps making and then correcting a deliberate mistake to emphasise the point. The child can then try. Conversation need only be about 'same' and 'different'.

The pace of this type of activity and the amount of conversation has to be determined by the individual child. As she shows she is ready, larger containers in yellow and then in green and same-colour small objects can be added. As children learn, they will not need the larger containers as a comparison point: they will be able to discriminate colour differences in the midst of other differences between objects. A collection of bricks may be sorted into different colour towers, a box of different toys may be sorted by getting out all the red toys and then the blue, etc. Paper cut-outs can be sorted into the Green family and the Blue family.

Colour names can be introduced into the conversation, but as information for the child, *not* as the pressure of 'Tell me what colour this is.' Adults' comments might be 'I'm building a red tower. Can you find me more red bricks like this?' (holding up a red brick) or 'I think you've got one of my Green family.' A sensitive adult can judge when a child reacts with interest to 'Where are the red ones?' or 'What colour are my trousers?' At this point, the child will be linking colour words more consistently with what she sees — and will be curious to know more.

Learning about number

Just as some adults start with colours at the point of 'What colour is this?', so some start numbers at too complex a level. Children gradually build up an understanding of number, and adults can very usefully help at the pre-language stages of this concept. Some adults place much emphasis on the reciting of numbers — 'She can count up to twenty' — without realising that the child has learned the numbers much like a nursery rhyme: it is just a sequence of words without meaning. The child may not have grasped the idea of counting objects one at a time or understand a request such as 'Please give me three bricks.' Children have to learn about 'more' and 'less' and 'same' and 'different', so that words for number make sense in terms of tangible objects.

Many games which help children to work with sets of objects enable them to make a visual check of whether there are in fact 'more', 'less', or 'the same'. Children who are learning about number — as well as those who are confused — will enjoy games and involvement in domestic activities which encourage the understanding of 'Are there enough?' These could include putting hats on dolls, putting cups on saucers for a tea-party, helping to lay the table, building brick towers, planting bulbs in pots, and many other activities. The child can see that something is missing, and the adult can provide the explanation of 'We need one more hat' or 'We're missing two spoons.' The adult can encourage an interested child to count up 'How many children have we got for tea?' or 'How many bricks have I got in my tower?' Learning about counting means much more if children are encouraged to count actual objects or pictures, rather than to rattle off numbers. Children can begin to understand numbers changing through a game of 'I have a pile of ten cars' — children count the cars and then the adult takes two away and the children count again. Counting steps in the stairs or pacing out rooms can be yet another way to bring number words to life.

Helping children to learn abstract concepts

Adults are very familiar with the abstract concepts that young children are attempting to grasp. Unfortunately, this can lead us to believe that these concepts are obvious. This is not the case, and we often unwittingly make the children's task harder. Adults are often slapdash about their use of words for size and shape — for example, we use the word 'bigger' to mean taller, fatter, heavier, and even older ('When you're a big boy, you'll go to school'). Children's learning survives a great deal of adult laziness in speech but, obviously they will learn the labels to the concepts more quickly if adults use 'tall', 'short', 'fat', 'older', and so on in a consistent and accurate way.

Precisely because all these words describe abstract concepts, children need opportunities to link the abstract to what they can experience through their senses. It is a complicated process, and all children will be confused at some point, although perhaps it is only the very confused who will be noticed as having a problem. Children learn to recognise some abstract differences through sorting or matching games before they can label those differences. They need to relate other concepts to personal experience to begin the understanding of the abstractions of, for example, temperature, or the complexities of family relationships, or speed experienced directly or through watching others. It is a sobering experience to list all the abstract areas that most four-year-olds will have grasped in whole or part. Try doing this as an exercise — you will easily fill an A4 sheet with your list.

The nub of children's difficulties seems to be that they are trying simultaneously to grasp lots of new information *and* the framework into which to fit this. Children can be perplexed because different frameworks are equally possible in theory. This gives rise to some very endearing anecdotes about young children, and such anecdotes are also very revealing of a child's level of understanding. For example, when my son was four years old, he asked me out of the blue 'Are my T-shirts getting small?' Rather puzzled, I answered 'No'. Drew followed this with 'Well, am I getting bigger then? Because Zoë's got my red T-shirt now.' He was searching for an explanation of why his T-shirts now fitted his younger sister but not him. A world in which clothes get smaller would explain this just as well as one in which children get larger. From this, both Drew and I learned something about the business of what changes and what stays the same over time.

Concluding remarks

Many of the play activities suggested for help with problems are, of course, equally enjoyable for children whose development is progressing within the normal range. However, some children will really need adult help to benefit from those activities. With some problems — for example, a child whose attention control is immature for her age — the value of the special time with the child might be to enable her, for once, to concentrate on one activity. Another child's special playtime might be important because an adult takes her more slowly than usual through a common activity.

Some of the suggestions have been clustered around the notion that, if a child's level of understanding or ability is over a year delayed in some areas, special activities have to be planned which will move the child on from that immature level. This does *not* mean that the four-year-old whose attention level is more like that of a two-year-old has to be treated as a two-year-old in all respects. However, it does mean that the selection of toys to help the problem may be more typical of play material that would normally be offered to a two-year-old. Part of this approach has to be a positive attitude on the part of adults. It is not a question of babying older children: it is simply a sensible strategy of starting at the point where the child is at present — the level which she can understand and manage in this particular aspect of her development.

9
MAKING THE MOST OF CHILDREN'S LEARNING OPPORTUNITIES

Chapter 8 dealt with problems in language development and considered adult behaviour as helping or hindering this development. The present chapter focuses on aspects of the learning environment created by adults which can help children's language to progress.

The risks of overloading children with adult language

Many programmes designed to help children with language delay place a strong emphasis on adult language, including questions to ask the child and suggestions to help. A new emphasis has developed, particularly in nursery education, on the general value of spoken requests that adults make to children such that those children are required to use different intellectual skills. The argument has been that, by such questioning, adults can assess a child's ability and promote her further development. The work, for example, of Marion Blank and of Joan Tough utilises this approach.

However, a cautionary note about the effectiveness of adults' spoken demands on children's skills has been sounded in the work of the Thomas Coram Research Unit at the University of London. In reviewing other studies and reporting her own research, Barbara Tizard suggests strongly that the day-by-day use of a questioning style by adults in their interaction with children is not an effective technique to stimulate children's learning. A problem highlighted by her team's research was that children did not necessarily reply, or failed to reply fully, to their nursery teachers' questions. The same child would often make more effort in conversations with her mother, which the research team recorded at home.* One practical conclusion is that children who feel overloaded by adult language can learn very quickly to avoid answering questions or to respond with only a few words. Either of these reactions is a poor reflection of the child's true capabilities.

Adults who work with young children could quite reasonably throw up

*This research is described in an article by Barbara Tizard and colleagues, entitled 'Adults' cognitive demands at home and at nursery school'. This was published in the *Journal of child psychology and psychiatry*, April 1982, volume 23(2).

their hands at this point and say 'Make up your mind! What are we supposed to be doing?' Such frustration would be understandable. In trying to make sense of the different projects and pieces of research, several guide-lines seem to be practical. These are:

a) Children learn a great deal from adults, so how much adults speak with children and what they say is important.
b) Adults' taking an active role in children's learning through adopting a questioning style has made an impact in special programmes to affect children's learning in specific areas of understanding.
c) There is no evidence to suggest that making this questioning style a *major* part of adults' daily interaction with children actually helps them learn faster, and it may actually get in the way.
d) The more intensive questioning and exploration by adults is probably best kept for special play sessions with children.
e) There is every reason for adults to try to be sensitive to their own use of language. However, this does *not* mean that each and every exchange with a child should have a clear educational purpose. Children have a right to relax and enjoy themselves, as do the adults who spend time with them. An over-use of questioning techniques seems to make for a rather heavy atmosphere.

The building blocks of good communication between adult and child

It was mentioned that adults seem to depend over-much on spoken language when children are talking. It is helpful to recall what seems to be important in building a relationship of communication between adult and baby and to remember that much of this is relevant to communication with older children.

A number of professions — research and applied — have become very interested in the interaction between mothers and their young babies.* Several features keep emerging as being important in babies whose ability to communicate develops well. These are:

a) There is a two-way exchange between the mother and the baby — initially the exchange of smiling, and later the exchange of sounds.
b) An important element of this exchange is that the mother and baby take turns and the baby learns the rules of conversational turn-taking.
c) The mother responds to signals from the baby, and the baby learns a

---

*You can find more detail on this area in *Infant communication: development assessment and intervention*, by D. McClowry, A. Guildford, and S. Richardson, published by Grune and Stratton in 1982.

number of strategies to gain attention, to start an exchange, and to keep an exchange going.

These points about the building blocks for communication can be related to what was said previously about the risks of overloading children with adult language. When an adult dominates conversation and directs the context by questions, then the communication becomes more one-way — the exchange is unbalanced. Turn-taking is reduced or controlled by the adult, and the child's signals of wanting to communicate may only infrequently gain a response from the adult. Some children seem more able than others to tolerate restricted exchange, and some restrictions may be inevitable when an adult is working with a group of children, but it should not be surprising to the adult if the children are not highly motivated by such a limited exchange.

Learning to listen to children

Perhaps a defect of programmes that focus on what adults say to children has been a lack of emphasis on adult listening. Adults are often not very sensitive when listening to other adults, so it is not very surprising that neither do they listen well to children. The importance of adults' paying serious attention to children has already been stressed; it is worthwhile restating it here.

Even under-fives can sense when an adult is not really listening. This is not just in terms of adults' turning away when the child is talking: it is also a sense of when adults know the right answer or the point they wish to make next and lead into that almost regardless of what the child has said in the interval. Adults need to listen to themselves to check if they are being over-eager in this way, as the likely consequence is that the child will not learn so well. Even the best-intentioned stimulating speech from adults will in the end be counterproductive if adults do not give children the respect of their attention and demonstrate that they have listened, by adjusting their comments in the light of what the child has communicated.

Adults' sensitivity to their own speech

One of the major influences on children's language development is the speech of adults. This shows in several ways.

It makes a difference when adults take the trouble to talk *with* children rather than at them. This is as relevant for conversations with a child who does not yet talk as it is for a child who is expressing herself through recognisable words. It is a case of leaving space for the young child to reply in whatever way she wishes. Adults' talk with children, whether brief or longer exchanges, is most useful when it takes account of the child's language ability, both in terms of her understanding and her speech. Of course, adults' speech will not always be free of confusions for children. This does not matter, as long as adults are prepared to explain, to phrase something differently, and to pick up clues from the child which will tell them where her understanding or expressive ability may be breaking down.

Adults can also make a difference to children's language development by making conversation an enjoyable experience. There will be unavoidable times when adult speech will have to be about 'Don't!', but these should definitely be outnumbered by the times when conversation is a source of enjoyment and fun.

Adults can also help the children in their care by listening to themselves. One of the ways of making this happen is by becoming more aware of the different uses to which we can put our speech. The following discussion outlines some uses of speech which adults and children share.*

SOME DIFFERENT USES OF SPEECH BY ADULTS AND CHILDREN

Giving information

Adults are major providers of information to children, often in answer to a child's question. For example:

CHILD: Where's mummy?
ADULT: Mummy's working at her office.
CHILD: When is she coming?
ADULT: She'll be here after we've had tea.

The many answers to 'What's this?' or 'What's that?' provide new or confirmatory information for the child. However, adult information is not always given as an answer to a child's question. An adult's request to 'Fetch the dustpan and brush' may be followed with explanatory information to help the child to find it — 'It's under the chair in the corner.'

Asking questions

Adults often ask children questions for information — 'Have you seen my bag?' or 'Do you want another biscuit?' These questions

*A further source of ideas and a more detailed look at uses of speech can be found in Joan Tough's books, *Listening to children talking* and *Talking and learning*, published in 1976 and 1977 by Ward Lock Educational.

require a straight 'Yes' or 'No' from the child. They are essentially closed questions. An open question needs more than a one-word answer, and it is worthwhile adults' attempting to ask both sorts of question.

Undoubtedly, some of the questions asked require simple answers, perhaps one-word answers. This may be the most appropriate way to check on whether a child knows colours, can count, or has learned the name of an object. However, there are times when this is unhelpful — adults can potentially restrict a child to one-word answers when the child is capable of more. For instance, when adults admire a child's building or painting, the question is often 'What is it?' However, if adults also ask 'How did you make that?' or 'What did you do to get that lovely shape?', the child is encouraged to describe and perhaps to show you. Making the effort to ask children open-ended questions — such as 'Tell me more about that', 'What did you do next?' or 'How on earth did you manage that?' — gives children an opportunity to carry on a conversation as far as their abilities and interest allow.

Telling and describing

Telling a child about something is more than just giving information. It has a more detailed, descriptive quality. This may involve telling a child a fictional tale or recounting for the child's interest a special event in the adult's life. Many children are fascinated to hear time and time again about 'silly' or 'naughty' things that adults did as children, and to hear about their own earlier years.

An alert adult listener can encourage children's attempts to describe past and present events and to imagine or plan future events. Obviously the abilities of younger children tend to be restricted to the present. Children may be prompted to describe what they are doing at present — for example, the details of a picture that adult and child are looking at together. Alternatively, the description may be about the recent past, for instance the events of the weekend or television programmes. When an adult and a child can look back on shared experiences, this can be a rich source of conversation, started by either the adult or the child with 'Do you remember when . . .?'

Children also enjoy making up stories, which involves an imaginative use of language. They can sometimes be encouraged to describe what an adult is doing. The common question of 'What are you doing?' from a child can at least sometimes be answered by something like 'Go on. You tell me. What do you think I'm doing?' If the child answers and the adult's activity involves a sequence of tasks — such as changing a baby or mending toys — then the adult can follow on with 'What will I have to do next?'

Speculation and imagination

Children may need encouragement to use words as a channel for imagination. Adults can help by being prepared to use their speech as a prompt for speculation. This might include questions such as 'I wonder what's happening now . . .', 'What do you think will happen next?', 'What do you suppose she's thinking?', or 'What do you think will happen if I put these ice cubes in my tea?' This use of speech can emerge through many types of play activity — talking about pictures and story-books, games with cars, puppet plays, water play, or building. Speech as imagination may take place in a complete fantasy context. Tea-parties, domestic play with dolls, fantasy conversations about 'animals I've got in my garden' can all need speech to support the actions. Basically, the adult role here is to be available when children want an adult presence. Some adults have to overcome feelings that such pretending is silly or undignified.

Suggestions from adults and children

Adults can use speech to make suggestions to children — 'Perhaps if you tried it that way round. . . .' Questions can be implied suggestions — 'Would you like to have a more difficult puzzle?' Statements may include a suggestion — 'I think the baby would like a rattle — why don't you choose one?' Making genuine suggestions when talking with children can create an atmosphere in which adults and children are equal. Suggestions which emerge more like instructions can make a child feel that here is yet another example when adults have the know-ledge and she, a child, does not.

Children can also be prompted to make suggestions to adults, which again can make for a more equal atmosphere. Adults can say 'Where do you think would be a good place to stick the picture?', 'Have you got any ideas on what the baby would enjoy doing?', 'What do you think the man should do with that naughty dog?'

Explanations and justifications

Some answers to questions are explanatory as well as or rather than giving information. Explanations may be of the unhelpful type — such as 'Because I say so!' — or may actually help a child to understand more clearly — 'The bus isn't working. Look — all its wheels are broken.' Some explanations from adults may be justifications for action — 'No. I told you. No television until you've put your toys away.'

Without some prompting and guiding questions from adults, young children often find explaining or justifying very difficult. Without some patient help, children's explanations are often limited to 'Because' or 'I just did.' It surely does not help that children are often asked for explanations of wrongdoing — 'Why did you hit Sara?', 'Why didn't you tell me you wanted to go to the toilet?' It would probably help if adults made sure that some requests for explanations were not in a conflictful atmosphere. More positive requests for explanation could be questions such as 'What makes the wheels go round on that bike?' or 'What do you think has made the puddles dry up?' It is also enjoyable for children to feel that they have information or understanding that the adult does not have — it builds their self-confidence and sense of being valued.

Discipline and instructions

Adults' words are sometimes used to reprimand a child — 'I told you not to touch that paint!' We are usually not very aware of how we speak in anger or irritation; consequently, it can be a sobering experience to hear a child disciplining her teddy or doll with the same words and tone of voice that an adult is accustomed to use to her. There will be times when children have to be reprimanded, but adults need to watch that these are no more than really necessary.

Many times the atmosphere is not so tense and the words are to instruct or request — 'Can you bring me another fork, please?' It can be an enjoyable experience for children to have an adult as assistant rather than vice versa. For this to work, adults have to be prepared sometimes to accept instructions and perhaps to pretend to be unclear about something they actually do know. This can give children experience of using their language to direct the actions of another individual.

Words as encouragement or as criticism

Spoken words, as well as all the non-verbal messages, can be used to communicate positive or negative opinions and judgements. We, as adults, often use more energy making critical remarks and commenting on what other adults have done wrong than in looking for positive and encouraging comments we can make. In terms of adult speech to children, it is a case of watching out for the times to say 'Well done' or 'You really tried hard on that' and making admiring remarks about what children have attempted or have in fact achieved.

The type of remark that says bluntly 'You're silly' or 'That's the wrong way to do it' is not helpful to a child. It gives no information on how the child could do better next time. It is only discouraging, unless the adult adds a reason for the criticism or a suggestion for how the child should manage what she is doing. A good rule of thumb is to imagine how you, as an adult, would feel if someone dismissed your efforts with a derisory remark. Children are not so very different. They are also likely to feel angry or hurt and less inclined to try hard in the future.

Ways of taking an honest look at adult use of speech

It is very difficult for adults to become aware of their own use of language through ordinary conversation. You are so involved in what you are saying and in other contributions to the conversation that it is next to impossible to stand back to consider your own speech objectively.

There are several ways to gain a more detached viewpoint. It is possible to ask another person to observe you for short periods of time and to note down what you say, so that you can look back over your comments and perhaps divide them up according to use of speech. Another possibility is to tape record a session with a group of children and listen to the conversation later on. The aim would be to gain an honest picture of how broad your use of language is during an ordinary playtime with children. You might ask yourself such questions as:

- Am I spending my time saying 'Don't do that!' rather than 'Why don't you try such-and-such'?
- Am I saying 'Oh, yes. That's nice' rather than asking a child about her drawing or the experience she has described?
- Do I encourage children to continue with 'Tell me more' or 'What happened then?'
- Do I ask children 'What will happen if . . .' and help them to discover for themselves what will happen in a given situation?
- Do I spend my time controlling the children when a conversation with them would keep them interested and less difficult?
- Do I tell children the answer when they have a problem they cannot solve, or do I try to ask questions which will help them to discover the answer themselves?
- When I have to give children instructions, do I try to explain the reasons behind what I want?

Another practical way of exploring adult flexibility in the use of speech is through talking about pictures with children. This activity also shows a child's ability to use her speech. The idea is to have some pictures — either a book or a poster — which have enough detail to encourage conversation. Two sets of pictures are included in Joan Tough's book *Listening to children talking* (published in 1976 by Ward Lock Educational), and these pictures can also be bought separately. Many children's books include eye-catching pictures of domestic scenes, shopping, building sites, or traffic, which give scope both to see what the child can say about the picture and for the adult to see how far she or he can encourage more conversation from the child.

A practical start to an activity with pictures is to ask the child an open-ended question such as 'What can you tell me about the picture?' Initially, it is useful to see what the child can manage with basic encouragement such as 'Well done' or 'Anything else?' but with no direct prompts. Some children who should be capable of broader use of speech may restrict themselves to naming objects — 'That's a car. A boy. A mummy.' Some children may attempt to describe actions, but in a vague way — 'They going', 'Boy doing that', 'Shopping.' Other children will describe in more detail, without much prompting — 'That's a boy and girl with their mummy. They're doing the shopping. The mummy's got a hat on. There's a bus. I've been on a bus.' When the adult has some idea of what the child is able to say with very little prompting, then is the time to ask questions which may help the child to look more closely at the picture. It may well be that a child who has limited spontaneous use of speech can progress beyond just naming objects and people. Adult questions about 'What's he doing?' or 'What's going on in this corner?' may stimulate some descriptions. Some children can surprise adults in this type of activity — perhaps the child thought that naming objects was all that the adult wanted!

ADULT SPEECH WHEN CHILDREN DO NOT UNDERSTAND

There may be times when, because of the pressures on you or the nature of the problem, you want to give a child a direct answer or an immediate demonstration to clear up any lack of understanding. However, children will often learn more and gain in confidence if an adult watches out for the times to ask questions or make suggestions which will help a child to reach the answer herself. It is often difficult for adults to understand what it is that a child does not understand. Many times this is because something is so obvious to us that we have forgotten that once we did not know or understand this ourselves. Impatience, unwillingness to make the effort, or lack of confidence about how to help a child to understand can all discourage an adult from taking the less easy route of trying to help a child to see for herself.*

Children fail to understand for different reasons. One of these reasons can be that the child was not paying attention when the adult first spoke. The problem of children whose attention is delayed was discussed in

---

*Marion Blank has undertaken a great deal of work in this area. The practical suggestions for adult speech when children do not understand derive from only a small selection of her ideas. More details of her work can be read in the article 'Language, the child and the teacher: a proposed model'. This is included in a book, *Psychological perspectives in early childhood education*, by P. Robinson and H. Hom (editors), published by Academic Press in 1977.

chapter 7. However, failure to attend can be a reason why children do not understand even where the child has no overall problem with attention. Adults need to make sure they have a child's attention before they start and must be prepared to recapture that attention if it seems to have wandered. Some examples will illustrate this.

(1)   The most practical approach is often to delay children, by words and by touch, so that they do listen properly. Some children may need this more than others. For example:

ADULT: Pick up the . . .
        (The child starts seizing objects at random.)
ADULT: Wait a minute. Listen to me. I want you to pick up the lids.

(2)   Children who have become distracted need to have their attention focused on the original request. For example:

ADULT: Please go to the shelf and get me a tissue.
(Child goes to the shelf and reaches for the first thing she sees, which is a toy.)
ADULT: Do you remember what I asked you to bring?

(3)   Some games can be repeated if the child has not been watching with full attention. For example:

ADULT: Where did I hide the hat?
        (Child shrugs, looking blank.)
ADULT: Well, watch me. I'm going to do it again. Then you can show
    me.

Sometimes, children are attending as well as they are able. However, they fail to understand what is being asked of them. Part of the reason for this can be that the adult's language has been too complicated or has failed to emphasise the part of the request that is confusing to the child. The following examples are some simple suggestions for how adults can rephrase what they have asked of children.

(4)   Sometimes it can help to repeat a request, emphasising the key words. For example:

ADULT: Please put the books on the chair next to the table. No, not on
    the table. Put them on the chair that's next to the table.

This type of instruction would be too difficult for many younger children. They would register either 'chair' or 'table' and not the spatial relationship between the two. An adult would have to simplify to 'Put the books on that chair' (pointing).

(5)   If a child does not understand, it is possible to rephrase a request. This may be particularly necessary if the activity is unfamiliar to the child. For example:

ADULT: Let's stir up the cake mix now.
                        (Child does nothing.)
ADULT: We stir it with this wooden spoon.

If the child still does not understand what is wanted, the adult will need to demonstrate stirring.

(6)   Sometimes children can grasp a hint given by the beginning of a sentence or a word. For example:

ADULT: What is a bucket for?
                        (Child says nothing.)
ADULT: It can carry w. . .

ADULT: What did we do this morning?
                        (Child says nothing.)
ADULT: Well, first of all we got the shopping basket and then we went . . .

(7)   With some thought, it is sometimes possible to highlight a particular feature for a child. In the following example, the adult is trying to focus the child on size:

ADULT: The marble went in the box, didn't it? Why can't we get this sponge in? *(The box is very small.)*
CHILD: Because it's a sponge.
ADULT: All right, I've cut the sponge in half. *(Cuts sponge and puts one half into the box.)* That's still a sponge, isn't it, but it's fitted into the box. Why's that?

(8)   Offering comparisons or alternatives can sometimes provoke a child into looking or thinking more carefully. For example:

ADULT: Where did the ball go?
                        (Child says nothing.)
ADULT: Well. Let's see — did it go under the table or did it go under the chair?

(9)   In some situations, children need a concrete example as a model. For example:

ADULT: Can you go over there and fetch me another sieve, please?
          (Child goes to cupboard and looks bewildered.)

ADULT: Do you know what a sieve is?
CHILD: No.
ADULT: Look. This is a sieve. *(Holds one up.)* Get me another sieve like this.

(10)   Encouragement to children to expand or clarify their answers is worthwhile if a child has not answered a question fully or has commented at a tangent to what the adult wants. For example:

ADULT *(pouring hot water on to jelly cubes)*:   Look! What's happening?
CHILD: Its jelly.
ADULT: Yes, but what's happening to the jelly?

(11)   Sometimes an adult can help a child to draw on her own knowledge from past experience to make sense of a new situation. For example:

ADULT: Now the spaghetti is hard. How do you think it will feel after it's cooked?
CHILD: Don't know.
ADULT: Well, you remember when we cooked the potatoes? They were hard to start with. How did they feel when we'd cooked them?

(12)   Sometimes an adult can suggest a line of action to a child which may focus her attention on specific aspects of a problem. For example:

ADULT: How is ice different from water?
CHILD: Don't know.
ADULT: Let's see. Turn over the cup of water into the bowl. Now turn over the tray of ice.

(13)   An adult's questions may help a child to tune into feelings and particular experiences. For example:

ADULT: Why did you pull your hand away from the cooker?
        (Child says nothing, looks at her hand.)
ADULT: Well, what did the cooker feel like?

All these suggestions are practical and are what might be called common sense. However, like much that seems obvious, such strategies do not necessarily leap to mind when adults are faced with a puzzled child. Much of the sense comes through learning from those frustrating times with children when we as adults could not find a way through. The insight now of 'Perhaps if I'd said . . .' may help to solve a similar problem in the future.

Sometimes it is the adults who do not understand!

In chapter 8 there were suggestions for helping a child whose expressive language was hard for adults to understand, even when an adult was familiar with the child. However, sometimes adults may understand every word that a child is saying but are still unable to grasp the meaning. Sometimes this is because the adults have no knowledge of the people or events to which the child is referring. This may happen in an under-fives centre when a child talks about family outings, or at home when she talks about events in the centre. To encourage the conversation following the child's interest, adults often have to ask questions to which only the child knows the answer — a pleasant reversal for the child. Also, the different adults in a child's life can profitably get together in conversation to relieve the confusion that comes from ignorance of the other 'part' of that life. In conversation with adults, children often make heroic efforts to make sense of the inexplicable (Margaret Donaldson and her colleagues report some thought-provoking projects on this topic*): it is not unreasonable to expect adults to make some effort too.

LOOKING AT FAMILIAR PLAY ACTIVITIES AS A SOURCE OF LEARNING

Even the most experienced or enthusiastic adults can become stale. It can be stimulating to think creatively about familiar play activities and equipment — about how many ways there might be of using these, without worrying initially about what might be practical or not. It is possible either to focus this thinking on a particular play activity or to start from a particular concept that children might learn.

Different ideas to learn from the same activity — the example of water play

Children can have water in a large water tray, but it also comes in bowls, sinks, baths, through wet weather, in parts of buildings such as drains or pipes, and in expanses of water such as streams, ponds, and reservoirs. Water in some or all of these different contexts might be one way of learning about movement and speed, the force and strength of water, water under pressure, air and water, temperature and extremes of this, evaporation, floating and sinking, relative weights, concepts of full and empty, the process of filling and emptying, depth, mixing water with

---

*Margaret Donaldson wrote *Children's minds*, published in 1980 by Fontana, and she edited, with Robert Grieve and Chris Pratt, *Early childhood development and education*, published in 1983 by Basil Blackwell.

other substances, cooking, what happens when hot water is mixed with different substances, what will absorb water, how some things shrink in water, and many other ideas.

Readers might like to take other familiar play activities and make as long a list as possible of what children might learn through them. The activity might be a set of wooden bricks, the sand tray, a climbing frame, or perhaps a doll's house and its contents. When adults think of a range of ideas rather than using the same play materials in the same way, the experience can be much more enjoyable for adults and children alike.

If adults are prepared to be creative, it can also help them with children who are very fixed in the play activities they will do. It may not be feasible to try to move such a child on to a completely different activity; however, she may be more amenable to a slightly different use of the same play materials.

Different activities as routes to learning similar concepts

Another approach is to start from a particular concept or set of ideas and generate play activities appropriate to this. Learning about space, about relationships between objects, or about movement can emerge through many different activities. Children who enjoy indoor games may learn such ideas with the help of play with building materials, farmyards and toy farm animals, cars and mats with a marked-out roadway, toys which fit together, or doll's-house equipment. However, ideas of space, spatial relationships, and movement can also emerge through physically active play and outdoor games. These might include music and movement, imitating adult physical movements in a game, moving according to instructions (for instance, sidewards, backwards, close together, finger-tip distance), or simple obstacle courses on foot or on bicycles where children experience in their body movements what it means to go 'through', 'under', or 'over'.

Adults can refresh their stock of ideas and ways of looking at familiar play activities from books published by a number of practical educational projects. One such project is the Early Mathematical Experiences (EME) project, which was led by Geoffrey and Julia Matthews.

It is unfortunate that many older children and adults view mathematics as a mysterious closed book. The numbers and other symbols of this subject are, after all, only a language, such as the language we use in conversation. The value of the booklets produced by the EME team is that they present practical suggestions on how adults can help children to gain the basis of such concepts as number, the passing of time, or space and shape. At the pre-school stage, understanding of such concepts will be limited, but it will provide the groundwork for later learning that adults might more readily label as mathematics.

One example of this is learning about time. Few children who start primary school will have a confident understanding of time as read from a clock or watch. However, adults can have built some basis to this understanding in the pre-school years through play and conversation. Exploring a sequence in a story is one early stage in understanding time — what follows what. A set of three or four pictures which tell a tale can be placed in order by a child and a conversation can emerge from talking about the events of the story. An older child may enjoy sorting out two jumbled sets of pictures which make two distinct stories.

Many ordinary activities can help children to understand the passing of time. They go out to play after breakfast. They may have a nap after lunch. In nursery, parents may come reliably at particular times. Conversation with adults can help children to learn these regular patterns. The words to describe what happens when will initially be in terms of events rather than clock time. Children will understand 'There's time to do one more painting' before there is any meaning in 'We'll clear up in five minutes time.'

Children can be helped to discriminate days of the week if something special happens on each day, or on some days. Monday might be the day for watering the plants or rearranging the nature table. Tuesday might be the day everyone watches a children's programme on the television. Other days might be the days you wash the doll's clothes or clean the rabbit's hutch. Children may like to talk about what they did at the weekend, which will need words or phrases like 'last night', 'yesterday', or 'the day before yesterday'. The more interest an adult shows in these conversations, the more a child is likely to try to express experiences and ideas about time.

In a similar way, adults can build a basis to children's understanding of number, weight, relative distance, volume, and many other concepts about which children will continue to learn during their school years. The EME booklets* are a valuable source of ideas on this and, because they are so practical, may go some way towards allaying adults' own worries that 'I've never been any good at maths so I'd better not start anything with the children.'

Alan Graham has tackled the business of helping adults to unravel their confusions about maths so that they can help children. His book *Help your child with maths*, published by Fontana in 1985, is an excellent read for adults — whether parents or under-fives workers — full of suggestions for what to do with children at home or at nursery or playgroup, and with clear explanations of concepts in maths so that the adults can emerge from the fog!

---

*These booklets are published by Longman (Primary). They include a general guide and six booklets, each covering two major themes.

Approaching children's learning through themes

Several projects which have developed materials for use with under-fives have presented ideas through themes. The EME project was one; another was a project on 'Social Handicap and Cognitive Functioning in Pre-school Children' run by the National Foundation for Educational Research (NFER).* The NFER team took a broad view of what constituted social handicap. They were concerned about children who had a poor self-image (especially if they belonged to a minority group) and children who were limited in their use and understanding of language, had low levels of concentration or motivation, had poor conceptual and problem-solving abilities, or who were not adept in social skills.

The NFER team's suggestions are built around themes such as 'Myself', 'Homes', and 'Food'. Within each theme there are ideas for play materials, talking points, linked group and individual activities, and possible rhymes, songs, or short stories. The team's recommendation is that a small group of between four and six children should have daily sessions of about fifteen or twenty minutes with one adult. The benefits of this approach are that the children's activities on one day have links with the previous day and will also link with the following day. This continuity can be enjoyable for all children but is especially useful if the children's lives have limited predictability otherwise.

The value of themes relevant to the child's learning is not limited to small-group activities. It is equally appropriate as adults think about what individual children might enjoy and as they plan activities to be made available to larger groups. Children need opportunities both to choose completely for themselves and to follow adult suggestions. Although a reasonable range of play materials is helpful, the value of play for children still depends a great deal on how adults present and use the available equipment. Part of this is helping a child to explore an interest or theme, which will sometimes have been introduced by an adult.

The very great choice available now in toys and different kinds of play equipment can have the unfortunate effect of unduly focusing adults on how much equipment they have and the sheer variety this will provide. Children do need change and a range of play materials from which to choose; however, there are many occasions when there is very good reason to offer a child the same materials as were tidied up earlier in the day. The child may have a building or model to finish. She may still be grasping how something works. She may have finally come to grips with a new jigsaw before lunch and now she wants the pleasure of completing the puzzle a couple of times with obvious ease. Even younger children

---

*The material developed by the project team is presented in *My world*, by Audrey Curtis and Sheelagh Hill, published by the NFER in 1979.

can enjoy a scrapbook which is kept safe between play sessions and then brought out so they can stick another picture into their own personal book. A children's television programme may mean so much more if, afterwards, an adult helps the children to make the model or carry out the same experiments that they saw on the television. Overall, adults have to aim for a balance between what children gain from variety and what they gain from repetition and continuity through themes.

Final comments

This chapter began with the drawbacks to adults' flooding children with language and, more particularly, with searching questions in excess of what children can manage. The overall point has been about adults' sensitivity to their own behaviour and language with children. A child who is not being given the opportunity to reply shows through her behaviour that this is happening. She may withdraw or reply without much effort. She may learn to interrupt and be as poor a listener as her adult model. Either way, the signs are there for the adult to notice. If too many of adults' conversations with children are over-heavy with educational purpose, then the evidence is again usually present for adults to observe. Adults need to be alert to the signs and need to adjust their own behaviour as appropriate. This is equally true for adults who are not making sufficient effort to talk with or listen to the children in their care. The appropriate balance and approach will be slightly different for each individual child, and adults need to work towards this.

Adults can become very intense about their work with young children. The best-intentioned plans can be counterproductive if adults become more concerned about what they feel they ought to be doing and saying than about children's reactions and children's needs. When adults are coming to grips with the ideas of an educational project or with a new set of play materials, there may be a period when their attention is more on themselves. The new ideas have to become part of the adults' own style. However, this should be only a phase. The time should return when adults can find pleasure in how the new ideas help children's learning and both adults and children can enjoy the playtime.

PART 3
THE BEHAVIOUR OF
YOUNG CHILDREN

10
THE EMOTIONAL
DEVELOPMENT OF YOUNG
CHILDREN

As children are advancing in physical development and language, they are also changing emotionally. Their views of the world and of relationships between themselves and others change. Children's ability to recognise and control their own emotions progresses, as does their understanding of behaviour such as sharing with others or the idea of danger — areas which become important in adults' views of what is 'good' and 'bad' behaviour. Adults need to be aware of what are reasonable expectations for children, otherwise their judgements of children as 'naughty' can take little account of the limited understanding of certain ages. The relationship of an adult to a young child is ideally one of steady adjustments by the adult as the child's emotional development progresses and her individuality becomes ever clearer.

It would be a lengthy business to describe all the steps in a young child's emotional growth. This chapter will focus on just some of the changes.* There is much value for adults in making sure that they are aware of the ways in which a child's world and understanding do expand. This makes it more possible that they may see a situation from the child's point of view at least as often as from the standpoint of adult needs and wants.

The individuality of babies

A baby is an individual as much as a toddler, a four-year-old, or a school-age child. The differences are there to be seen from the earliest days for anyone who takes the trouble to look rather than blandly assuming that all babies are much the same.

Some babies are more lethargic or passive than others, some seem to be more responsive, some are more wakeful, some are more jumpy, some seem to be upset very easily, some cry more. Even if an adult has known and cared for many babies, a new baby is always a unique experience,

---

*More detail, as well as many practical suggestions, can be found, in Penelope Leach's *Baby and child* (published by Michael Joseph in 1977 and by Penguin Books in 1979). Mary Sheridan's *Children's developmental progress* (third edition published by the NFER in 1975) is also a compact source of information on the steps in emotional development, as well as other areas of development.

Babies are individuals from the very beginning.

since that adult has not known this particular baby.

   Since the baby's individuality is present and developing from early on, the match between adult behaviour and the behaviour of the baby is central to making life pleasant. If the two do match, then life is a little easier. If there is a mismatch, then life can be very difficult. For example, if an adult's preferred way of handling a baby is through plenty of movement and games right from the start, this will be fine with a baby who enjoys action and change and being carried about. However, if the baby is very sensitive, tending to be jumpy, then this kind of handling may really upset her. If an adult feels that babies should be quiet and lie in their pram or cot for much of the time, a placid or fairly sleepy baby will fit the picture. However, another person might be upset and disappointed by what is seen as a lack of responsiveness in the baby. Babies vary and so do adults — hence the combination is a unique one each time, and adults have to learn a little more.

Balancing the needs of babies and the needs of adults

Caring for babies and children is demanding and tiring. Adults have needs, just as children do. Even adults who really enjoy being with children have days when patience and understanding run out. Stressing the importance of adult sensitivity to the baby's or child's point of view is not asking adults to deny all their own feelings and wishes: it is rather that with many adults the balance seems to be too much in the direction of their wants and their adult viewpoint. Care of children can be more enjoyable and less tiresome if a baby or child is given some respect for her needs and moods.

For example, many adults expect that babies should tolerate being handed round from lap to lap, and should even welcome the sudden attentions of complete strangers. If an unknown adult came very close to you, smiled, and tried to touch you, your reaction would probably be to move quickly out of reach. Many people expect, however, that babies will not mind a similar sudden intrusion into their personal world. By six to seven months, babies often have clear preferences about contact with familiar and unfamiliar adults. In fact, babies much younger than this will often be upset by an unfamiliar way of being handled or carried.

As babies become toddlers, adult needs for affection sometimes take the form of expecting that a child will be equally pleased to see you as you are to see her. Adults may expect the child to be prepared to give affection at the time when they need it or, as the child becomes slightly older, expect gratitude for 'all I've done for her'. There are many times when the needs of adult and child coincide. These can be very joyful times, but other occasions can be made less stressful to both adult and child by remembering that each has his or her own needs.

Children being 'demanding' of adults

By twelve months, children who have had experience of a few familiar adults will clearly show the importance of these adults to their world by wanting them in sight or hearing for much of the day. The reassurance of a familiar face is often necessary — even if the child seems to be busy in her own play. The frustrations of the second year of life also mean that a child of this age often needs the reassurance and comfort of an adult, as well as the adult's help in activities too difficult for the child alone. For some time yet, an adult caring for a child must accept that, while the child is awake, her needs and calls for attention will mean that the adult will not have long uninterrupted sessions for adult activities. This does not mean that the child is being naughty or is spoilt. She will learn to spend time enjoying her own activities if an adult has built up the reassuring feeling that — as far as practically possible — adult attention, help, and encouragement are there for the asking.

The eighteen-month-old child is still emotionally very dependent upon a familiar adult, but her behaviour often swings from one extreme to another. She will cling to and retreat to a familiar person in times of stress or difficulty. At other times she will resist and be angry with the adult when she wants to do something by herself or something forbidden. Such sudden changes can be most confusing, especially if the adult is not aware that such apparent inconsistencies are normal for this age group. The child is not being inconsistent from her own view.

For example, you may want to talk with another adult without interruptions. However, the child may be unsure of the surroundings you are in and become petulant and demanding because — from her point of view — you are not giving her enough of your familiar presence. At home, on her own ground, she feels confident to climb up on to a wobbly table and then throws a tantrum when you take her down. In the first instance she wanted your protection and in the second instance she did not, so she became cross each time.

Being able to play 'properly'

Children's behaviour in their play is as much a reflection of their personality and experience as their behaviour at other times. There are differences, however, which are related to age. Individual children vary in their willingness to play alone, or to play at length with other children. However, at eighteen months or two years, most children are not really capable of cooperative play with other children. They may play near other children but not really with them. At this age they may well be interested in older children; they may want to watch them or, frustratingly for the older ones, carry off some of their toys.

Although not capable of cooperating in play with others, children of eighteen months to two years are able to copy and often really enjoy imitating the actions of older children and adults. The limited understanding of this age group can make life worrying and frustrating for adults, especially if they do not learn to see the world at least sometimes from the child's perspective. At eighteen months to two years, children cannot understand that it is all right for the builder to knock holes in the living-room wall because the house is being rewired, but that this is not normally acceptable behaviour. Similarly, it is all right to paint on walls which are being redecorated, but not to paint or crayon on walls generally. The child's ability to imitate is not yet matched by an ability to understand that 'It's only all right if. . . .'

The understanding of danger

Two-year-olds have learned so much that adults can find themselves surprised at the large gaps that exist, and will exist for some time, between a child's and an adult's view of the world. Especially if the child's language has developed well, adults may sometimes expect too mature an understanding.

Children can be very curious, and yet the beginning of a sense of danger really does not develop until closer to three years of age. The physical abilities of two-year-olds can carry them into trouble with devastating speed. Children learn that certain actions are not allowed long before they understand that these prohibitions are because the action could be harmful to them or to someone else.

It simply does not occur to young children that they might be physically hurt as a consequence of what they are doing. It may help adults to think back to their own childhood. Many have looked with horror on a favourite play area of theirs when they were children. Often, it would seem, the child's inability to see danger in climbing a rickety tree has meant that her climbing has been safe and not made shaky by fears of falling.

Even children of school age can feel frustrated by adults who can see potential danger where the children see none. With older children, adults often have to walk a worrying middle course between trusting a child to know the limits of her own physical abilities and stepping in when they judge that there is a real danger. Younger children — the under-fives and especially the under-threes — need to be protected from their very limited understanding of the possible dangerous consequences of their own actions. It is unreasonable for adults to become angry with young children over this — a child simply does not understand 'But you might fall and hurt yourself', since 'might's have no more meaning than 'danger'. If the child does fall, this might be one experience which will slowly add to her understanding. However, adult reactions of the 'I told you so' variety are neither helpful nor reasonable, since the child's emotions at the time will be about feeling shocked and in pain. She needs comfort, not criticism.

Adults can help children to learn to take care of themselves by steadily teaching them how to deal with potentially dangerous situations — crossing roads, using sharp knives, developing respect for fire. It should not be a straight leap from 'No, you mustn't' to 'I suppose I ought to let you do it on your own.'

Understanding the hurt and upset of others

Another aspect of learning about danger is the risk of hurting other people by certain actions. Children will learn that waving sticks about or throwing stones is not allowed before they appreciate that such actions can lead to gouged eyes or serious cuts. Younger children are also limited by their lack of understanding of the physical and emotional sensations of others. Young children often hurt people because they cannot understand that slapping or punching hurts the other person as much as the same action would hurt them. Adults do not usually blame uncoordinated babies for where their little fists land. However, a physically coordinated toddler is often blamed, unless the incident is viewed as a genuine accident.

It is obviously important to teach toddlers not to lash out or to bite. However, they have such limited understanding of another's pain that they are only likely to be puzzled by appeals to think about others. They will, however, learn that adults disapprove of slapping or biting and that the child who receives comfort and attention after such an incident is the one who has been hurt. Children's understanding gradually develops so that, by four or five years of age, a child will often move to comfort or protect someone who has been hurt or who is not feeling well.

Living in the present

Babies and toddlers live very largely in the present. A child of eighteen months to two years shows clear evidence of remembering and hence of learning from her past experience. She can remember where toys are kept, where the biscuit tin is stored, how to open cupboard doors. However, this reference back to past learning is firmly rooted in present needs — she wants a biscuit or the favourite toy now. However, the wishes of the moment can overrule what the child has previously learned. She may have become adept at walking round a particular table; however, one day her eyes and mind may be firmly on reaching a favourite toy before another child and she runs straight into the table.

Children of two and three years old have only limited speech to describe the past and future. This reflects their level of understanding of time. There is little point in adults' telling children 'But you promised this morning', since it is no longer this morning, and a child this age probably does not really understand the notion of a promise. Four- and five-year-olds do have a much wider understanding of the past and discussions of what will happen in the future. This can be the basis of enjoyable adult—child conversations. However, adults cannot assume that the child's understanding is equivalent to their own. This is often shown by children's descriptions of what happened 'a long time ago'.

Two-year-olds have very limited ability to 'wait until later'. From the child's viewpoint, what is worth having must be had now. However, if adults are patient and prepared to be flexible, two-year-olds can sometimes be distracted, learn to wait a short while, or be satisfied by an alternative offered by the adult. However, the alternative is not likely to involve waiting quietly while the adult completes a lengthy task or another child finishes playing with the favoured toy. Three-year-olds usually show some ability to wait, if adults have helped them to learn this by making sure that promises such as 'You can have the bike when he's finished' are actually honoured. A child who has learned that 'waiting' means 'not getting' has no incentive to learn to postpone her immediate wishes.

Understanding sharing

An ability to look towards the immediate future seems to be important in learning to share. A two-year-old cannot genuinely share, and it is pointless for adults to expect this behaviour from her. She may hand over a toy on request and the adult may then give it to another child; however, the first child is cooperating with the adult's wishes, not sharing with the other child.

With appropriate experience, children can learn to share sometime after about three years of age. A child needs to have learned the difference between her own and others' possessions, experienced that her own possessions are returned, and learned that group possessions, for instance in a nursery or playgroup, are toys which she can enjoy like everybody else but does not possess. However, like so many other developments, the idea of sharing does not automatically appear. If a child's experience is that her own possessions 'shared' with other children are not returned or return broken, she will learn to resist adult requests to share. If she finds that nursery toys, like bikes, are used mainly by the children tough enough to resist attempts to take them away, then the child is not going to learn to 'share' these toys. This is hardly surprising from the child's point of view — if all the connotations of sharing are unpleasant, there is no incentive for the child to learn this behaviour.

This is an area where adults need to take a considered look at what they are asking of children. It seems to me that there are three kinds of behaviour that adults ask of children which are quite distinct and yet are all labelled as 'sharing'. We ask children to 'share' their own toys when friends come to play, or with brothers or sisters at home. The rules of this are that the toys are returned, so we are really asking for a pattern of *lending* and *borrowing*. In a nursery or playgroup, we ask children to 'share' toys which belong to no one individual — here we are really asking them to *take turns*. A third way in which adults use 'share' is when we say 'Share your sweets, please.' Now, sweets or crisps are one-time possessions of a child — she does not get them back once 'shared', so we are actually asking her to *give*. These are all hard behaviours to learn. Adults can help if they appreciate the different requests that they are making and if they avoid the emotional pressurising of 'You must learn to share!' and 'Don't be so selfish — share!'

Limits to a child's 'good' behaviour

By three years of age, a child's emotional development and social behaviour will have progressed to the extent that she can behave more like a model of what adults see as 'good' behaviour. However, she will not always behave this way. Three-year-olds are more able to play together, with toys or in make-believe games, than younger children. They are more able to cooperate with each other, to help adults, and to be sensitive in a limited way to the feelings of others. They are more able to share, to wait for something, and to be rather more amenable to changes in plans. However, children will not always behave this way. Like adults, they will not always feel cooperative or thoughtful of others. The fact that they are more capable of what adults judge to be 'good' behaviour does not mean that they will always behave this way.

A toddler often shows frustration by tears, tantrums, and shouting. Although an older child may be much less likely to throw tantrums, her sense of self and wish to be independent are strong. A four-year-old may not need to throw a tantrum if she has the language to argue. However, if adults will not answer her demands to know 'Why must I?', she may resort to tantrums. A four-year-old who is very tired or who has experienced a particularly stressful day may react with behaviour that was more typical of her when she was younger. This is information to an adult that for this child, at the moment, everything has become too much to bear. She most probably needs an outpouring of reassurance and comfort that will allow her for a short while to act like a younger child.

Behaviour with other children also varies from one child to another. The four-year-old is capable, if she has had the experience, of playing with other children in cooperative and imaginative games. Four-year-olds can also learn the idea of taking turns — with a favoured toy or in a game which involves one person at a time making a move. Children can also show concern for younger children or for animals, and sympathy for children who are distressed. Although this is what a four-year-old can manage, it does not mean, of course, that all children of this age play cooperatively all or even most of the time, show sympathy for upset children, and so on. Children vary in their personalities, and their experience will have coloured their outlook on the world and people. By four years of age this experience will have given them some definite expectations about what life is like and how other adults and children are likely to behave. A four-year-old's experience does not mould her for life — much depends on what happens in subsequent years — but her life so far will make a substantial impact on her behaviour.

Adjusting to primary school

The entry into primary school may mark a very great change from a child's pre-school years or it may be similar in many respects. A child who has spent some time in a nursery or large playgroup may be unworried about the number of unfamiliar children. She may have become used to getting to know new adults, may be familiar with the type of activities and used to the routine. In contrast, a child who has spent most of her life at home with one parent is more likely to find the numbers of children and adults at school worrying. The building is likely to be very different from the smaller-scale home environment, and the rules and routine will be alien. The ease with which children settle into school is influenced by their previous experience, by their own personality, by the sensitivity of the teacher in charge of the reception class, and by the efforts of the adults who are responsible for them pre-school to ease the transition into school life.

By five years of age, children's emotional and social development will have reached the point where they can understand and follow a daily routine. Within this, they may have the beginnings of an understanding of clock time. They have a greater understanding of adults' wish for order and tidiness and will cooperate to some extent. In short, they understand that adults have rules about children's behaviour. However, their experience will determine whether they believe that adults are people who are inconsistent about rules and can be persuaded by sufficient whining or tantrums or that adults are reliable people who mean what they say. Until she has understood the new set of rules, variations in adult behaviour from that which a child has learned in the past are likely to cause concern and confusion.

Conclusions

Much of a child's learning in the early years and the work of adults with the child and baby is towards encouraging behaviour which adults feel will be acceptable in the family and in the world outside the child's family. Adults vary considerably in the details of what they judge to be appropriate behaviour, different communities vary, and the differences between cultures can be striking. The child's social development is very strongly influenced by the specific ways in which we train children in our culture.

In general, our babies learn to eat progressively more like their adult family members and to sleep the sort of pattern that their adults do — for instance we train children out of an afternoon nap, but many hot countries plan their day around just such an afternoon siesta. Children learn ways of behaving which are more or less acceptable to the adult community. In our schools, we stress the importance of time limits on many activities, the importance of getting the right answer, and the importance of getting that answer on your own and not usually in unofficial cooperation with others, which we call 'cheating'. Some cultures would find these rules alien and incomprehensible. There are cultures in which it would be judged the height of bad behaviour to keep the right answer to yourself and to fail to help those who do not understand. Other cultures find the concept of having a restricted amount of time to complete a task very strange. Our babies and children learn the social codes of their culture. They do not learn them perfectly all the time, or else they learn to prefer a different set of behaviours which causes them trouble within the family or school.

Within one culture, adults' views vary considerably about the details of how to treat children. Adults need to remind themselves of how much a child's emotional and social development depend on learning and, therefore, on the child's experiences. The appearance of behaviour such as sharing or the passing of the awesome two-year-old tantrums does not happen automatically. Such changes are influenced by how adults, and other children, treat a child and how the adults deal with the frustrating aspects to the development of the under-fives.

11
ADULT BEHAVIOUR WITH CHILDREN — SOME GENERAL APPROACHES TO DEALING WITH PROBLEMS

Personality and experience

A practical approach is to work from the basis that children learn the ways in which they behave. They learn from people around them as models. They learn from the experience of what happens when they behave in certain ways, from the limits or sanctions that other people impose as well as from what emerges as approved behaviour. They also learn from experience of which behaviours seem to work — which achieve the desired aim. The process of learning is not necessarily conscious, although there may sometimes be a rather deliberate experimenting. The end result in terms of how children — or adults — behave will not always seem to an onlooker to be either rational or sensible, but behaviour that irritates or surprises other people is often achieving a goal for the individual concerned. There may, of course, be other ways of reaching the goal — ways which do not irritate others.

Both children and adults learn ways of behaving, but the end results are very different, even for individuals who appear to have been in the same situation, for example children raised in the same family. The reason is that the impact of experience is filtered through the child's or adult's personality. Babies show differences in their reactions and responsiveness from their earliest days. Undoubtedly, these differences lead the adults who care for them to behave differently. So, from the beginning, the individuality of a baby is mingling with the experiences she is having.

It is important that adults remind themselves of the individuality of children. However, there are serious pitfalls to taking a view of personality that fixes a child as rigid. The child's individuality will colour her reactions but it does not make her into a robot, fixed in her behaviour. Just as she has learned certain behaviours, she can not only learn new ones but can also unlearn ways of behaving that are no longer effective. The probable reason that children, and adults, can seem so fixed is that other individuals and circumstances have combined in such a way that there seems to be no incentive to change.

For example, a child who wants to gain an adult's attention may have learned from previous experience that threatening or actually attacking younger children brings adults running. The consequence is a dramatic situation, and the child feels that she is at the centre of events. The fact that the adults are cross with her may count for little when set against the pleasure of having their full attention. The child has learned to be satisfied with the attention of an angry adult, so there will have to be some definite incentive for her to change, and such change will take time. The motivation for change may come from an alteration in how the adults react, both to her attacks to gain attention and to her behaviour at other times. Some positive action from adults to encourage other ways of seeking attention may redirect the child's energies and provide her with the opportunity to experience attention from a pleased rather than an irritated adult. With older children, teenagers, and adults, it becomes more possible to talk about the consequences of certain ways of behaving. The motivation for change may be stimulated by such discussions. However, for under-fives, adults' actions will often speak more loudly than their words.

Since learning to behave in certain ways combines with individual personality, similar feelings may emerge in different ways. There are, for example, many ways for angry feelings to be expressed. Through a combination of personality and experience, some adults and children tend to express their anger outwards. The feelings burst out in angry words, perhaps through physical aggression to others, perhaps through hurting other people. Some adults and children may feel equally strongly but the feelings emerge in a different way — they are turned inwards on the individual who feels the anger. Children or adults may feel angry with themselves, perhaps anxious about having such fierce emotions, and may develop nervous or compulsive habits through this concern. Within any attempts to generalise, there has to be allowance for variety between individuals.

Adults treat boys and girls differently, in many subtle and not-so-subtle ways. Attitudes are expressed which encourage certain kinds of behaviour from children and discourage others. Boys are often allowed to be noisier and play more roughly than girls. A boy may be allowed to have an untidy room at home with the almost admiring excuse of 'He's a real boy.' A young boy and a young girl may be equally sensitive, easily hurt or moved by the plight of other people. The girl will probably be allowed to cry. Most probably, the boy will soon be discouraged from this — told that 'Big boys don't cry' or criticised for being 'soft'. He may learn to hide his feelings, perhaps to cover them up with a show of bravado. Alternatively, he may be unable to stem his tears and come to see himself in a negative way if the adults around him do not value male gentleness or sensitivity.

People who feel strongly that personality determines behaviour and outlook on life are likely to judge that there is little hope of changing anybody. People — adults or children — are as they are and they are not likely to change. This can lead to very rigid judgements — 'He's always been a bad 'un' or 'You'll never change her — she's just an evil-tempered little girl.' People's personality — the core of what makes them individuals — is most unlikely to change: it is best seen as a given. Attitudes are also very resistant to persuasion, although people's attitudes do sometimes change if the jolt is strong enough. However, the way that personality and attitudes are expressed through behaviour is much more amenable to change. This is the reason for the focus in this and the following chapter on dealing with how children behave.

Approaches rather than solutions

In dealing with children there is rarely, if ever, a perfect match between a problem arising from a child's behaviour and something particular for the adult to do as an effective solution. Adults trying to deal with a child they find difficult often hope, quite understandably, that someone somewhere will be able to tell them precisely what to do and that a short application of this will remove the problem. The comments of unhelpful, although perhaps well-meaning, other adults often perpetuate this myth of the simple answer — 'If only you'd been firm with him when he first started all this', 'It's too late now of course, but what you should have done . . .', 'It's all this spoiling when they're babies that does it.' The fact that much of this so-called advice is after the event only adds to the unhelpfulness — there is no way of knowing now whether the approach offered so categorically would have made any difference at all. People so often hope for a behaviour 'prescription', like a pill for a headache, that is applied once for the problem to go away. However, even the most simple suggestions for handling a child usually imply some change in the approach of the adult. They are not one-off solutions of 'You do this and then she won't do that anymore.'

Emphasising adults without trying to blame

The discussion in this chapter focuses on adults as much as on children. There is certainly no intention of blaming adults for the problems that children present. It is instead a realistic view that adults' feelings and behaviour are a major influence on children and so some attention has to be paid to that side of the problem. Furthermore, adults should be able to take a rather broader perspective and a longer-term view than a child. Adults are more able to think about their feelings and modify how they act. The stress is on 'more able' rather than 'always able' because we, as adults, are often so involved in what is happening that it can be hard to see ourselves as a possible influence on matters becoming better or worse. We often need a breathing space for thought, or a chance to talk over the problem with someone else who is not so closely involved. Whatever the details of the events, there is nothing to be gained by trying to apportion the blame for why relations have become as dire as they have. Everyone has to deal with the situation and individuals as they are now and not as they might have been had something else been done in the past. 'If only's such as this get everybody nowhere fast.

Accepting that change will take time

Adults have to be prepared to persevere in how they deal with the more difficult aspects to the behaviour of young children. This is as true of dealing with children who are passing through temporary difficult phases as it is of trying to influence a child who has learned a particular way of behaving that is driving everyone to distraction. There is no need to take the defeatist view of 'It's too late now, the child is so set in her ways.' Undoubtedly, the longer the difficult situation has continued, the harder it will be to change ways of behaving. However, it is not impossible — just harder. The adult concerned may have to realise, perhaps helped through the support of other adults, that his or her behaviour is affecting what is happening — it is not just the child, although that child has also become relatively fixed in her ways of reacting. The adult will have to be prepared to live through what may be a very difficult period of adjustment while the child learns that the ground rules have changed. The relationship between adult and child may become worse before it improves.

For example, a child who has learned that whining, griping, or destructive behaviour brings attention fast may increase this sort of behaviour initially, while the adult is trying hard to reduce the attention given to this and increase attention for more constructive behaviour. The child has already learned that whining and griping succeeds, so the adult has to be willing to tolerate the change-over period as that child learns that the adult has changed or that what she previously learned about adults does not apply in this new environment. Adults need strength, patience, and support to persevere through this most difficult period and give their approach time to succeed.

Even when a problem has not developed over a long period, adults need to accept that children's behaviour will not necessarily change quickly. Even when it emerges in the end that the adult's approach is the best one to help, it may be some time before the effects are seen. So, none of the suggestions discussed in this chapter is a solution in the sense that it will swiftly 'cure' a difficulty with a child. Many have implications for long-term changes in how a child is handled.

'It's just a phase'

Some problems which arise with children can reasonably be seen as part of their normal development. A common example is the ease with which many rising-twos and two-year-olds go into a temper tantrum. At this age, an emerging sense of self and clear notions about what they want to do are combined with limited ability to express strong feelings through words or to redirect themselves. Two-year-old's tantrums can therefore be called a phase. The knowledge that such outbursts are not unusual with this age is some comfort. However, this does not remove the fact that adults still have to deal with a kicking screaming bundle of fury — often in front of other people! Many of the approaches to dealing with difficulties with young children are applicable to problems which are associated with a particular stage of development. Saying that a particular behaviour is 'just a phase' is not an answer in itself.

CONSISTENCY IN ADULT BEHAVIOUR

Being consistent over our own rules

It is important that adults are consistent with young children, because children are learning from adult behaviour. Adults are a model for children, and a child who has experienced adults as inconsistent will see no point in keeping promises or trying to be consistent herself. There is no obvious benefit to her. Furthermore, inconsistency from adults confuses children. Instead of learning about limits to what is allowed and which limits are flexible, the child learns that adults are generally unpredictable. At one time they will allow certain behaviour and then, without warning, on another occasion become very cross about it. For example, it is difficult for children to learn what adults want if a child's cheekiness is sometimes seen as amusing and then the adult punishes what in the child's view is the same clowning around that was seen as a joke yesterday. Adults often protest that they have their reasons — 'I just wasn't in the mood today' or 'It was all right yesterday, we were on our own, but today she showed me up in front of the doctor.' There will be times when a child can understand that circumstances alter cases — perhaps that there are certain sorts of joke that are just for within the family, or that today the adult has a bad headache and so will not feel like leaping about. However, children need these circumstances explained, so that they can learn to adjust their behaviour accordingly. Adults have to appreciate that for younger children the changes will make no sense, so the adult just has to try to be as consistent as possible.

A further reason for adults' learning the habit of being consistent in their own behaviour is that this is so important when dealing with children who are proving very difficult to handle. The child must come to understand that clear consequences follow certain sorts of behaviour that adults are trying to discourage. If the ground rules vary, children are less likely to change their behaviour and more likely to keep pushing against any unclear boundaries between what is and what is not allowed. If a child learns that sometimes an adult can be nagged into giving way on what has been presented as a hard and fast rule, then she will be tempted to try nagging and pestering on future occasions.

Consistency between adults

Consistency on limits to what is allowed is particularly important when a child whom adults find difficult is being handled by more than one individual. A child is less likely to change if one adult allows her to reach one level of, say, aggression or destructiveness before intervening but another adult steps in at a much earlier stage. Particularly with a child who is always pushing adults to the absolute limits, it is crucial that those adults discuss and reach an agreement on how the child's behaviour will be handled and what are the limits to be set. Sometimes, however, the inevitable individual differences between adults are less of a concern, and children learn that adults do not all react in similar ways.

It is preferable that home and nursery, or home and childminder, should be consistent in major principles of handling the child. It is not realistic to seek 100% consistency. Adults vary in many small ways as to how they feel comfortable in dealing with young children. Many children learn that different rules of behaviour operate at home and at their grandparents' house. As long as the individual adults are consistent in their own rules, children learn the fact that people differ. However, if the differences are wide, a child may be very confused until she reaches this conclusion.

A source of difficulty between adults who have very different views on dealing with the same child is that this can lead to antagonism between the adults. Perhaps with a younger child this might be 'I spend all week on toilet-training her and her mother just doesn't bother at the weekend, so it's back to square one every Monday.' With another child it might be 'She plays so contentedly at home, why do you see her as such a pest at nursery?' This is not the child's problem — it belongs squarely to the adults concerned. It might be a matter for discussion about different views of toilet-training or ignorance about what the other adult is trying to do. It might be a case for considering that the child plays contentedly in one environment because there is an adult who is close by to help and who responds quickly to comments from the child, whereas at this particular nursery or playgroup the child has learned that only serious

Children will often look to you for a clear 'Is this allowed?' ▶

pestering brings an adult's undivided attention.

Children often learn different ways of behaving at the meal table, in line with the expectations of different adults. The concern of 'She eats her dinner for you at nursery but she won't eat it for me' is again not the child's problem, although it may be seen in terms of her 'naughtiness'. The child may have learned that different rules operate for mealtimes at home and at nursery, and she is conforming to these on the basis of her past experience. If the child's parent wishes her to behave at home as she behaves at the nursery, then that parent's own behaviour may have to change — perhaps making meals an enjoyable social occasion and not interpreting the rejection of food as rejecting the parent's concern and effort that have gone into cooking it.

LOOKING FOR ALTERNATIVES

The possibilities of diverting children

It is important to remember that adults do not have to stand by waiting for a situation to become worse. There are many times when a well-placed adult may be able to divert a child from an aggressive attack, a tantrum, or from hurting herself. Distracting a child does not always work, of course, but it works sufficiently often to make it a method well worth having towards the top of a list of possibilities. Some adults, it seems, cannot be bothered to anticipate difficulties — they sit back with a self-satisfied 'There she goes again!', or call 'Stop it!' ineffectively from a distance.

Obviously, the success of diverting children from one course of action into another depends on knowledge of individual children. Some children may be distracted from fights over favourite toys by being offered another which the adult knows is also highly prized. Sometimes the suggestion that a child 'Come and help me with this' may be a more tempting prospect. A sensitive adult may be able to show two children how they can rearrange an activity so that they can both participate. Sometimes the diversion may be away from the squabbling towards telling the adult about what has happened. This role of referee and general releaser of tensions is something that often needs an adult — children can only sometimes do it for themselves.

Offering children a choice

Another way of diverting children from one course of action is to offer them a choice between two other alternatives. Adults have to be careful

Children can sometimes sort out the rules of play for themselves. ▶

not to over-use this approach, otherwise the novelty of choosing wears off. The rising-twos and two-year-olds who have developed firm ideas of what they want can sometimes be distracted by a choice. When my son was nearly two years old, his demands for a biscuit could sometimes be diverted by an offer of 'No biscuit. You can have carrot or raisins.' He would then ponder on the choice between two foods he enjoyed and would often happily pick one of these. Older children may more readily accept an explanation of why they cannot go on a shopping trip today if an attractive choice is offered for what they might do indoors.

Encouraging a particular alternative

With some kinds of behaviour that adults wish to discourage, there is a definite alternative way of acting that literally cannot happen at the same time. The two ways of behaving are incompatible. For example, a child who throws toys or spoonfuls of food at other people cannot *give* these things at the same time. It is worthwhile for an adult to persuade the child into the habit of giving rather than throwing. Initially, the adult will have to contribute a lot towards making this giving action happen, for instance by catching the child's hand as she moves to throw. The adult thanks the child, although at this stage the child was not intending to give. A more acceptable pattern of behaviour can be set in motion since the child is being thanked for the giving rather than being reprimanded for the throwing. It may be useful at mealtimes or play at table to take the giving action a step further and to place the object on the table, the adult keeping his or her hands around the child's throughout this action. This can also be repeated until, hopefully, the child places the object on the table of her own accord.

The idea of adults' looking for actions which are incompatible can be a very constructive approach. A child cannot bite and kiss at the same time, cannot be patient and impatient with a younger child at the same time. The incompatible alternative may not be in itself a straightforward behaviour to encourage, but this approach can help adults to think about what sort of behaviour they would like to see. The result of a more positive orientation to a child — perhaps supported by observation to look for the positives — can often be a realisation that the child does show patience sometimes, does not always respond aggressively to frustration, or sometimes shows a flicker of interest in amongst the general withdrawal.

Acceptable needs, unacceptable outlet

As adults coping with young children, we can easily get stuck with the behaviour that we find hard to handle and not consider what could be motivating a child. A good example of this is the behaviour which adults call 'attention-seeking'. Children's methods of getting attention can have a disruptive effect; however, it is right and proper for them to want attention — being 'attention-seeking' is not in itself something reprehensible. Children have a number of basic emotional needs — to feel recognised and noticed, to feel important and special in some way, to feel liked and accepted for themselves, and to feel competent in their own world*. The difficulties arise from some of the ways in which children learn to satisfy these needs, or to cope with feelings of not being valued or not feeling able. It is the responsibility of adults to recognise the likely underlying need and to help children to learn other ways of satisfying it.

Looking for other ways to express the same feeling

Children have strong feelings, just like adults. They too feel anger, humiliation, fear, distress, sadness, depression, excitement, the wish to retaliate. Sometimes the strength of the feelings can seem overwhelming to children. Children whose anger has spilled over into a tantrum or into cross and hurtful remarks can be quite frightened after the event and need reassurance that what they have said or done has not caused permanent harm.

Sometimes adults need to reassure children that having these feelings is all right, that everyone sometimes feels angry or tearful or afraid. It will not help a child if the adult approach is to try to make the child suppress the feelings altogether — 'I don't like bad-tempered children', 'Big boys don't cry', 'Don't be so silly, nobody's afraid of a little worm.' A more sensitive adult would look towards what seems to give rise to these strong feelings, seeing if there is any way an adult can help before the child reaches a strong emotional pitch. The other, equally important, approach is that of helping the child to express the strong feelings through a different channel to the one which is being used at present.

Sometimes young children express strong feelings through violent action, when a less harmful way — to others or to themselves — might be to express the feelings through words or through gentler activities. A child who gets very excited — described from the adult viewpoint as 'over-excited' — can have this energy directed into active outdoor games where shouting and rushing around can be part of the fun. In this way, an adult can gradually calm the child down. Inside a room, the same physical activity and noise may seem unbearable to the adult.

Some children become angry easily, and their anger spills over into

---

*These are discussed in more detail in *The parents' handbook — STEP, systematic training for effective parenting*, by Don Dinkmeyer and Gary D. McKay, published by Random House and available in the UK from the Adlerian Society of Great Britain, 11 Osborne House, 414 Wimbledon Park Road, London SW19 6PW.

aggression against other children or against themselves. An adult needs to take as a starting point that these angry feelings exist and then help the child to learn that anger can be expressed in other ways — for example, by stamping her feet rather than kicking someone — and that saying 'I'm cross with you!' can be as effective as lashing out. Of course, if adults want children to learn to express strong feelings through words, then they must be willing to listen to the children and to encourage them to talk about their feelings. Part of this may be to introduce the words needed by children to describe their feelings — 'Do you feel all cross about that?'; 'You don't look very happy, what's the matter?' A depressed or very unhappy child may need very sensitive adult help to express feelings of extreme sadness or hopelessness. That adult may need to give a lot of time to encouraging the child gently out of her shell with reassurance and steady affection.

A trap for children who have been encouraged to speak up rather than to lash out is that they may unwittingly cross the line into what an adult judges to be 'telling tales'. It is very difficult to protect children from this, since the judgements of different adults vary so much. However, an adult does need to keep a fair balance for children in terms of his or her own behaviour. It is possible to deflect children whom adults judge have become rather griping, or reporters on what other children are doing. Possible comments from adults include 'I think you can sort that out between yourselves' or 'I'd rather wait until one of them comes to tell me.'

Looking for alternatives through changes in the situation

Sometimes a cool look at the environment in which adults and children are spending their days can produce an idea which does not involve a specific change in adult or child behaviour.

In one nursery, I visited a room in which books were displayed by being propped up, overlapping, on a window sill. The arrangement looked tidy until a child wanted to have a book — as one book was removed, several others tended to fall on the floor. Staff were getting exasperated with continually tidying the books until someone realised what an impractical method of display they were using. As an interim measure, they laid the books out flat on a little table, so that children could sort through easily. As a long-term solution, they ordered the kind of bookcase in which books are held upright by restraining slats.

In a similar way, an objective look at the daily routine can sometimes point to simple changes which will ease the annoyance of an adult and the frustration of a child. A baby who tends to play noisily in her cot before settling down to an after-lunch nap can be the first one of a group to be prepared for sleeptime. There is then a chance that she will have quietened by the time the older children in the group are ready to sleep.

The physical layout of a room can influence children's behaviour, and sometimes the most effective way to influence a noisy, very boisterous group is to rearrange furniture. Some nurseries and playgroups have buildings with very large rooms. It is possible to arrange tables, bookcases, etc. so that children do not have the opportunity to hurtle from one end of the room to another. The furniture can instead be used to create quieter corners and to make partly separate sections to the room.

Rethinking the daily routine or room layout does require willingness to step back and think afresh about something which has become very familiar. This is not always easy. It is worth trying because there is sometimes an answer to a problem within the working situation.

LOOKING FROM THE CHILD'S POINT OF VIEW AT WHAT ADULTS SAY

Explaining rules

There are occasions when children genuinely do not understand what is expected of them. The rules and limits may be so clear in adults' minds that they may not appreciate that an individual child has not grasped them. Although children can learn that rather different expectations are held by different adults, this process is slowed down if the adults concerned are not clear in their explanations to the child.

Sometimes, the child is adjusting to a set of rules that are alien to her but which are part of normal routine to the adult. For instance, a child attending nursery school for the first time may be surprised to learn that she cannot have a drink whenever she wants but that there are definite times of the day when milk or juice is available for the whole group. If she has been allowed to draw on her own books at home, she may do this at nursery school, without even thinking about it — she is not being deliberately naughty or destructive. Learning to do otherwise may be part of learning the new idea that possessions shared by the nursery group are treated differently from possessions which are solely hers.

Asking 'Why?'

Adults often place importance on explanations from children as to 'Why?' they have done something that the adult judges as 'naughty' or perhaps very surprising in the light of adult expectations. The frequent response from children — young or well into the school years — to 'Why?' questions is silence or a muttered comment of the 'Because I did' type. The lack of an explanation satisfying to the adult often makes that adult even more cross or perplexed.

Some consideration of the child's viewpoint is really helped by thought about what happens to us as adults when faced with 'Why?' questions. In a tense or confusing confrontation with another adult, most people do not respond very coherently to 'Why on earth did you do that?' or 'Why don't you stop nagging me?' The type of reply is usually a fairly blunt 'Because that's the way I do it!', which offers no explanation, or a rising to the attack with 'I'll stop nagging you when you start behaving reasonably!'

The overall problem with 'Why?' seems to be that it has such an accusing ring to it. Children sense that they have already been judged, so the reaction tends to be an anxious silence or a belligerent attempt to justify, often by putting the blame elsewhere — 'He started it!' Nobody is satisfied by this. With children, as with adults, a question or request which is less accusing may encourage a far more helpful description of what has led up to the incident — what the child was trying to do and what feelings have been prompting the behaviour. So it is well worth-while trying to avoid 'Why?'s and replacing them with questions begin-ning with 'What?' — for example, 'What were you trying to do?' or 'What did you think was going to happen?' Alternatively, a request to 'Tell me what's been going on here' asks for information without accusing anybody.

The 'If you're good' trap

The words 'good' and 'bad', referring to children's behaviour, are always placed in inverted commas in this discussion. This is because the words are judgements from the adult viewpoint. They are not absolutes. They are an adult shorthand which covers a wide range of children's behaviours and adult feelings about those behaviours. No two adults will have identical views on exactly what constitutes 'good' and 'bad' behaviour. Even for individual adults, there is often a degree of incon-sistency depending on the stresses of a particular situation. As such, the words 'good' and 'bad' are really not at all helpful. They give very limited information to the child. The problems of seeing a child as 'bad' are discussed in the following part of this chapter. Some space will be given here to the problems of being 'good'.

Many adults use 'good' as a compliment and as praise — 'There's a good girl', 'You've been very good today, so we'll have your special story.' Sometimes the compliment is to someone else — 'Why can't you be good like your brother?' The child who is being exhorted to be 'good' is likely to remain confused by the last comment — of all the 'good' things that her brother does, what is it that the adult wants this time? Is it being quiet? Is it answering promptly when asked a question? Is it not making a mess with the toys? Is it playing 'properly'? Actually, for giving a child clear information about adult expectations and words, talking of 'goodness' is worse than useless. The fact that adults have made the pronouncement, 'Be good, or else!' makes them feel that they have given fair warning to the child. However, so often the child is muddled.

A useful example of the unhelpfulness of 'good' is the trap of 'If you're good, then. . . .' This is rarely, if ever, said to adults and it can be a sobering lesson to do precisely that. Say to a colleague 'If you're good, then I'll wash up the cups after coffee', or promise a friend or spouse 'If you're good today, I'll take you to the cinema this evening.' The other adult will probably look surprised and make some comment like 'What do you mean "good" ?' or 'What have I got to do to make you think I'm "good"?' Children (and adults, if you try that experiment) have to guess what is wanted on the basis of how that adult has reacted and what has been demanded in the past. This is a long-winded detective job.

It is much better to be specific about what you would like to have happen — to give people information on which to work. Instead of saying to a child 'There's a good girl', it is better to be definite about what has pleased you — 'Well done, you've finished all your dinner', 'Thank you for helping me tidy up', 'You were very patient to wait. I was talking for such a long time on the telephone.' It is better not to contrast at all in the manner of 'Why can't you be like your brother?' — it does not help anybody. The 'If you're good . . .' threats and promises are far better given as concrete requests — 'Please try to be patient. I must write this message before I forget, and then I can help you.' Allowance has to be made, of course, for the limited ability of younger children to wait, however well you phrase your request.

Reasonably intelligent children can and do take advantage of adults who use the 'If you're good' method. A two-year-old boy, whom I now know as an adult, had worked out that special treats came if he was 'good'. He had logically progressed from that to the idea that a promise of being 'good' in the future ought to be a method of obtaining things he wanted now. He tried to excuse his seizing of special sweets, and on one occasion trying to prise away another child's book, by cries of 'Gonna be good! Gonna be good!'

'GOOD' AND 'BAD' BEHAVIOUR

The risks of seeing a child totally through problem behaviour

When a child is seen by adults as difficult or irritating, there is a danger that the child will come to be viewed almost totally in terms of the disliked behaviour. The adults notice the irritating behaviour more than any more positive moves on the part of the child. They tend to react quickly to the annoyance, failing to notice the glimmers of other possibilities. This can lead to a serious risk that the child herself will be seen largely in negative terms. She will be described as a bad-tempered child or an un-cooperative child, rather than as a child who sometimes loses her temper or who sometimes needs to be persuaded to cooperate. The behaviour that the adults dislike has become the child's whole personality to them, and there is then a strong chance that the child will begin to see herself in this way. If the child develops a negative view of herself, the unhappiness and dissatisfaction that this generates will hinder her learning to behave differently.

Adults need to be very sensitive about seeing a child in terms of her 'bad' behaviours. At a purely emotional level of judgement, an onlooker may say that this is not 'fair' to the child. Apart from whether adults are being fair or unfair, a very sound reason for trying to avoid the 'child = "bad" behaviour' trap is that this usually makes matters worse. The child will be steadily learning that adults mainly pay her attention when she is behaving in ways that irritate them. Although adults see this attention as negative, if it is the only sort of attention the child receives, she will work to get it. There is little incentive to behave in any other way. It will not matter to that child that other children receive attention that is kindly for other sorts of behaviour that the adults see as 'good'. The 'naughty' child has learned through her experience that her limited efforts in the 'good' direction do not bring as much adult attention as her 'naughty' behaviour. A vicious circle has been set in motion, and the labelling of that child may travel with her as a report or a reputation if she moves on to a different nursery or when she moves to infant school.

Keeping behaviour separate from personality

It can help avoid the build-up of 'child = "bad" behaviour' to work hard not to label any children, either for 'good' or for 'bad' behaviour. Children are individuals — with varying interests and aptitudes, and with variations in qualities like patience, willingness to cooperate, inclination to persevere, curiosity, and helpfulness. Once a child is labelled — 'hyperactive', 'spiteful', 'considerate', 'patient' — the implication is that this is an unchanging part of that child's personality. Adults' feelings about the negative labels then tend to be fairly hopeless, since how can you change the way a child is?

In thinking about the dangers of labelling children, adults are usually more sensitive about the consequences of critical labels. However, children given the positive labels are not necessarily benefiting from the all-over glow that these give. A child who is told that she is 'such a patient little girl' or 'always so considerate to the younger ones' may begin to see herself as only valued because of these qualities. She may become something of a 'goody two-shoes', perhaps not liked so much by other children because she is praised so often by adults. The child may also become worried about the feelings she has that do not fit the 'good' image, perhaps worrying that, if the adults realised that sometimes she wants to say spiteful things or feels very cross, they would not like her any more. Adults do unthinkingly encourage these worries when they make comments like, 'Now that's not like you, is it? You're always so patient.' This is imposing an adult judgement on the child which effectively says 'I know you best' and which denies this child the right sometimes not to feel patient.

It is not always easy for adults to separate a child's behaviour from feelings about what the child is like as an individual. Our reactions to children are, of course, influenced by what the children do. However, it is better to deal with 'good' or 'bad' behaviour as the single incident that it is. This means thanking a child for particular examples of helpful behaviour rather than making a personality judge- ment — saying 'Thank you, I finished that much more quickly with your help' rather than 'You're such a helpful boy.' This leaves children space not to feel like being helpful all the time. By concentrating on a child's behaviour, an adult is also providing some specific information for the child which will help her to make more sense of adult reactions to her behaviour.

When adults want to discourage particular actions, it is more con- structive for them to describe the behaviour that concerns them than to assign a label to the child. This means thinking of a child as one who has firm notions about what she wants to do and when she wants to do it, has little patience about being offered alternatives, and often lashes out physically at the adult or child whom she feels is in her way. This gives many more indications for how an adult might need to work with this child than simply saying she is an 'aggressive' child.

A final point on keeping 'bad' behaviour separate from personality is that it is possible, and often helpful, to make this difference clear to children. You, as an adult, are trying to view the situation as one where you are frustrated or infuriated by the child's behaviour but are not dis- missing the child. You still value her. To the child you would be clearly signalling, by your words and behaviour, that you are very annoyed with what she has done. However, you still care for her as an individual. Comments such as 'I like you, John. I don't like your swearing' focus on the behaviour. They can gradually show this child that his personal value to you is unchanging but particular ways of behaving from him annoy or upset you, and you will be trying to discourage him from these. All children misbehave in adults' eyes sometimes, but they deserve to be reassured that adults still care about them, even though, at the moment, those adults are angry or hurt.

TRYING FOR BALANCE BETWEEN THE POSITIVES AND NEGATIVES

Looking at the 'do's and 'don't's

An adult who has worries and stresses or who is trying to work with a group of particularly demanding children may expend much more energy on stopping children doing things and saying 'Don't do that!' than on encouraging children in constructive activities. There does not seem to be the time to comment when children are managing well, helping each other, or sharing. It is often easier for an onlooker to see this imbalance, although sensitive adults may realise from their own feelings of annoyance and frustration that most of their exchanges with children are tending to be negative.

It is important to watch out for this, as imbalance towards the 'don't's leads to a miserable and dissatisfying atmosphere for adults and children alike. The adults can feel that being with children consists of annoyance and interruptions, with little enjoyment. The children can feel, not necessarily consciously, that they only ever hear nagging, so why bother to try to behave well? Children also learn that behaviour that an adult finds naughty or irritating is the most reliable way to attract that adult's full attention. There is then a strong incentive for children to increase this behaviour and little or no incentive for them to behave in ways that the adult would like. This is a vicious circle which is likely to be broken only by a change in the adult's behaviour.

It is necessary to reduce the 'don't's, perhaps through thinking clearly about what behaviour from children really must be stopped and what can reasonably be ignored. Hand in hand with this, an adult needs to increase the 'do's. This can be through making sure that as many 'don't's as possible are balanced by a positive. Adults might offer an alternative to a child who wants a toy another child is using, or might draw the child into another activity. With older children, a promise that they will be next in line for the favoured toy — a promise which the adult must keep — or, in some cases, an explanation of why some activity is impossible may soften a blunt 'No.'

It is sometimes possible to offer children a choice in terms of behaviour. This can sometimes be a positive strategy for adults who are becoming frustrated with saying 'No' and 'Don't'. A child who tends to dash off in a busy street may be given the choice of 'holding my hand like a big girl or having the reins on like a little girl'. Rushing off into danger is not one of the choices on offer. If the child's choice happens to be the option of having reins, then the adult does not make any critical comments about being a 'baby'. The child can be offered the two alternatives each time the adult and child go out. At some point the child will probably choose to hold the adult's hand herself. The adult can then comment positively 'It's nice to walk together, isn't it' or 'I can talk with you easily when we walk like this.' This sort of choice can be offered to younger children — but with the emphasis on actions, not words. A younger child who finds that she is taken away from the play when she pinches other children will learn in time not to pinch. Choices can be used elsewhere. For example, children who are refusing to go for their evening bath can be given the choice of 'Would you like to climb the stairs yourself or shall I carry you?' Again, the possibility of escaping the bath is not an option.

So long as the giving of choices is not over-used, it can be a constructive way of focusing child and adult on to what *can* happen, rather than what is forbidden. It often works for the child because it gives her a feeling of responsibility and some control over events. The offer of choices is ruined if there is any atmosphere of punishment about the offer.

Trying to encourage children seen as very difficult

It is very easy for an adult's attention to be drawn to a particular child mainly when she is being a nuisance, but it is so important to know what the child is doing when she is *not* being a problem. She may be in activities where an adult can become involved and provide attention and, therefore, encouragement for constructive play and cooperative behaviour. It happens so often that adults heave a sigh of relief when a child they find difficult is out of sight.

In order to encourage more positive behaviour, adults need to become clear about what they would like a child to do, rather than concentrating all their energy on the actions they would like to stop. It can be a constructive exercise to write down in clear descriptive terms what it is that an individual child does that you find irritating or disruptive. Then, against each negative description of the child's behaviour, write a concrete description of how you would prefer the child to behave in the same situation. This is not an easy task, since adults have often become so absorbed by their concern about the 'bad' behaviour that they have lost sight of what would please them, beyond a hope that the child will stop what she is doing. There is no helpful direction for adult encouragement if adults have no thoughts about what will take the place of the 'bad' behaviour. Attempting to envisage the positive alternatives may reveal that the child does behave in that more positive way, at least sometimes, but that the adult is failing to notice because the positives are buried in the general adult feelings of frustration and annoyance. This is why making observations of children for instances of non-problem behaviour can bring about a lightening of the load for adults.

The limited usefulness of punishment

Punishment is not generally an effective way of helping anyone to learn. This includes all the negative reactions — physical punishment, spoken abuse or recriminations, and the range of unspoken looks and gestures which say just as clearly 'What a hopeless effort!' or 'Stupid boy!' Used as a way of controlling children's behaviour, punishment gives only the negative information 'Don't do that!' It does not say clearly 'I want you to do this instead.' The child on the receiving end of the punishment is often left confused — guessing as to what the adult does want. Because the positives are not clear — however much the adults claim 'Of course, she knows what she ought to do!' — the end result is that the punished behaviour will, at best, be suppressed. A child who is trying to please or who is cowed by the punishment will stop doing what is punished; however, it is unlikely that new ways of behaving will easily emerge. A child who enjoys the drama may only increase the behaviour which so annoys the adult.

Another major drawback to punishment is that — physical, spoken, or unspoken — it tends to arouse feelings that do not help new learning. Children, or adults, who are punished tend to feel anxious, humiliated, confused, or angry and vengeful. The exact feelings and the strength of those feelings depend on personality and how the punishment was given. However, none of these feelings merges at all well with efforts to behave differently.

It can be a useful exercise for adults to remember when they have been trying to learn some new skill — for instance, driving a car. Driving instructors — professional or amateur — who spend more time criticising than encouraging are not helping their pupils. People learn far more quickly with plenty of 'You did that very well' and 'You're still having trouble with the three-point turn — let's talk that through again.' A barrage of comments such as 'Don't crash the gears!' and 'You'll never pass your test like this!' is useless without suggestions on how to avoid crashing the gears and comments on good driving as well as not so good.

Punishment is often satisfying to the person who is giving it. Shouting at a child or slapping her expresses the frustrations and annoyances of the adult. It is a way of letting off steam, perhaps of expressing the very real fear that the child is in danger, or perhaps of paying the child back for 'showing me up in front of everybody'. It is often, therefore, a release for adult feelings. Because caring for and raising children is a job with many frustrations as well as pleasures, it would be unrealistic to say that adults should never say a cross word to a child or should never punish a child for wrong-doing. What is so important is that adults should realise the very limited value of punishment for changing children's behaviour. Children do need to know what is not allowed or what is dangerous.

However, they also need to know clearly what is allowed and to be encouraged in their efforts to fit in with adult rules and regulations. When punishment is thought to be necessary, it is best to make it brief, and clearly linked with what the child has done. This is particularly important with under-fives, who will have quickly forgotten an incident about which an adult is still fuming. If it seems most appropriate to take the child away from her play, or to remove a favourite toy, this should be done immediately after the incident and the punishment should not last long. For under-twos especially, the point can be made in the few moments it takes to hold them steady, look directly at the child, and say something like, 'No! No biting!' Even older under-fives are best dealt with by reprimands or sanctions which last no more than a few minutes; otherwise, resentment and confusion set in.

With four- and five-year-olds, it can be possible to use some future sanction as a punishment, since they will remember over a longer period. However, this has drawbacks. For example, suppose a four-year-old hit the baby an hour ago. She is now informed 'I told you if you hit the baby again, you couldn't help me at tea-time.' The child will probably remember the incident. However, since the baby-hitting episode, she has possibly been cooperative and helpful at least sometimes. Yet all that is being ignored in the light of one action now held against her, yet again. So, even with the older children, it is better to deal with each incident as it arises and then continue with a clean sheet. This is not always easy from the adult viewpoint, but it is well worth the effort.

Adults do become impatient and annoyed with children. Sometimes the most patient adults lose their temper or slap a child in sheer desperation. Such incidents will not harm a child forever. With an adult who rarely shouts or slaps, the sheer surprise of it may jolt a child into realising that she has gone too far this time. However, adults do need to remind themselves that such reactions do little good from the point of view of the child's learning. Used as a regular way of controlling children, physical punishment and spoken abuse can be harmful. What starts as a few slaps can get seriously out of control when an adult has formed the habit of unloading feelings through this treatment of the child. The child is also learning that this is the way to behave and may well start hitting and shouting at other people as soon as her own feelings are aroused.

Using the consequences of a child's action

The most effective use of unpleasant events for children is for adults to be calmly consistent about certain consequences following on certain actions of the child. There are two different ways of using consequences.

The first way is to allow a child to experience the inevitable 'natural' consequences of her actions — if she leaves her books out in the rain, they will get wet and probably spoil; if she does not eat her lunch, she will get hungry before tea-time. The experienced pressure of reality can be an effective way for children to learn that their choices have consequences which they may not enjoy. A child is, of course, denied the opportunity to learn this if an adult rushes out to get the books when a request to the child has met with a blank, or if the child is allowed snacks between lunch and tea when she starts to complain of hunger. However, there are, of course, some natural consequences which no responsible adult would allow a child to risk, such as the likely consequences of dashing out into the road.

The other type of consequence is that determined 'logically' by an adult — for example, removing toys that a child is misusing. For this to be an effective way for the child to learn, she needs to be warned of the consequence the adult is going to impose, and the adult must follow through calmly. It might be, for example, that a child is not allowed to rip up the pages of her books. If she starts to rip, then the book is taken away. A little while later, if she is interested to have the book, it is given back to her, but as soon as she starts to tear pages the book is taken away again. An older child can have this explained in words — 'When you're ready to look at the book without tearing the pages, you can have it back.' A younger child will understand, especially after a few repetitions, a firm 'No', and the removal of the book, with all the head-shaking and annoyed adult look which support this. The child is learning that certain consequences follow on certain actions. Other examples might be that the child's ice cream is taken away if she is pushing it into another child's face, her bike is temporarily removed if she insists on riding it into the family cat, or she forfeits her turn at pushing the dinner trolley if she deliberately rams it into the doorway. Clearly, with such incidents, it would be appropriate to try telling the child first. However, persistence by the child would be followed by particular consequences.

Use of consequences really helps children to learn, if adults resist the temptation to nag or hark back to the incident later. The idea is that the child starts with a clean sheet each time. Snide remarks or recriminations will spoil this. In the example of the child and the bike, an adult might say, after a break, 'Are you ready to ride the bike now?' If the child says 'Yes', then she has the bike. If she rides it over the cat, the bike is once again removed. However, the child needs to be given the chance to show that she can use the bike without damage. The child has a choice in the matter, but not a completely free choice — if she chooses to ram the cat, then this means no more bike. It is a matter that certain behaviour is followed by particular consequences.*

---

*There is a useful discussion of using consequences in a non-punishing way in *Happy children*, by Rudolf Dreikurs and Vicki Soltz, published in 1970 by

A number of strategies that adults use in a punishing way can be better applied as consequences. The difference is in the adult behaviour. For many years, one of the ways in which adults have dealt with unacceptable behaviour has been by removing children — putting them in corners, on 'naughty' chairs, or outside the room. If this is done with adult anger — when the adult snaps at the 'last straw' — it operates as punishment, especially since the child is often left for an indeterminate length of time, until the adult cools down. This strategy can work effectively as a consequence. (The organised use of this strategy was developed within behaviour-modification methods and is known as 'time out'.) It is, however, crucial that adult removal of a child follows consistently on particular behaviour from the child, the removal is calm, and the child stays removed for only a brief period of time (a few minutes) on each removal. The child then returns to the action without any adult nagging. The aim is that the child becomes progressively able to control her own behaviour and, when she cannot or will not stop herself, the removal is viewed as a 'fair cop'.

In my home, we have used this method with our children (since they were about three years old) for a small number of clearly defined behaviours all to do with keeping the living-room as a peaceful room. The removal is known as 'going in the sin bin'. If either of them persists, after a warning, in forbidden activities (for the living room) such as bouncing on the sofa, yelling, or running round the room, he or she is put outside the door for 2 minutes — timed on the cooker timer which beeps when the time is complete. Recently, our four-year-old Zoë (who since birth has disproved the sugar-and-spice notion that girls are easier) told me 'I like going in the sin bin.' If I were trying to punish her, this would be disastrous — punishment is not supposed to be at all pleasant! Since I am applying a consequence, however, this does not matter — all that matters is that she gradually learns to help us keep the living-room peaceful.

Encouragement and rewards

The value of encouragement and how it differs from reward were discussed in chapter 7. Many of the practical suggestions offered throughout this book depend on encouraging children's efforts at least as often as praising their achievements. In the discussion in this chapter, there has been an emphasis on encouraging children towards how adults would like to see them behave, or towards one method of coping rather than another. The focus on encouragement is not meant to suggest that rewards should never be used as a way of changing children's behaviour.

Souvenir Press and in 1972 as a Fontana paperback. This was written primarily for parents, but it has many practical ideas for any adult responsible for children.

Rewards, used sparingly, can be effective in changing some behaviour. One method of helping older children to deal with wetting or soiling accidents is to build in simple rewards for success but avoid punishment for failures. The reward might be immediately tangible, such as a penny for every dry night. Alternatively, the reward might be in terms of a star to stick on a chart, when the understanding is that a certain number of stars can be traded in for a special treat. (It would be children of four or five years and older who could understand the symbols of a star system.) The emphasis is on rewarding for success. The money or stars are not taken away if the child fails. Part of this type of approach has to be a plan for gradually moving on from giving a reward every time. The adult wants the child eventually to be motivated by the satisfaction of having a dry night, not by the promise of reward. So, there needs to be a steady progression from a reward for every success to a reward for a certain number of successes until child and adult can be well pleased that there is no longer any problem to solve.

The risk of over-using rewards is that adults can be trapped into 'You gave me five pence last time I took the medicine — I want five pence again now.' It is a less hazardous course to be very supportive and encouraging about how well the child took an unpleasant-tasting medicine and to follow this with some enjoyable and distracting play-time. She will have to manage this in the future and it is better that her reward comes from inside, from her feelings that this was unpleasant but necessary and she managed it — 'Well done!' Providing five pence, or some increasingly inflationary rate, from the tooth fairy is unlikely to cause problems, since a child has a limited number of teeth to lose. However, giving financial or other rewards for 'good' behaviour can have unfortunate consequences.

I was struck by the story I was told of a family friend who, as a child, was promised sixpence whenever he told the truth. Painters were working in the house and had returned from lunch to find two different-coloured pots of paint well mixed together. Suspicion fell on this young boy. His father had a conversation with him but the boy said 'No', he definitely had not done it. His father reminded him that the house rule was sixpence for telling the truth. The boy still said he had not mixed the paint pots. An hour or so later, the boy rushed into the house and up to his father. 'Daddy', he said, 'You know the pots of paint. Well it was me. And now I've told the truth, can I have my sixpence straightaway, because I've told the ice-cream man to wait?'

The story illustrates how a child can manipulate a parent's well-intentioned system of rewards. There is much less trouble in giving children money on a clearly understood weekly pocket-money basis. Special outings and treats, ice creams or sweets are given because they are fun and enjoyable, not as variable events dependent on the child's behaviour. Adults as well as children like a change and something special. Everyone likes to be cheered up after something unpleasant. However, all this is in the context of making life enjoyable and bearable and is not dependent on 'good' or 'bad' behaviour.

Concluding remarks

There is no perfect way of dealing with young children. There are some general approaches which work more readily than others, but there are no simple solutions. The themes and principles which have been discussed in this chapter have implications for how adults behave and for how they think about their relationship with young children. If adults follow some of these general approaches, it often means making more effort in the short term with a child. However, this will ease matters in the long term. Sometimes it is a question of adults' taking a cool look at the consequences of a particular way of handling a child. It is a great advantage if adults can admit to themselves that what they are doing or saying could be worsening the situation. It does not mean that most of what they do with the child is misguided — it is simply that, with this particular combination of child, adult, and circumstances, the first reaction of the adult to dealing with the situation was perhaps not the most constructive alternative. If adults can allow themselves to be flexible in this way, their lives with children can be more enjoyable and less of a battleground.

12
COMMON BEHAVIOUR PROBLEMS WITH UNDER-FIVES

A child alone does not make a problem: somebody has to experience her behaviour as a problem. Because adults are different individuals, their judgements will vary as to how difficult a child is or whether she is more of a problem to them than another child. Some adults find particular kinds of behaviour hard to tolerate — perhaps they can remain patient and calm while a child makes hurtful remarks but become incensed if a child spits at them. Not all potential problems are noticed equally quickly. For example, in a group of children, the noisy problems of aggression or destructiveness may seem very obvious; however, the distress of a depressed child or the lack of interest of a very lethargic child may be missed, especially by less experienced adults.

The aim of this chapter is not to suggest that some problems are more serious than others — instances of all the examples discussed can range from minor to very serious with different children. The discussion is, however, restricted to problems which are relatively common in the under-five age group. Many of these problems are faced by adults dealing with children whose development is progressing within the normal range of behaviour for young children.

PHYSICAL AGGRESSION

Many young children act aggressively at some time. Their lives are full of frustrations which seem minor to adults but which can become all-absorbing to children. A physical reaction may seem to be the most satisfactory solution to a child, especially if she has limited ability to express herself in words.

There is a wide variation in how children express physical aggression. A child may be indiscriminantly aggressive, lashing out at anyone who is close at hand. Some children may attack other children younger than themselves, including babies. It may be that they sense the power of being larger and the limited chance of being attacked in return. For a harassed youngest child in the family, the younger children in her nursery or playgroup may be the first opportunity ever to unload her aggressive feelings on to someone smaller and weaker. Some children turn their aggression against adults, some against animals.

158

Physical aggression is a problem which tends to bring adults running. In some cases, the sheer noise of the confrontation brings attention. In the case of a child who is sly in her pinching and biting, the 'sneaky' nature of the action may outrage adults. It is a problem which is hard to ignore completely, although different standards may be applied by different adults — some certainly tolerate higher levels of aggression from boys than from girls.

Many of the problems discussed in this chapter benefit from the techniques of observation discussed in part 1, particularly in chapter 4. The problem of aggression is no exception. Labelling a child as 'aggressive' says very little about what the child does. It is certainly no basis for an adult to work out what could be the best approach. Observing such a child can be the beginning of seeing whom the child attacks, under what sort of circumstances, and how often this really does happen without any provocation. Some careful observation can sometimes help adults to identify the warning signs of an imminent attack from this particular child.

Stepping in before an aggressive outburst

There are undoubtedly times when it can be better to leave children to deal with the situation themselves. Children are capable of sorting out some disputes and, if an adult is keeping an eye on events, it may be a useful experience for the children to learn that they do not always need an adult as referee. When adults judge that it would be better to intervene before a child's aggression is expressed, it may be possible to distract the child into some other channel of behaviour. This can be offering a favourite toy — something to substitute for whatever the children are squabbling over — attention from the adult in the form of energetic activity, or perhaps providing a toy that the child can legitimately kick or bite. Unfortunately, there will be many occasions when this is not possible: the child is unwilling to be distracted or a physical attack is clearly just about to happen — the hand is drawn back or the child's face shows that she is just about to bite. In these circumstances, physically preventing the child by catching her hand or holding back her entire body, so she cannot reach to bite, can be the best immediate action, especially if reinforced with a sharply spoken 'No!' If the adult is too far away for this, a shout may also halt the child who has learned from previous occasions that this aggression is not allowed.

Handling children after an aggressive attack

There will be many times when the aggression cannot be stopped. The aim is then to act after the event to bring home the lesson that this sort of behaviour is not acceptable. The approach of a sharp word to the aggressor and plenty of loving attention to the victim can show a child very clearly that she loses out through such unpleasantness. It is, of course, very important that the aggressor receives this sort of loving attention at other times, when she is not being aggressive. An approach of making children apologise is of limited use on its own. Some children simply learn the formula of 'Sorry, sorry' in order to escape from the unwelcome adult attention.

There are definite risks to adults' replying to aggression with further aggression, or encouraging young children to do this. The suggestion to 'Go and hit him back' may be taken by a child as a general permission to pummel this aggressor or to hit back with gusto at any frustration. The threat from an adult of 'I'll bite you, then you'll know how it feels!' also has some serious drawbacks. The problem of retaliating in this way to a child of any age is that the adult is doing, as punishment, the very aggressive action that the child has been told not to do. Some people do claim such an approach as very effective. The very real risk, however, of starting an adult biting-back or slapping-back campaign comes if it does *not* work first time. The adult is then left with the decision of what to do on subsequent occasions — do you bite harder, do you bite the child twice for every one bite, do you slap her as well? Such an approach can get seriously out of hand, and it is better to avoid that option. It can become a dangerous channel for the expression of adult anger and frustration.

It is important with aggression, as with other problems, to be consistent over the limits to what is allowed and what is not allowed. This is part of a longer-term policy of encouraging the child towards other ways of expressing strong emotions. The action that adults take immediately after an aggressive attack benefits from some thinking time when the problem is not occuring, as there is usually very little time to think as the attack unfolds. The specific point about dealing with aggression from under-fives is that the action taken by adults should be brief and to the point.

Adults sometimes choose to send a child who has been aggressive into a quiet corner to calm down. This can be an effective way of marking the incident for the child and expressing strong adult disapproval. It is also sometimes important to remove the child for a brief period while you, the adult, calm down! However, removing a child in this way rapidly loses its effect if the child is left for more than a minute or two. The younger under-fives are likely not to understand the link between what they have just done and being banished. It is better to hold them securely to face you and say a very firm 'No hitting!' or 'Absolutely no biting!' The attention the aggressive child receives is limited and negative: the victim receives plenty of comfort.

Ideally, adults need to make their point every time the aggression happens and have the incident over quickly. Lengthy explanations or recriminations are not very effective — even if the child could understand, she is probably not listening. If an appropriate consequence of an aggressive attack seems to be the removal of favourite toys or privileges, then this again should be as immediate as is possible; otherwise, the punishment for an incident can be dragging on for much of the day. The child will quickly forget the reason for this — all she will focus on is that she is now being stopped from doing favourite activities or is being pointed out to others as a 'naughty' child. Her resentment at this treatment will reduce the chance of her learning to behave differently.

AGGRESSION EXPRESSED IN WORDS

Aggression is not necessarily expressed through physical attacks — the difficulty sometimes arises out of what is said rather than what is done. Some children may be frequently shouting abuse, taunting other children, or swearing. It seems to be the swearing that concerns many adults in nurseries or playgroups, and this is often because of the fear that other children may copy the swearing child and angry parents will want to know why.

Insults and other unpleasant remarks

When adults are on the receiving end of hurtful comments from children, they need to ignore as far as possible what is being said to them. There is little point in rising to a child's verbal attack, and it is better to try hard not to feel hurt. However, it is worthwhile trying to deal with the emotion underlying the child's attack. As always, there is an element of guesswork in judging what is leading the child to make such remarks. It may be a wish to hurt others as she has felt hurt herself. It may be the delightful sense of power at succeeding in upsetting adults or other children. Sometimes children say vicious-sounding remarks — 'I hate you', 'I wish you were dead', 'You're an ugly old ratbag' — because in their anger they do not know a milder way of expressing their feelings. Their remarks cannot then be judged as you would an adult's comments.

There is scope for simply ignoring a child who has made a habit of insulting people. If other children also learn to ignore the child when she is being hurtful, she may find that there is little point in continuing. If children on the receiving end of insults are very distressed by it, there can be good reason for adults to provide them with some verbal ammunition in reply. If a child finds that her victim returns with 'Well, I think you're a heap of old rubbish', the inequality that gives satisfaction to insulting others may well be gone.

Adults can sometimes turn insults from a child into a comical exchange if they reply with silly remarks to make an atmosphere of trying to cap what the child has just said. Penelope Leach (in her book *Baby and child*) gives the example of replying to a child's shout of 'You're a stupid old cow' with 'What does that make you, then — a silly little calf!' Whether the comical approach will work depends on how the child's remarks are made. A child who regularly says very hurtful things and expresses them with some venom might need to be told firmly 'I like you Sandy, I don't like it when you say. . . .' A long-term approach would have to include an attempt to meet the child's needs to feel powerful or to get back at others for her own hurt — if adults judge that such feelings may be underlying the verbal aggression. The child may discover in time that she can be liked — in fact, adults have persisted in liking her, despite what she has said — and that she can have responsibility or a special role in a group of children without resorting to insults.

Swearing

Children swear for a number of different motives, and this obviously affects what may be the most useful method of stopping them.

Some children undoubtedly swear in complete innocence. They do not know what the words mean and are not intending to shock. In these cases, it is often effective simply to tell children that this is a rude or unpleasant word and you would rather that they did not use it.

Some children may not know the meaning of the words but are very well aware that these are forbidden. They are using them to create an effect — to upset or annoy the adults present. Ignoring a child when she swears but giving her your attention at other times may help — the child may become discouraged from swearing if she is not getting the dramatic reaction she wants. However, just ignoring the problem may not discourage a very persistent swearer. It may be necessary to reprimand the child, especially one who is aware of which are swear words and which are not. In this case, sharp disapproval along the lines of 'That's enough!' tends to work better than a tirade. It is certainly better than showing upset or shock. Adults also need to avoid openly calling other adults' attention to the swearer. Comments such as 'Did you hear what she said!', made in front of the child, usually provide an audience and attention which will encourage rather than discourage the swearing.

Children need to express their emotions as much as do adults. Consequently, it can be helpful to provide children with alternatives to swear words — words which can be said with feeling if a child hurts herself or gets frustrated, words with which to answer teasing, and words to emphasise what she says. The range of words introduced should be ones that adults use themselves, such as 'Sugar!', 'Rats!', or anything else. The behaviour of children who use swear words without even thinking — perhaps copying what they have heard elsewhere — can be gradually changed in this way. For instance, an adult might repeat for a child a sentence in which a word has been replaced. If the child says 'Look at that bloody big dog!', the adult might reply 'Yes, look at that e— nor — mous dog!' If the adult manages to ham it up a little, the child may feel that this new word can be said with more dramatic emphasis than the swear word.

DESTRUCTIVENESS

For some children, physical aggression takes the form of being destructive with things, rather than aggressive to people. This might include tearing up books, emptying packages of food, or throwing toys around. It may extend to potentially very dangerous actions such as setting fire to objects. Obviously, there are times when destructiveness and aggression to people become one and the same thing, for instance when a child is throwing toys at other children or adults. Many of the points which have been made about physical aggression are equally relevant to children whose fiercer feelings are being expressed through destructive behaviour.

The age of the child concerned is an important part of making sense of the problem. For example, once a young child has learned the physical skill of throwing, she will throw objects indiscriminately. It will be some time before she understands that balls bounce but china plates smash. Likewise, a young child has to learn that, although it can be all right to rip up old magazines, adults expect her to treat picture books with more care. All this is part of a young child's learning about what adults see as acceptable behaviour.

A great deal of drama can become associated with children whose anger or frustration emerges in destruction. It is important for adults to remain as calm as they can manage and not to return anger with anger. This is far from easy when chairs and toys are flying around your head! If children's behaviour is being fired by a wish for attention, drama, and a sense of power, then signs of panic and strong emotions from adults may only encourage those children.

Adults' feelings and reactions

Adults need to be aware of their own feelings in a situation such as the above. A physically strong and destructive four- or five-year-old can be frightening to adults. Not only is there the real danger that the child will hurt you, but the unpredictability of the outbreaks can make adults feel that they are sitting on a tinder-box. Adults really need to support one another in dealing with these feelings and, despite the unease or fear, to help one another hold to a consistent way of dealing with the destructive attacks.

Much of what was suggested for dealing with physical aggression from children is equally relevant to dealing with destructive outbursts. It is worthwhile stepping in to prevent such an outburst if knowledge of a child indicates that she is about to hurl something. Firm but brief words or physically restraining her actions are better than shouting matches or flurries of adult activity. After the child has been destructive, brief expressions of adult annoyance will again make a more effective point than tirades. It is worth offering the child the opportunity each time to help clear up any mess she has made. She will often refuse, but there may come a day when she will respond to an approach which says 'You're big and strong enough to make this mess, so I'm sure you're capable of helping me clear it up.' If clearing-up is presented as a punishment or the child is forced to help, then this is very unlikely to change her destructive behaviour — it has to be in the context that an adult believes she is enough of a 'big girl' to take some responsibility for the consequences of what she has done. If the child does help clear up, she should, of course, receive a genuine 'Thank you' and no recriminations — the incident is now over.

Just as adults need to support one another in how they deal with destructiveness from a child, so they need support in attempts to behave as normally as possible towards such a child when she is not being destructive. There is a real risk that a very aggressive or destructive child may be hedged round with many prohibitions in order to guard against the chance that she may break out into an attack. It is very important, although not necessarily easy, to give such children experience that there are other ways of exercising power and gaining an audience and that these other ways can, in the end, be more enjoyable, because of the different adult reaction. It may be very significant for such a child to experience the enjoyment of demonstrating a skill she has in front of an appreciative audience, or the fun of making other children laugh rather than run for cover. She may respond well to being given some simple responsibilities or being allowed to lead a group of younger children.

Being aware of the drama of 'problem' children

Sometimes adults are unwittingly drawn into the excitement and drama created around children who pose the noisier problems — aggression, destructiveness, tantrums. Even experienced adults can become more absorbed in the awful aspects to a child than in looking for good points. The child becomes a topic of conversation — 'You'll never guess what Billy did today!' — or becomes fuel for exchanges about 'My children behave far worse than your children!' This attitude will not help the search for an effective way to deal with the child. The dangers of becoming absorbed into the problem can often be identified more easily if you are an onlooker.

For example, some years ago several colleagues of mine were working with the family of a three-year-old who was developing into a serious fire-raiser. My colleagues felt that the parents of this child were enjoying the excitement of having a child with a really dramatic problem. There seemed to be some satisfaction for the parents in getting the professionals to admit that they had not seen anything as bad as this before. The involvement of the parents in the drama was seriously hindering improvement in the child. On a purely practical level, in a home where this child had already caused several fires, matches were still easily available.

Adults often have to help one another — with tact — to see how far they might be becoming involved in the dramatic aspects of a child's behaviour and perhaps making matters worse than they might be.

TEMPER TANTRUMS

Part of making sense of temper tantrums from children is taking some account of the children's age. It is not unusual for the rising-twos and two-year-olds to have tantrums on many occasions. A wide range of events can spark off minor or major outbursts of temper — from the inability to make a toy work to being refused sweets; from a change in expected routine to the end of a special treat. As children grow older, they tend to become more amenable to reason, and to being offered alternatives. They can more clearly understand explanations from adults and prior warnings, such as 'We're going home when this cartoon has finished.'

Some older children still have many tantrums as a reaction to frustrations in their lives. There can be many different reasons why children do not grow out of frequent tantrums. When the children were younger, adults may have given in to their wishes at the first sign of temper. Their lives may be so confusing and unpredictable that tantrums are more an expression of distress and feelings of lack of control than temper as such. The adults the child knows best may also fly into a rage at the slightest provocation, and so the child has learned this as a means of communication, never having experienced that there are other ways of getting a point across.

Handling a two-year-old's tantrum needs patience and a willingness to see the world from the child's standpoint. For instance, she has been very patient in four shops — is it really crucial now to go into a fifth? Adults need to be willing to say 'Sorry' with words and a cuddle when the realisation dawns that they have fought over some issue that was really not important. You also need to be honest to yourself, often after the event, to admit how much your feelings of pride or embarrassment at the time affected how you handled the situation.

A major difference between dealing with a tantruming two-year-old and a four-year-old is that, because of her size, the younger child is likely to be easier to restrain physically or to lift up and remove. The other difference is that an older child should be more able to talk about her feelings afterwards. Despite these differences, there are some general points which apply to tantrums from any child in the under-five age group.

Trying to avoid tantrums

It is sometimes possible to see a tantrum building up. This, of course, is part of getting to know children as individuals. If an adult recognises the pattern, it can be possible sometimes to distract the child. Alternatively, it is sometimes sensible for the adult to leave the immediate situation, so that there is no audience. An older child might be encouraged to express her feelings through words.

Part of the sequence of events leading up to a potential tantrum may be the child's sensing that the adult is undecided, for example, whether or not the child can have another ice cream or have the special books out. The value of setting definite limits and being consistent can be seen clearly in dealing with children likely to tantrum. Wavering between 'Yes' and 'No', and being seen to waver by the child, provides an opportunity for her to influence an adult's decision by a tantrum. Young and older under-fives are less likely to tantrum if a 'No' is firm and adults look as if they mean it. However, part of thinking about the definite prohibitions has to be a willingness from adults also to think, in a calmer moment, about whether they are fighting any battles over issues that are not really important. It is possible to be drawn into a confrontation solely on the grounds of 'He's got to learn who's boss!'

Dealing with a child in a tantrum

Once a child has gone into a tantrum, she is beyond immediate comfort or reason. Calming words from an adult may slowly have an effect, but it is the emotional tone of what is being said that calms, not the words themselves. The child needs to be safely contained — in some cases physically prevented from hurting herself or others. Some children may be able to shout and kick out the tantrum in a corner without being restrained. As she emerges from the tantrum, the child will need comfort, especially if the fierceness of her emotions has frightened her. At this stage, an older child may be able to put some of her feelings into words or to listen to an explanation from an adult.

Adults will help the situation — before, during, and after — by remaining as calm as possible, doing what has to be done in terms of restraint, but not answering anger with anger and so adding to the dramatics. It does not help for the child to be removed from the room by another adult if this means that the child in any way receives special attention as the result of a tantrum. Children will quickly learn to throw tantrums for this, just as they will if they learn that adults give in to them easily. Basically, if a child sees that she is gaining some benefit from tantrums, she will learn that they are useful to her and the tantrums will increase, rather than decrease.

Breath-holding in tantrums

Some children learn to hold their breath in a tantrum, and their faces may actually turn blue or purple. This can be a very frightening experience for adults. However, medical opinion is that it is impossible for a child to hold her breath long enough to do harm — she faints before that point, and her body overrules her and starts breathing again. In this situation, therefore, the best course for adults is to remain as calm as possible and not take desperate measures to try to force the child to breathe.

As the child emerges from holding her breath or a faint, she is likely to need comfort. As with temper tantrums and general shouting matches, the violence of the child's feelings may well have frightened her. Equally as with tantrums, it is unwise for adults to give in to the child solely for fear that she will hold her breath. This is only likely to make the problem worse.

DEFIANCE AND GENERAL LACK OF COOPERATION

Behaviour which adults label as 'defiant' tends to cover a wide range of actions on the part of a child. Perhaps the child flatly refuses to eat certain foods, perhaps she is always the one to take out special toys without permission, or perhaps she can never resist the temptation to have the last word in an argument. Adults' tolerance over such behaviour varies considerably.

There can be many reasons behind behaviours which seem uncooperative. Some children may enjoy defying an adult and then watching the reaction. In fact, the family experience of some children is such that the only time they have had an adult's undivided attention is when that adult has been angry with them. The child has then learned a reliable way of getting attention but has not learned that attention through play or for cooperative behaviour can, in the end, be more enjoyable. Another form of uncooperativeness, which can also be linked with attention-seeking, is that of the child who is very slow in everything she does. Some adults find this very irritating and feel unable to leave the child to carry on at her own pace. They take over with a 'Come on, slowcoach, I'll do it.' A child who has little motivation to try is then encouraged to act in a hopeless, helpless manner. Such a child may well need some help, and it is worthwhile dividing up a task, such as dressing, so that she completes part of it and then is helped with the remainder. If the child receives a genuine 'Well done!' for what she has attempted, she will be encouraged to try.

Dealing with a child who appears uncooperative

A child who has been labelled as 'uncooperative' is often given many more instructions than other children, since adults are assuming — perhaps without being aware of this — that the child will not react without a great deal of persuasion. A child who has also come to be seen as the 'naughty' child of the group is often chided for actions that might be ignored from another child. Banging her spoon on the table is seen as yet another example of how irritating this child is and how she will not behave reasonably even for a moment. The same behaviour from a child who is not labelled as 'naughty' might be seen as high spirits, excitement over the coming mealtime, or just pleasure in making a rhythmic noise.

It is important for adults to monitor themselves if there is a child in the group who is seen as uncooperative. It is a good idea consciously to reduce the number of instructions given to such a child. Adults should make sure that they have the child's attention the first time by being close to her and talking directly to her. A child may be encouraged to follow an instruction if adults make the time to accompany her through the movements or towards the place the child is supposed to go. For example, the adult tidies up with the child or walks with her to another play activity away from the play she is interrupting.

If adults become sensitive to their own behaviour, they will also realise if a compromise can sometimes be reached by meeting the child half-way on some potential confrontations. It is very worthwhile discussing with other adults who deal with the same child ways in which you all might let some of the smaller issues be ignored and save any confrontation for times when the child must follow what you say. For instance, you might agree that drumming of feet beneath the dinner table should be ignored, but that the child has to conform to the rule that bikes should not be ridden through the part of the garden used by very young children.

It is important to look for behaviour that an adult can encourage in a child who is experienced as defiant. Children who seem constantly to be testing your limits and setting off power struggles with adults may respond well to being given some responsibility. For example, if the child seems interested, she might be given the opportunity to take messages or to assume a more mature role at lunchtime — perhaps handing out plates. She might be flattered if adults take the trouble to ask her opinion on choice of toys or rearranging a room. Basically, adults need to give the child attention for behaviour they would like to encourage. They can do well to ignore the backchat and to remove themselves from a situation in which the child appears to wish to provoke a confrontation.

Lack of cooperation over eating or drinking

Refusals to eat or drink often become an issue for an adult dealing with·a group of children. There is the anxiety that other children will also start to refuse to eat. However, the flat refusal to eat does not seem to spread, whereas messy behaviour such as flicking food does spread if one child is behaving in this way without reprimand. In this context, there are several points which are worth remembering.

Some children may enter a nursery without much experience of sitting down to knife-and-fork meals. If their family lives a great deal on 'take-aways', or if the family pattern is to eat from a plate or tray on the lap, the notion of sitting down at a table will be new. Furthermore, children have food preferences as much as adults — it is not reasonable to expect them to eat everything they are ever given. In an area with various ethnic groups, some children may be used to different foods and ways of eating it than are judged 'normal' in their nursery. Having tried to settle a child sensitively into new mealtime patterns, an adult may well find that the child very quickly learns alternative ways of behaving in different settings. It is the responsibility of under-fives workers to make sure that their expectations of mealtime behaviour and the menus offered reflect the different cultures represented by the children.

Children who do not eat much are better given a smaller helping than the larger helping eaten happily by other children. Adults can then be encouraging about the fact that the small-eaters have enjoyed their meal or have been willing to try a portion of something new. Adults who allow children to serve themselves do sometimes find that children become more likely to finish the meal which they themselves have chosen for quantity. This obviously needs supervision, but the principle of providing some choice for a child can make mealtimes less of a battle between adults and children.

Mealtimes at home or nursery can be times when adult tempers run high. Some adults lay themselves open to uncooperativeness from children by making mealtimes a thoroughly miserable event. I have had many meals in nurseries, and have seen considerably fewer eating problems and adult — child conflicts over food when the atmosphere has been that of a social occasion. Happy meal tables have been those where conversation was encouraged, children were allowed to express preferences over food, there was not the insistence that children finish every last morsel, and there was not the constant threat of 'No pudding!' I have been at a few meal tables where, from practically the first spoonful, there was a barrage of 'Well, I hope you're going to eat up properly today', 'Come on, hurry up', 'If you don't eat that cabbage, no pudding for you.' This has been, to me, an example of adults' simply not putting themselves into the children's shoes for one moment. This sort of continual nagging would make mealtime a misery for an adult — and the most patient individual would probably feel like saying 'You can keep your dinner!' — yet some adults seem to feel that this type of approach will improve children's eating habits. This hope is seriously misplaced.

Unfair judgements on children seen as uncooperative

Adults sometimes feel that a particular child is being deliberately difficult over issues like toilet-training or some aspect of learning through play. For example, an older child who sometimes wets herself but is generally dry may be seen as causing trouble, even as doing this out of spite or naughtiness. Similarly, a child's difficulties in learning are sometimes seen as a mixture of stupidity and pig-headedness. This is generally not only unfair to the child but also tends to worsen the situation.

In the case of a child who wets or soils intermittently, there is very little point in getting angry with the child. If the accidents are happening because of nervousness or over-excitement, adult anger is only likely to make the child anxious. It is quite reasonable to show that you would rather that wetting or soiling did not happen, and it can help to involve the child in washing out her pants or trousers on the grounds that she is old enough to help in this way. However, shouting at children or humiliating them about such events is unhelpful. It can also be cruel. Very few children are behaving in this kind of way in a spirit of defiance. Some children who become very absorbed in play activities ignore, until it is too late, the physical feelings which tell them that they need to go to the toilet. Some may even be so busy that they seem genuinely not to notice. It can help to take the child to the toilet at regular intervals, to be encouraging whenever she goes of her own accord, and to be calm when accidents do occur, although quite reasonably communicating to the child that you would rather she had reached the toilet in time.

When a child is having difficulties in learning, there is no point in adults' becoming irritated or telling her she is silly. It will only make the child more anxious and less likely either to answer questions or to join in learning games at all. The most likely explanation is that the child does not understand. Children do tease adults sometimes. However, mistakes over ideas that you judge the child should have learned almost always mean that she is confused. She is not setting out to annoy.

VERY PASSIVE OR WITHDRAWN CHILDREN

Some children can be a worry because they are too quiet. These may be children who are unhappy or depressed. They may spend a lot of time rocking alone or thumb-sucking. They may be children who wander aimlessly around, perhaps staring or just following other children or adults. There are undoubtedly children who enjoy playing alone, and many children go through temporary unhappy times when such behaviour is characteristic. However, observation of the children for whom you are responsible will soon distinguish the self-sufficient child, or the one who is temporarily out of sorts, from the child who is frequently withdrawn and isolated. It is important to keep an eye on the overly quiet child. Some people who work with young children are not sensitive enough to see this type of behaviour as a problem — thinking of the quiet child in their care as a 'good' well-behaved child, or perhaps as dull and boring because the child does not react to adults.

Very quiet children may be feeling a number of different emotions. They may be unhappy, depressed, or very shy. They may be disconcerted by the numbers of children and adults in a large nursery or playgroup. If a child in your care seems to be very unhappy, it can help to talk with the parents, if only to sense whether the unhappiness is a short-term or longer-term problem. In the case of disoriented, apparently withdrawn, children it may be simply that they do not know how to play — their parents may have failed to appreciate children's need for play, especially if the parents themselves had a very restricted unbringing. If a child enters nursery or playgroup with very limited play experience, she may not know what to do with play materials which are very familiar to other children. She may react by wandering around without purpose or by looking rather perplexed.

Clearly, a great deal depends on the personality of the child. Some children, faced for the first time with a wide choice of novel toys, go a little wild, rushing from one activity to another. They may earn themselves the label of 'hyperactive'. They need as much help as the very quiet child in learning how to play.

Bringing out the quiet child

It is very likely that adults' approach to an overly quiet child will have to be gradual. Adults also have to be very patient and prepared to give a lot of time to the child before a response may follow. If a child's main difficulty is a lack of play experience, regular periods of time spent with her may build up that experience. This might involve only a short period each day, with the aim of showing her how to use one toy or activity at a time so she can enjoy her play and join more easily in the play of other children.

A child whose extreme quietness is a response to neglect or a continuing unhappy home life may be very unresponsive to adults' friendly overtures. This can be hard for the adults, and they can come to feel inadequate since the encouragement and play approaches which have worked with many other children are failing to work with this child. It may be necessary, initially, to give the child time to get used to and tolerate an adult physically next to her. The adult's best move might be to make sure that some time is spent playing alongside the child each day, but that no pressure at all is placed on the child to join in. A friendly presence, interesting activity, and then friendly chat, without any pressure on the child to reply, may gradually build up feelings of trust.

A very quiet child may be one who does not know how to approach an adult or may be feeling nervous and threatened when adults are close — especially if adults have previously been unkind to her. Physical affection and cuddling may win her confidence, but the child may not ask for this and some children may not want close physical contact. Adults who are trying to help such a child really have to accept that part of the help may be that the child will become very attached to the adult who brings her out of her shell. Part of that adult's task will later be to help the child to approach and have confidence in other adults and to mix with children. However, this process is likely to be a slow one. The child has to gain the confidence to leave the protection of the single trusted adult.

Emotional problems reflected in behaviour which isolates the child

Some children who are passing through a distressing time withdraw into the kind of repetitive and self-absorbing behaviour which isolates them in their own personal world. Some of these behaviours, such as thumb-sucking, are not worth worrying about when they do not absorb much of the child's waking hours. Others you would want to stop even if the incidence rate was not high, for instance head-banging.

Some children who are disturbed by their strong emotions start to spend much of their day withdrawn in rocking to and fro or thumb-sucking. They may show nervous habits such as picking their skin or pulling out their hair. They may masturbate a great deal. Some children's behaviour can become a danger to themselves, for example frequent head-banging. Many children suck their thumbs or fingers at some stage or retreat to a favourite blanket in times of stress or tiredness. This is a perfectly reasonable way for a child to cope, and adults can be pleased that the child has her own resources to turn to as well as the comfort of adults. Many children go through times of being very interested in their genitals and find pleasure or comfort in playing with themselves. With all these behaviours, the worry comes if the child is spending much of the time distractedly thumb-sucking, rocking to and fro on her own, or masturbating. Then there is a real need to distract a child from this withdrawn behaviour, to encourage her to accept comfort from someone else, and to help her to express the feelings in other ways.

Simply telling a child to stop rocking or masturbating is unlikely to achieve much — you are asking her to give up the one thing that is enabling her to cope at present. It is, therefore, more effective to do something with the child that will help the expression of emotions. The child needs to discover that she can find comfort in an adult and enjoyment in activities that are not so withdrawn and compulsive. Initially, an adult needs to make time to be close to the child. If she will tolerate it, sitting the child on your lap and talking quietly with her will provide one way to distract her. If you continue to spend regular periods of time with such a child, you will gradually be able to interest her in yourself, what you are saying, and then some play activities. This may be looking at pictures with you — cuddling a toy for comfort while she listens — or becoming involved in a small way with your own activities. The important point to remember is that this process is likely to take a long time. Children do not just snap out of sad and depressed states any more than do adults. Such a child needs an adult's time and caring attention in a consistent way, so that trust can be built. She certainly does not need any criticism or harsh words — these will only drive her further into herself.

A child who is harming herself through head-banging or pulling out her hair needs to be stopped, but this means offering more than just saying 'Don't do that!' The feelings underlying head-banging may be anger or frustration. For some children, it seems to be the most satisfying way of expressing very strong feelings. Even limited head-banging is best discouraged, as children may hurt themselves. Serious head-bangers can badly harm themselves and are possibly very disturbed children.

The aim of adults is to stop the head-banging and hair-pulling by words and physically preventing the child. With a head-banger, it is usually possible to place a hand between the child's head and whatever she is banging against. This both protects the child and is a means to lift her up. A sharp 'No!', as you put your hand under her head, often gets a child's attention quickly. It is important then to comfort the child, if appropriate, talk with her, and ideally involve her in some distracting activity with you. A sharp 'No!' and a handclap can often get a child's attention from a distance. If you persevere, there is a good chance that the child will begin to stop herself, often with the same words that you have used. However, this will take some time.

In the same way, an adult would want to discourage a child from pulling out her own hair or regularly picking at her skin. It would be important to try to find out what events might have distressed the child to this extent. Some information can help an adult to offer the best kind of comfort for that child. Depending on the age of the child, it might be feasible to try to encourage her to express her feelings through words or through make-believe play. If the child seems seriously disturbed, then it may be necessary to ask the advice of someone who specialises in the psychological problems of children.

REGRESSION IN CHILDREN'S BEHAVIOUR

Children who have achieved certain milestones in their development sometimes regress in their behaviour, such that for a short or a long period of time they behave again as they did when they were younger. Children who are adjusting to the arrival of a new baby sometimes demand to return to some of their previous baby ways, perhaps wanting a bottle when they have managed well with a cup for a long time. This change in behaviour is not very surprising — the older child sees the baby receiving lots of attention for being helpless and dependent. The older child may feel for a while that the compensations of being the big one — the one who can do many things that the baby cannot — simply do not make up for the costs in terms of adult attention. Sensitive help and encouragement from her parents and other adults in her life can help the child to see the benefits of being able to do a lot more than the dependent baby. If her regression to baby ways is tolerated without criticism and all her more mature accomplishments are encouraged, she will come to see that being more independent than the baby does not mean that she loses out.

Regressions can happen in toilet-training, eating, or any other area in which a child is learning to cope more on her own. It does not help to take the blunt approach that the child is being 'naughty'; it is worthwhile instead trying to pinpoint what might have led a competent child to regress. It may be emotional upset, possibly someone putting too much pressure on the child to act like a 'big girl', or a temporary illness which makes the child want to retreat into more babyish ways for a short while. With adult tolerance and patience, the wish to regress will usually pass.

It is worthwhile remembering that, for all their leaps in development, the older under-fives are still young in many ways. There will be times when, although they can manage something on their own, at that moment they really want to have an adult do it for them. As long as this is not becoming a helpless attitude of 'I can't' for much of the time, there is every reason to indulge children sometimes. After all, most adults are capable of making themselves a cup of coffee and a snack, but it is very pleasant to have someone else do this for you as an occasional treat.

FEARS AND PHOBIAS

Children, like adults, are frightened sometimes and, just as with adults, the fear of some things or some people can become a major influence in a child's life. Adults need to be aware of their behaviour with children who have a specific fear. It does not help at all to be brusque or dismissive of the fear on the grounds that it will go away. If a child is frightened of worms or caterpillars, it is no use telling the child not to be silly — explaining logically that such little creatures cannot hurt her — and it is certainly no use thrusting them at her on the grounds that 'She's got to get over it.' Silliness really does not come into the matter — after all, many adults are frightened of creatures such as mice, spiders, earwigs, or snakes. If a child is frightened of something, then that has to be the starting point.

It may help if an adult tries to understand what it is about the source of the child's fear which makes her frightened. It may then be possible to tell her definitely that worms are not the same as snakes or that caterpillars will not be able to climb up to her bedroom. If the child is prepared to try, then some gradual coming together with the thing that frightens her may allay her fears. This might not always be the best course. For instance, if a child is frightened of dogs, you might want to deal with the fear by reassuring her of your presence to protect her but leaving the child with a healthy respect for unknown dogs.

Quite a few children are frightened of the dark. Again, there is no point in trying to dismiss this as something 'they'll have to grow out of'. Making a child's bedroom a warm and safe-feeling environment is important. For example, providing a night-light or a low-wattage bulb in a table lamp is useful for as long as she wants it, together with making sure she understands that you are close by and will come if she is frightened. Related to fear of the dark, children also sometimes need reassurance about vague fears such as burglars or things under the bed. There is no reason for adults to agree that such things are a possibility — in fact, you would want to reassure them that they could not happen. However, this need not stop you doing a ritual checking of under the bed and in the cupboards each night, if that makes the child feel better.

For some children, fears turn into phobias which can disrupt their lives. The difference between a fear and a phobia is that, with fears, children or adults are frightened of something which they are facing at the time. If the feelings become worse, then their fear can be aroused by the possibility of the source of their fear, so their actions begin to be hedged around by fears of 'in case'. A child who will not pick up worms, backs away from them, and does not want to garden where she has seen worms is showing a fear. A child who will not even venture outside the back door, in case the worms are lying in wait for her, may be developing a phobia. A child who hesitates in dread by the front gate in case there are dogs hiding up the road may also be developing a phobia. However, a child who hesitates to pass a gate where dogs have leapt out barking on previous occasions is showing a more concrete fear.

If a phobia does seem to be developing in the life of a child for whom you are responsible, you may need the advice of a child psychologist. A gradual approach to facing the source of a phobia or fear is feasible with children, and it may be possible to talk with the child. Obviously, the level of discussion with a child about her fears would be very different from that with an adult. However, children's feelings do sometimes emerge through their play, especially fantasy play. This may provide some clues as to how the fear has developed and also give a context for talking about the feelings.

Sometimes, children with many fears have lives which realistically are full of frightening events and threatening people. This may lead them to become very nervous twitchy children who are always concerned that an apparently friendly gesture hides danger. Some children react differently — responding with indiscriminate aggression on the grounds of strike out before you are struck. When a child has learned to behave in this way, adults have to be very patient in building trust and creating a secure atmosphere for her. Adults need to discourage the aggression, but some knowledge of the child's life may help them to see that the attacks are not personal.

ATTACHMENTS AND SEPARATIONS

The experience of separation on entering nursery or playgroup

Children need a settling-in period to provide continuity between their earlier experience and the new world of the nursery or playgroup. Different children need different amounts of time to adjust, and it is not always the parent who is the best person to help in this transition. For example, if a child has spent more time with her grandparent or a child-minder, this might be the more appropriate person to help her. The adjustments required from a child on joining a day nursery can be particularly high, since the child may be very young and the day can be long. However, a three- or four-year-old who has been at home with one parent may find the experience of a nursery school baffling — with new adults, new children, and new expectations and routine. Children have a limited concept of time, and a full day in a nursery school or day nursery can be confusing. They may be genuinely frightened that their parent will not return. If they are expected to take a rest during the day, some children believe that they are going to spend the night at the nursery.

Under these new and unexpected conditions, you would expect a child to need some help in settling or in some cases to show distress. It is worrying, in fact, if under-fives take too readily to new people and places. Some children have experienced so many changes that they accept further changes with little obvious reaction and attach themselves superficially to any new adult. However, the attachments are not deep, because they are not based in the belief that the adult will continue to be present. This kind of behaviour is a matter for concern and is not evidence of a 'good' or 'well-behaved' child.

There are many ways in which a sensitive adult can help a young child to become accustomed to bewildering new surroundings. Nursery or playgroup staff should make sure that the mother or father explains to the child where they are going, reassures the child that they will come back, and takes an affectionate farewell. If staff know that the parent has gone to work, they can talk about this with the child, explaining that 'after tea' — or whatever is the appropriate time — the parent will return. Over the first few days, some children are reassured if they can keep a parent's bag or gloves by them, as it gives them confidence that their parent will return both for the bag and for them.

Some children attach themselves to one particular member of staff. Admittedly this can be difficult, since staff have a responsibility to other children as well. However, if a child has chosen you as her safe place, it is important to make time to comfort her and to involve her in what you are doing. Children who are distressed often follow one adult around for days. It is useful to think of ways in which such a child can help you with little tasks, carrying things for you and coming with you to various parts of the unfamiliar building. This not only familiarises the child with the layout of the nursery or playgroup but also gives her the reassurance of knowing one adult to whom she can turn. With a particularly distressed child, it may be some time before you will be able to interest the child in play with other children. However, before this stage it should be possible to plan activities which mean that the child is alone with toys or with a group of children in an activity for an increasing length of time before you return to show an interest in what has been done.

Problems of jealousy

It is unreasonable to expect young children to get on well together all the time. Adults who work with under-fives come to expect some disagreements and arguments, especially over new toys or when children are tired. However, sometimes there is a particular problem of jealousy between children, perhaps by competing for the attention of a favourite adult. Sometimes this happens between younger children in a group. For instance, the 'baby' of the group feels pushed out by the arrival of a younger child. It may be noticeable that the second youngest is being aggressive to the new child, who is now the youngest in the group. It often happens that sudden expression of jealousy is particularly noticeable in certain places or at certain times. For example, in the bathroom or at mealtimes, the youngest child needs the kind of attention that the other child may feel should belong only to her. It is important that adults attempt gradually to encourage the 'jealous' child towards more independent behaviour and encourage the child both in this and for any friendly overtures to the second child.

Adults may have to look out for aggressive behaviour as an expression of jealousy. It is obviously necessary to stop the aggression, but it is as important with jealousy as with any other problem to bear in mind what it is you are trying to encourage as well as the behaviour you want to stop. In this instance, you might want to watch out for friendly behaviour and any cooperation or patience between two children who are sometimes at loggerheads. By being encouraging about this behaviour, you make it much more likely that children will gradually change away from the jealous behaviour. A major part of adult help for a child who feels jealous will also be reassurance that she is liked and is special to you, although your time and caring has to be shared.

PROBLEMS AND PLAY

Boredom

Some children are judged to be very demanding, in that either they want an adult's attention a great deal or their behaviour is such that an adult is often intervening to stop them from doing something. Sometimes the reason behind this is boredom — children may have become tired of familiar toys and activities which are repeated. The answer does not have to be expensive new toys. A bored child may be excited by the involvement of an adult in what she is doing. She may be fascinated by a chance to take part in domestic activities which the adult finds boring and repetitive. For the child, clearing out cupboards, running messages, and helping to make decisions about everyday events may be a fresh experience. In a nursery or playgroup, the older children will benefit from a chance to have their own projects which last over several days and which they know are kept safe from the clutches of younger children.

Adults may need to take an honest look at whether they are providing activities which are sufficiently challenging to older under-fives. This can require some thought about practical arrangements in day nurseries or centres where adults are coping with a wide age range. Small-group work with rising-fours and four-year-olds may be possible if one adult can be freed for short periods on a regular basis. There is also time for attention to the needs of older children if the younger ones take a nap after lunch. Many of the play activities discussed in part 2 of the book would be useful here.

Bored children, especially those of average intelligence and above, can be a real thorn in the side of adults who are not prepared to take a serious look at what those children need. It may be a very constructive approach to look carefully at what a bored child can manage — perhaps through using a developmental guide as discussed in chapter 3. This will probably give some pointers to activities and the level of difficulty which the child will enjoy.

Inability to play or very limited play

Lack of previous play experience, the problems of poor concentration (discussed in chapter 8), and adult frustration with a child whose play interests are very limited all benefit from observation of the child. If such a child is to be helped, then adults need to know how she plays and what are her current interests, however limited. Children who are only enthusiastic about football, or who always want to play outside, can be encouraged to extend their play by adults who are prepared to start at the point of the children's present abilities and interests. Cars do not just have to be pushed about with a 'Vroom, vroom' — they can be part of wider activities such as building, drawing, and imaginative play. Outdoor play is limited if it just consists of dashing around on bikes. However, there are many physically active ways of learning if adults use their imagination — chapters 8 and 9 have many ideas which can be built into outdoor play.

Expressing feelings through play

As children experience very strong emotions and their time perspective is limited, their frustration, distress, anger, and other feelings can erupt over events which an adult may feel are insignificant. There may be times when adults feel confident that a child will get over an emotional outburst quickly and that there is no long-term problem. However, there are other children who may have frequent outbursts of strong emotions. There is a need to help children express these emotions, although not necessarily through the channel they have chosen so far. One approach is to encourage them towards play which will help this expression.

Children sometimes frighten themselves by the violence of their emotions, yet these are feelings that need to be expressed. It is not wise to try to clamp down on an emotion altogether — it is better to help children to develop ways of expressing the emotion that do not hurt themselves or others. Some children can be helped just by learning the words to express feelings. An adult can encourage them to describe what they feel in a simple way, by asking 'Do you feel unhappy?' or 'Are you feeling really cross? Tell me what has made you cross.' Children need to be encouraged to feel able or allowed to say that they are angry with another child, or to tell that child that they are cross as an alternative to lashing out. Energetic games sometimes help a child who is struggling with angry feelings. Toys which can be kicked, bitten, or thrown about may help to express feelings. There is satisfaction sometimes in pummelling floor cushions or shouting at teddies.

Children often express their fears or worries through imaginative play. Toys such as dolls and teddies, figures of families, toys for domestic play, and others can be used to help a child express through play her emotional upset or particular worries. An adult listening to imaginative play or becoming sensitively involved in it can often hear — expressed perhaps through the dolls — a child's concern about events at home, fears about other children, or thoughts about a particular experience. This can help adults gain an insight into the child's feelings and can lead to ideas about how to help.

Sometimes a child will accept reassurance through imaginative play. For example, a three-year-old who was embarrassed and upset by occasional accidents of wetting his bed at night expressed these feelings to me when we were playing at putting teddy to bed. As he picked up the sheet and pillow, he told me they were wet and that teddy had wet himself in the night. The boy seemed reassured by my comments that 'Never mind, we'll put the sheet in the washing machine' and 'Everyone has accidents sometimes.' Sometimes a child may work through fears of a past event. The three-year-old daughter of a friend of mine was in a car crash. She was badly shaken, although not physically hurt. In the following weeks, she played out the incident again and again with her toy cars, until the memory did not haunt her any more.

In their fantasy play, children can act out having the power which they never have in their non-fantasy lives. They may boss around their dolls and teddies, the way that they feel they are controlled by adults. They may treat their toy monkey in the rough way they would like to treat that intrusive new baby but are managing to resist. Through hospital play or being dentists, children may voice the fears or lack of understanding that they have not managed to communicate to the adults in their lives. They may deal with such fears completely through play, but often adults need to look for ways to reassure a child or to explain what she does not understand. This may be by becoming involved in the play or by chatting with the child on another occasion, perhaps using an appropriate book as a starting point.

CONCLUSIONS

In talking exclusively about difficulties in this chapter, there is a risk of painting a picture of under-fives as problems waiting for a place to happen. This is not true, of course. Some adults do have to deal with children who have learned ways of behaving which are particularly disruptive or worrying; however, in many instances, children show more minor expressions of the range of problems discussed. Often, a similar approach will help whether an individual example would be judged as a minor or major problem. However, the longer the child has behaved in that way, or the stronger the feelings underlying the behaviour, the more persistent an adult may need to be in coping with the problem and in pointing the child firmly towards alternative ways of behaving and coping. This is hard work, although very satisfying. Being responsible for children's well-being and development is a challenging and sometimes difficult task. We all need support from time to time in our relations with children. We need thinking time to ourselves, but also the opportunity to talk matters over with other adults. Other people's ideas and approaches are not necessarily more appropriate than our own; however, out of such a discussion, an idea often develops which is best suited for an individual adult to use in handling a particular child.

PART 4
WORKING TOGETHER AS THE ADULTS IN CHILDREN'S LIVES

Part 4 differs from the rest of this book in that it concentrates more on adult relationships, whereas previously the focus has been on children. These chapters are about adults who come together because of the children. They are about adults who are parents and adults who are working in the services that deal with young children. The adults have not chosen each other as individuals. They are meeting over the heads of the children, and their particular roles in this meeting are different from adult relationships in other parts of their lives.

Many books on parent involvement are presented almost solely from the standpoint of the staff. I wanted to write for parents too. Staff and parents share their 'adult' status as well as the children for whom they are, in their different ways, responsible. I want to stress what staff and parents have in common and how both can benefit from looking from the perspective of the other.

In chapter 13 I take an overview of what is going on in parent involvement in under-fives centres. The aim is to make some sense of a diverse group of activities and to provide a framework on which readers (staff and parents) can place their own experience of parent involvement. Chapter 14 is geared more towards staff and looks at effective planning of parent involvement. Chapter 15 starts by highlighting the different perspectives of staff and parents and, from a reminder that both share their 'adult' status, goes on to discuss those skills important in making contact between adults as constructive as possible.

13
PARENT INVOLVEMENT AS A DEVELOPMENT IN WORK WITH YOUNG CHILDREN

Most young children have several key adults in their lives. Some of these adults will be within the family; some will be family friends. In different ways, the adults whose lives touch those of particular children are faced with the business of working together. They are also faced with the consequences for themselves and the children of *not* working together. As parents stop taking sole responsibility for their children, then other adults also become involved in the children's lives. They share the 'adult' status, yet, in this relationship, the adults wear different 'hats'. The adult as parent has other roles — for example, within the family, in friendships, and in paid employment. The other adults working with young children will have their own professional 'hat' — nanny, child-minder, nursery nurse, nursery teacher, playgroup worker. They too take on other roles in their lives — one of which may be as parents themselves. However, it is in the child-care role that they meet other parents during their work.

Adults as professional workers in children's lives

There is much variety in how families are made up and in the ways in which they may change over the years. However, most children have one or two parents to share their daily life. Any other adults who are involved with other people's children have to decide on how much contact they will have with the children independently from their parents. These adults may be workers in the under-fives field or in the medical establishment and health services; they may come from specialist areas like speech therapy, physiotherapy, or child psychiatry. For all these people, the initial reason for contact is the young child. However, every professional will need to determine his or her relationship to parents — how close or distant this should be. For some, this will be a personal decision; others will simply follow current practice in their area.

PARENT INVOLVEMENT AS A DEVELOPMENT

Why the push towards parent involvement?

During the 1970s and 1980s there has been a great deal of sometimes heated discussion about the appropriate relationship between adults as professionals and adults as parents. There has been something of an explosion of books about this contact and about how different services for children and their families are developing parent involvement. Later in this chapter I will be summarising what is happening in parent involvement: at this point I am going to look briefly at possible reasons why people are pouring energy into it.

Any historian will tell you that it is a very hazardous business to try to pin down the causes of a broad social change. This does not, of course, stop people trying. In this case it is worth the effort because the different likely influences on development in parent involvement represent some very different perspectives. I believe it is important to grasp these differences in order to make sense of what is happening in the area.

There seem to be five major approaches — three broadly from the professionals' side and two from the parents' side. Of course, these are not mutually exclusive.

1 Professionals concerned to help 'disadvantaged' children

From the 1950s onwards, it was increasingly accepted that children's measured intelligence is strongly influenced by their environment and is not solely a matter of inheritance. Over a similar period, it became politically acceptable to argue that children should have equal opportunities to reach their potential. So, believing that some children were disadvantaged by circumstances, professionals felt obliged to do something about it. Additionally, the message from some of the intervention projects with 'disadvantaged' families was that the projects' impact on children lasted longer when their parents were also involved. This work therefore gave professionals — particularly in education and related services — sound reasons for wanting to work with parents as well as children. Notice, however, that this approach was motivated by a desire to help children. Parents are being involved because they are seen as important in improving the prospects of their children. Parents may additionally be seen as part of the problem.

2 Children's difficulties seen as family difficulties

In the 1970s there was a growing emphasis in social work and in some branches of medicine, such as psychiatry, that difficulties experienced by children could not sensibly be seen in isolation from the family. It was not just a case of making sense of children's problems — professionals also argued that, without awareness and change in other family members, the likely causes of the problems would not go away. Notice that this source of influence on parent involvement also started from the perspective of wrestling with problems in order to help children.

3 Professionals being realistic about what they can achieve

In the 1970s, it dawned on professionals in many specialist areas that they were unlikely to progress far with children on the basis of infrequent specialist sessions unless parents understood and continued the work at home. Once professionals attempted some tentative involvement of the child's parents, they found that this could speed up progress, rather than parents interfering and blocking the work. This approach to parent involvement does not necessarily view parents as part of a problem: it assumes rather that they may instead be part of the solution — that parents can learn additional skills and have the strong motivation to do so in order to help their own children.

4 Parents as people with rights as well as responsibilities

A different source of pressure towards parent involvement has resulted from parents claiming the right to be informed and consulted — to have an effective say in their children's lives. In education, for example, parent 'consumer groups' such as the Advisory Centre for Education and the Confederation for the Advancement of State Education have aimed to change the attitudes of professional staff and to ensure that parents have some control of their children's education.

5 Parents viewing themselves as skilled adults

Discussion about services for children seems to be moving steadily away from assumptions that parents have nothing special to offer — that they are 'just parents'. Some parents have made this shift in their view of themselves.

There are many different ways for adults to gain confidence in themselves as parents; however, an influence for many women as mothers seems to have been the playgroup movement. The 1960s saw a tremendous expansion in this type of under-fives facility. Playgroups vary a great deal in how they are run and to what extent they are staffed or managed by parents. However, for all the variety, the playgroup movement seems to have given many women an experience which boosted their confidence in themselves as organisers, planners, and providers for young children.

You might like to consider which of the above influences have probably affected the development of parent involvement in establishments and services with which you have personal contact — as a parent or as a professional.

FROM REASONS FOR CHANGE TO DEVELOPMENTS IN PRACTICE

The focus in this book is on children and their families in under-fives centres. I will therefore look in detail at what is happening in this area with parent involvement. However, it is worth briefly outlining related developments:

- There has been a growth of home visiting schemes (see, for instance, Willem van der Eyken's report, *Home Start — a four-year evaluation*, published in 1982 by Home-Start Consultancy, 22 Princess Road West, Leicester LE1 6TP.
- Structured work to help children with special needs has been taken into the home (for example, read Gillian Pugh's *Parents as partners*, published in 1981 by the National Children's Bureau).
- There have been some moves in the medical and related services to involve parents more in work with their children, both through individual professionals and through the style of work of centres (such as the Hester Adrian Centre in Manchester or the Wolfson Centre in London).
- Another expanding area is that of 'education' for parents or prospective parents. (The very different services and approaches here are documented by Gillian Pugh and Erica De'Ath in *The needs of parents: practice and policy in present education*, published by the National Children's Bureau in 1984.)

What is the range of activities involving parents with the establishments attended by their young children?

I have compiled a list of 'activities' that I have read about, heard about, or myself seen in action that represent a full range of what is happening in parent involvement in different kinds of under-fives establishments (nursery schools, day nurseries, playgroups, combined centres, family centres). In my experience, there is little point in trying to group activities by type of establishment, since these vary so much. Instead, I have grouped by different kinds of involvement.

1 The first contacts between families and establishments

Many establishments have some kind of contact between families and the establishment before the child's first 'official' day. This may be any of the following:

- An invitation for parents, with or without their children, to visit the establishment before taking up the child's place.
- A visit by staff to the family's home.
- Some written information for parents about the establishment.
- A meeting to clarify the conditions under which the child (and perhaps the parents) will attend — the agreement to a contract of attendance.

2 The continuing contact and communication between parents and staff

- Daily face-to-face contact as parents bring or pick up children.
- Informally arranged conversations about children ('Can I have a word about . . .?') or scheduled meetings with parents to discuss progress, independent of particular problems.
- Some procedure on parents' access, or lack of it, to written material on their child.
- Invitations to attend medicals, reviews, etc.
- A notice-board for parents.
- Open days or open evenings for parents to see their own child's work and/or the general work of the establishment.

3 Parents' involvement in activities to support the establishment

Again, there is a wide range of ways in which parents may be invited or offer to become involved:

- As organisers or supporters of fund-raising events.
- Sharing responsibility for a continuing activity such as running a toy-library.
- Collecting materials for use by children.

4 Parents present during the daily activities for children

- Parents staying to settle their child into the establishment.
- Parents welcome to stay with their (now settled) child, join the children for tea, or similar.
- Parents offering or being invited to stay in order to help out in the daily activities for the group.
- Helping out on special occasions such as outings.

5 Parents' contributing to their own child's learning

● Parents working with their child in the establishment. (This tends to be in the context of staff concern that parents need to learn how to help their child.)
● Parents' continuing programmes of work or projects at home, or being part of a home—school reading scheme.

6 Parents in policy and decision-making

● Parents having a role in decisions made about their own child.
● Parents on management committees, users committees, or as parent governors, taking part in decisions about the running of an establishment.

7 Social activities for parents as adults

● Hospitality for parents to stay and have social contact on an ad-hoc basis or as arranged, such as coffee mornings.
● An on-going parents group or club.
● Social events for parents as adults (not about their children or the work of the establishment).
● Access to sessions on craft, literacy, or outside speakers on anything of interest to parents (again, not necessarily about children or parenthood).

8 Help for parents as adults

● Help in parenting, aspects of child care, or management.
● Resources of information and practical advice.
● Help with problems (not necessarily in parenting) that moves towards counselling or coping with crisis.

How much of this is actually happening?

Every type of parent involvement described can be seen in some under-fives establishment. There have been a number of surveys of parent involvement, but these have not produced information to confirm that certain percentages of different kinds of establishment undertake this or that type of involvement — different questions have been asked, and this makes comparison of different surveys very difficult. A further problem in sensibly answering the question 'How much is going on?' is that developments that sound alike ('Yes, we ask parents to settle in their children') can operate very differently in practice.*

*If you want more information on 'how much is going on?' there is a survey reported in my discussion paper (written under the name Jennie Lindon) *Parent*

Looking for good practice in parent involvement

Services for young children and their families are not alone in tending to present 'good practice' in terms of what people have done in their establishments. Descriptions typically offer 'model' nurseries or playgroups to copy. I do not see this as a constructive way to approach good practice.

The essence of good practice in parent involvement is not so much the chosen programmes of action but

a) how people have reached the decision about what they will do, and
b) exactly how they carry out the programme.

What might be a very positive programme in one establishment could be irresponsible in another with different resources, staff skills, and parents. Two establishments might be carrying out plans that sound the same in terms of action, yet the two staff groups might differ considerably in how they view and act towards parents — a lack of respect for parents would create what was effectively a different programme for parent involvement from one in which parents' views were taken seriously.

Good practice allows for adequate thinking and planning, and the key aspects to this are discussed in chapter 14. Read on!

involvement — developments in pre-schooling and the early school years, available from the National Nursery Examination Board, Argyle House, 29—31 Euston Road, London NW1 2SD.

14
MAKING PARENT
INVOLVEMENT WORK
WELL – THE PLANNING

It is very important to be realistic about parent involvement as a development. Parent involvement in its many different forms is not an optional extra, easily slipped into existing commitments: many aspects of parent involvement require hard thinking by staff and a possibly painful reappraisal of their professional role. Reorientation to parents as well as children can be hard for staff whose thinking and planning has so far been appropriate to full job involvement with children. Furthermore, work with young children provides a full and busy day in itself.

If staff are asked to make substantial developments in parent involvement then there are implications for how many staff will be needed, if the number of children is to remain the same. If staff attempt to cram more into the day with the same people resources, the quality of work may decline. If there is no money for more staff, serious consideration needs to be given to what development in parent involvement can realistically be achieved within available staff time. Sometimes, committed staff will pour energy into activities and manage by using their non-work time to complete reports, prepare material needed for the children, and so on. This is not a low-cost alternative: the individual staff pay the cost, along with their families and people important to them in their personal lives.

Even very committed staff can become disillusioned if their current resources are insufficient for what they wish to achieve and the way in which they are attempting to achieve it. Thinking and planning time are necessary so that individual establishments move at a pace and in a direction that is appropriate for them. I appreciate that the time needed to do this well could be used as an excuse for staff to drag their feet. However, a rush into action with confused goals and a poor assessment of the necessary roles and resources leaves the chance for staff with low commitment to parent involvement to argue 'We tried it and it doesn't work – don't ask me to try again.' If you believe it is worthwhile trying, then read on.

How do you look at parent involvement?

I will start with what might be called the different 'philosophies' of parent involvement.

There is a great deal of variety in what actually happens about parent involvement in under-fives establishments. Some of this variety comes from the differing people and space resources, but some undoubtedly comes from the differences in how adults (both staff and parents) view parent involvement.

It seems to me that there are two large clusters of beliefs that influence how staff — and probably parents too — approach parent involvement:

i) beliefs about *power* and the balance of power between staff and parents;
ii) beliefs about the nature of the *exchange* between staff and parents.

These beliefs influence the judgements made by staff and parents about how relationships between them *ought* to develop — what is appropriate.

I suggest that you think about *power** in parent involvement. Think about your own attitudes and what appear to be the attitudes of fellow-staff and fellow-parents. In the under-fives centres that you know:

- Who decides whether written information on children is available to the parents of those children?
- Whose views count in the methods used in helping children to learn?
- Who determines the activities offered in parent involvement, and who judges whether these are successful?
- Who determines the role of parents as helpers in the centre?
- Who decides to what extent the answers to these questions, and many other possible questions, are public information?

I do not have a hidden list of 'correct' answers to these — it is likely that for every under-fives centre a slightly different balance of power is appropriate. However, I do believe that staff and parents need to think about the business of power, otherwise beliefs about what is and is not appropriate will influence everyday actions and planning for the future without those beliefs being closely examined themselves.

I suggest that you also think about the nature of the *exchange*† between staff and parents. Do you see this as mainly one-way or as a two-way exchange? Does the way you behave — as a member of staff or parent — reflect your beliefs? Again, look at the following questions, turn them over in your mind, and consider 'Where do I stand on these?'

---

*Power and the balance of power are discussed by Gillian Pugh and others in the National Children's Bureau *Partnership paper 2*, published in 1985.
†The question of one-way or two-way exchange is discussed by Barbara Tizard, Jo Mortimore, and Bebb Burchell in *Involving parents in nursery and infant schools: a sourcebook for teachers*, published in 1981 by Grant McIntyre.

- What do you believe parents could learn from the professional staff? What do you believe staff could learn from parents?
- What information would staff like from parents which they are not sharing at the moment?
  What information would parents like from staff which is not being shared as yet?
- What do you think parents really need to understand to be in tune with the everyday life of an under-fives establishment?
  What do you think staff really need to understand to be in tune with the everyday life of parents?
- As a member of staff, what would you like parents to respect about you as a professional?
  As a parent, what would you like staff to respect about you as a parent?
- From the staff perspective, to what extent do you feel parents contribute to difficulties in the everyday life of your establishment — how could they make life easier for you?
  From the parent perspective, to what extent do staff contribute to difficulties in your everyday life — how could they make life easier for you?

Where you stand on these will influence how you approach the planning of parent involvement, as well as how you behave from day to day.

PARENT INVOLVEMENT NEEDS PLANNING

Developing parent involvement in under-fives establishments needs careful thought and detailed discussion. Your starting point is *not* 'What shall we do and how soon can we do it?': the process is better seen as a journey which starts with the question

'Where do we want to go?'

The next sensible question is

'How shall we get there?'

And a question which must not be forgotten is

'How will we know we have arrived?

These questions look deceptively simple to answer. They are not. In my experience, the questions can lead to a great deal of heated discussion within groups of staff who share a general commitment to parent involvement, let alone among staff who have doubts about developments in this direction.

Where do you want to go in parent involvement?

There are two steps in answering this question. The first is to get in touch with your *aims* for parent involvement. Then, you need to move from these aims to concrete and specific *goals*. I am describing only briefly a process which takes a lot of thinking about and discussing.

Identify your aims for parent involvement

Aims give an overall direction, but they are not in themselves achievable. They are not goals, nor are they plans for action. They are an important start to planning, and it is helpful to commit aims to actual words (preferably written down), whether you are planning as an individual or as a group of adults (staff or parents) planning together. Commitment to actual words can really clear the air on 'What are our reasons for getting into parent involvement?'

I approach this business of identifying the aims in three ways, depending on the group with whom I am working. Sometimes I work through all three ways.

I may ask a group of people who work with young children and their families to write down their personal aims for parent involvement. The mix of replies often illustrates some different starting points. Aims may be expressed such as:

- 'I want parents to understand better what we are trying to achieve with the children here.'
- 'I want mothers and their children to have a better relationship.'
- 'I want to be able to help parents with their problems.'
- 'I want parents to be more involved in their children's development.'

and sometimes, if people are extremely frank,

- 'I want to get my senior management off my back by showing that I am doing something in parent involvement.'

With staff who work in the same establishment or who are in establishments supposedly offering the same service, I ask them to reach agreement on a poster that would be fixed at the front door. They have to imagine that this poster is weatherproof and built to last (at least five years), so a group is committing itself to a statement of 'What we are here for'. I limit the poster to fifteen words, which must include 'we' but not words like 'try' or 'perhaps'. I find this exercise makes people think hard about the assumptions underlying their aims. It may seem appropriate — even professional — to discuss in a family centre or day nursery how 'We want to help mothers to have a better relationship with their children.' This seems incredibly arrogant when turned into a weatherproof poster saying 'We are here to help you get on better with your child.' Different under-fives centres may come up with statements such as

- 'We welcome children and parents here.'
- 'We offer a safe and caring place for you and your child to learn together.'
- 'We run this nursery in partnership with parents.'

The third way that I approach overall aims with groups of adults is to ask them to sum up the nature of their work in two words — a verb and a noun. For example, a group of firefighters might say that the core of their work was 'saving lives'. Using the same format, I have found different groups of under-fives workers have given such statements as 'encouraging change', 'preventing breakdown', and 'supporting families'. In the discussion that followed, we found that the choice of words was important: it was a window into the nature of the different services.

Of course, all these overall aims can be interpreted in different ways. They would be almost useless if planning ended with a statement of aims; however, they are just the beginning.

Identifying the goals that will achieve your overall aims

Aims may well be vague. Goals *must* be specific. They need to be worded in such a way that you can tell whether or not the goals have been achieved. They define a particular point you intend to reach (an end state), not how you reach it. Goals are not about a particular plan of action — we are not yet at the step of 'Let's have a coffee morning.'

You need to put your statement of overall aim in front of you and ask yourself 'How will I judge that I have succeeded in achieving this aim? How will I know success when I see it?'

For example, suppose the poster for your under-fives centre is 'We run this nursery in partnership with parents' and, working together as a whole staff group, you keep asking yourselves the pointed question 'How will we know this when we see it?' You might come up with the following five descriptions as a starter to working towards goals. You agree that:

'We will be running this nursery in partnership with parents when

i) there is a change in how we run the nursery which comes from an idea contributed by a parent;
ii) we try to have at least one parent in the building all day long for every day;
iii) staff ask parents for their views and really listen;
iv) an event in the nursery is planned and run completely by parents;
v) parents understand what we're trying to do and we understand what they are trying to do.'

These five descriptions are not yet workable goals. Goals need to be specific, with no room for misunderstanding.

In point (i) you would need to ask·'What sort of change do we mean?'

In point (ii), the word 'try' reduces the force of the goal — goals are about achieving an end, not trying to achieve. If 'try to' is removed from point (ii), it is then a goal.

In point (iii), it is unclear what 'really listen' means — you need to ask how you would recognise it if you saw somebody 'really listening'.

Point (iv) might well be something you could observe happening or not happening. However, is it an appropriate goal? Supposing parents plan an event that runs counter to a basic principle of the centre? Some basis of cooperative discussion may be necessary.

Point (v) needs clarification because you cannot observe 'understanding', you can only deduce it from people's behaviour. This point therefore needs to be attacked with the question 'How will we recognise "understanding each other" when we see it?'

You work away like this until you have a set of shared and workable goals. There is a shorthand to help you remember the characteristics of a good goal — this is SOAP IT. An effective goal should be:

- Specific (not general or vague)
- Observable (to you and to others)
- Achievable (you realistically can succeed in this)
- Performance-directed (about achieving an end, not trying)
- Involving (you have to want it)
- Time-bound (you commit to 'When' and 'By when?')

How shall we get there?

Once an individual or a group of staff has specific goals, then it is possible to look at each goal in turn and, in an open-ended way, explore the possible courses of action that could be taken to achieve this goal. As with any kind of problem-solving, it is better to consider a range of possible plans of action before deciding on the particular route you will take.

Take point (i) from the earlier example. Let us suppose that in a particular under-fives centre this has been worked into 'We will know the views of all parents on major changes under discussion in the centre' and that plans for the spare room are to be the first 'major' change. There are several different ways in which the staff could achieve this goal. They might ask each parent face-to-face. They might set up a parents' notice-board and put up a sheet asking for suggestions. They might hold a coffee morning or an evening meeting to discuss what to do with the spare room. The staff might decide that some regular forum is needed to discuss changes and set up a users' committee, or get parents' representatives on to a management committee.

For any goal, there will be a number of possible plans of action. In any one under-fives centre, staff need to consider each possibility and ask themselves:

- What resources do we need for this?
- What roles will staff need to take on?
- What skills will staff need?
- Overall, what will help us achieve this goal?
- Overall, what will hinder us in achieving this goal?

The resources of any centre will provide positives and negatives. It is very important not to highlight the negatives — 'We haven't got a spare room for a parents' room' — at the cost of the positives — 'The parents come from six different ethnic groups and between them have more specialist knowledge of these cultures than do the staff.'

You need to consider your resources in terms of

a) the building(s) and the space available;
b) the people: staff and parents — skills, talents, time, energy;
c) the broader network reached through staff and parent contacts;
d) finance — how much money is available and the options for raising further funds;
e) access to additional facilities, equipment, transport, etc.

You may find that there is a gap between your current resources and what you realistically need for your preferred plan of action. This may mean that a different first step is more sensible.

The different plans of action will require particular skills from staff, and require them to take on particular roles if a goal is to be achieved. You need to ask yourself: does a course of action need staff as friends, as instructors, as facilitators, as referees? Who will fulfil these roles? Who will do it, where and when? Do the required roles go contrary to how staff currently view their professional input?

Example: asking parents to help in the normal daily activities of an under-fives centre

You will need to check your *resources* of space (how many adults can comfortably work with the children) and your 'hospitality resources' (providing coffee etc. for parents, somewhere for them to take a break if they stay all day, toilets that are easily accessible).

You will need to think through the *role* that staff will take on vis-a-vis parents, and this will have implications for *skills*. Staff need skills of organisation (how many parents and which day) and planning (what will be the parents' role and the limits to how they may work with the group). Social skills will be important in helping parents to feel at ease in somebody else's 'territory'. Good communication skills will help in explaining to parents in what way staff would like them to work with the children, and in discussing any of the ground rules of the group or the centre. Staff will benefit from some skills of self-awareness (in making sense of their comfort or discomfort with having parents present).

You might like to try a similar breakdown for resources, roles, and skills with other activities in parent involvement — perhaps home visits or running a parents' group.

How will we know we've arrived?

If you set yourself 'SOAP IT' goals, then you will recognise when you have achieved them. If they are specific, if they are observable, if they are about achieving something and not about trying, then there will be no room for argument about whether the goals have been achieved. The more vague the goals, the more difficult it will be for you, and your colleagues, to say definitely 'We have achieved the goal we set ourselves.'

It is not just a question of whether you have achieved a goal: there will often be lessons to learn. However careful your thinking and planning, there will often be some unexpected developments. Looking back, you may learn that enthusiasm to get going led you to brush over potential difficulties that could have been foreseen. Similarly, there may be some unexpected positive results.

It can be valuable to keep track of how many staff and parents have been involved. This is not because high numbers are a necessary sign of success — some forms of parent involvement may be heavily used by only a small number of parents, and this may be judged to be appropriate. It may be decided to adopt some form of parent involvement which effectively excludes any parents who are also employed. This may be a disadvantage that staff choose to live with, because of other factors involved in the decision, but this should be done with awareness of the consequences.

WHAT DO PARENTS THINK ABOUT PARENT INVOLVEMENT?

Staff approach the issues of parent involvement from a different perspective to parents. This is probably inevitable and need not be a problem if staff consult with parents. Staff need to ask themselves questions like 'What would parents like?', 'What do they think is needed?', and 'In the parents' judgement, how well did the activity go?'

The initial answer by staff to the questions may well be an honest 'I don't know.' If you do not know, then ask parents directly. This genuine effort to find out means that parents are consulted before plans for

Dario Mitidieri

Parents means fathers as well as mothers.

involvement reach anything like a final stage. They may be asked in what way they would like to be involved with the establishment. As experienced 'consumers', they can be asked for their informed opinion on such issues as how the first contact between establishment and home, or the early weeks of their child's attendance, might have been eased. Parents' views on changes in an establishment provide another perspective. However, these views do not provide a blueprint that must be followed willy-nilly, anymore than staff should expect parents to apply advice uncritically to their own home and child-rearing.

Meeting some of the parents' wishes may not be feasible once the establishment's resources are seriously considered. Some parents may make proposals that go directly against values that staff regard as non-negotiable. For example, many under-fives centres operate with principles of non-sexist (and non-racist) child care. Parents might want to arrange an activity exclusively for girls or exclusively for boys, regarding this as appropriate. When incompatible views are held with equal strength, a discussion between staff and parents will not be easy. However, honesty, tact and an insistence on respecting others — though not necessarily agreeing with them — may help to bring about a working acceptance of one another's positions.

The adults involved (staff and parents) may have quite distinct reasons for promoting or joining activities. Different motivations are not necessarily incompatible if they are honestly expressed. However, if they remain as the unspoken hopes of the different adults concerned, then misunderstanding and disappointment can be the result. For example, the staff of a nursery school may encourage parents to join the group of children on a regular basis with the unspoken hopes that parents will understand more about nursery aims and methods and will also, as additional adults, help to provide better-supervised activities for the children. Parents may accept the invitation in order to achieve their unspoken hope of seeing how their own children behave during nursery time, and perhaps also with the general wish to help. These different general hopes may or may not be incompatible — if parents and staff talk about them, they will soon find out!

The situation in the example above is not unusual. I would comment that an understanding of the philosophy underpinning nursery practice will probably be achieved more directly through adult conversation, supported by what parents see, rather than by leaving parents to deduce the philosophy from samples of daily nursery activities. Some parents

Daisy Hayes

Between them parents and staff will have a wide range of skills and knowledge.

may be happy to provide another pair of hands for the nursery; however, if they choose not to meet a need defined by the staff, this is not evidence that parents are uninterested or that parent involvement as a whole 'does not work'.

Planning for parent involvement — a summary

Much thinking and planning needs to go into parent involvement. I sum it up in the diagram below. In working your way through this process,

A planned approach to parent involvement

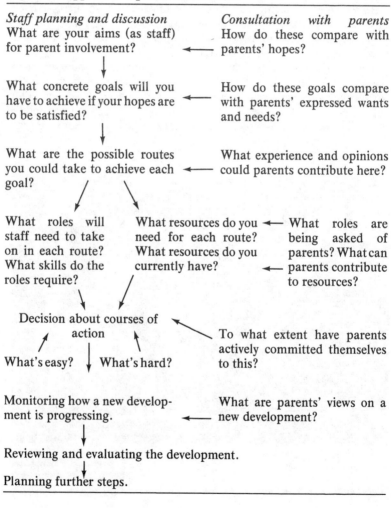

Staff planning and discussion
What are your aims (as staff) for parent involvement?

Consultation with parents
How do these compare with parents' hopes?

What concrete goals will you have to achieve if your hopes are to be satisfied?

How do these goals compare with parents' expressed wants and needs?

What are the possible routes you could take to achieve each goal?

What experience and opinions could parents contribute here?

What roles will staff need to take on in each route? What skills do the roles require?

What resources do you need for each route? What resources do you currently have?

What roles are being asked of parents? What can parents contribute to resources?

Decision about courses of action

What's easy? What's hard?

To what extent have parents actively committed themselves to this?

Monitoring how a new development is progressing.

What are parents' views on a new development?

Reviewing and evaluating the development.

Planning further steps.

you can reach decisions about first steps in parent involvement which are sensible for your under-fives centre. Your next steps will be likely to follow a different pattern to those of other centres, since you will have a unique combination of staff and parents and centre resources. However, all centres have in common the necessity of following these planning stages.

When my son was three years old, he was given to encouraging slow adults by jumping up and down shouting 'Do it! Do it! Do it!' I am reminded of this strategy whenever I talk with staff who feel obliged to plunge into parent involvement — usually because somebody else is saying that the staff 'must' get on with it. In any development there is always a time for 'Do it! Do it!'; however, this must follow thinking and planning. If you take the 'Do it!' route, this can make a nonsense of any attempt to evaluate what you have done — in any development in your work.

*If you would like to read further, you could look at the practical section in *Including parents in nursery and infant schools: a sourcebook for teachers* by Barbara Tizard, Jo Mortimore and Bebb Burchell, published by Grant McIntyre in 1981. They offer some sensible questions for staff to ask themselves about different activities. I would also recommend the resource pack on *Working with parents*, edited by Erica De'Ath and Gillian Pugh (published by the National Children's Bureau in 1986) for use in discussions about planning parent involvement.

15
MAKING PARENT
INVOLVEMENT WORK
WELL — THE PEOPLE

When adults have a group label attached to them (like ethnic group, sex, or social class), other adults are sometimes far too quick to leap to conclusions about individuals because of an overall picture assigned to the group. This can happen between adults-as-parents and adults-as-workers in the under-fives area. The generalisations may be positive, but are more often negative — 'The parents simply aren't interested!' or 'The staff are an unfriendly bunch of know-alls!'

Under-fives workers sometimes lose sight of an essential fact:

Parents are people *who have children of their own.*

Parents have the same mix of personalities and worries as other adults. The same basic rules of communication apply as in other adult relationships. The parent — staff relationship is a particular kind, but it is still a relationship between adults.

In the same way, parents need to remind themselves that

Staff are people *who are working with young children and families.*

PARENTS AND UNDER-FIVES WORKERS — THE ADULTS INVOLVED

Does being a 'professional' get in the way?

Plenty of arguments have started with attempts to define 'professionalism' and what occupations can or cannot be classified as 'professions'. I am not joining these arguments. The term 'professional' covers, in practice, beliefs about particular adults being able to offer in their work a package of expertise, knowledge, experience, and attitudes which combine commitment with detachment. At this point, I wish to use the term 'professional' in contrast with 'parent', as a label, without any assumptions about either having more or less to offer than the other.

Sometimes staff believe that their professional role justifies a one-way view of parent involvement (remember the discussion in chapter 14) — judging that they have the knowledge to advise parents on how to deal with their own children but not that the 'professionals' could usefully

204

listen and respond to parents' suggestions. A sense of shared professional status with colleagues can lead to a closing of ranks, a sense that only fellow-professionals are competent to comment on your work. It can also encourage an unwillingness to share skills or admit ignorance to 'lay people'. All professions have areas of uncertainty and ignorance, and a distance between the profession and the people it serves can sometimes be used as a protective barrier. In turn, parents may themselves conspire in losing the individual in the child-care role, preferring to assume that the staff are 100% experts or have a hide like a rhinocerous to deal with hurtful remarks. Both parents and staff do not have to act like this: they are choosing to do so. You can choose to relate to the person behind the role label and still maintain a reasonable working relationship.

Staff may well aim for a friendly relationship with parents. However, staff and parents have not come together because they have chosen one another as friends. There may well be difficulties to be ironed out in the difference between friendly professional and friend. They are all individuals and will feel more comfortable with some individuals than others. However, staff have a responsibility to judge priorities in their work and not to have favourites among the parent group.

Bringing expectations to a relationship

No one comes cold to any contact with another adult: everyone has expectations about how other adults are likely to react and ways to make sense of behaviour. When there is a role label like 'parent' or 'teacher', adults additionally bring some specialised expectations from previous experience or even hearsay.

Staff may have built up a picture of 'parents' as a whole from their training, from the input of other staff, and from generalisations developed in contact with a few individual parents. Anyone working with young children, however experienced, will have some areas of relative ignorance and may feel threatened by some parents' detailed knowledge of child-rearing and expertise about their own child.

Parents may be affected by memories of their own schooldays, whether the staff they are relating to are actually teachers or not. If those memories are unhappy, parents are more likely to be suspicious of staff and ready to defend themselves and their child against criticism. If the memories are happy, relations should be easier, although parents' behaviour can still be influenced by the 'child within them'. Some parents may be eager to cooperate with staff and to please in a way that is more reminiscent of a child than appropriate for adult relationships.

Parents who have continuing difficulties with authority in various guises may view under-fives workers as another example of 'them'. It is appropriate that staff see this as a perspective. However, parents as well as staff share a responsibility for distinguishing this adult relationship from others with which they may have problems.

In short, parents and under-fives workers are all adults. They each have a role. Focusing on being adult helps to overcome the worst problems of viewing the individual through the role.

Making sense of the behaviour of other adults

'Parent' and 'staff' are roles that adults take on. Their behaviour follows rules for adults — neither group is a special breed. A major rule here is that it is risky to generalise from people's behaviour — what they do — to what they are like as people or to their intentions towards you. Behaviour you can observe: the rest is guesswork. It is especially important to remember this when the roles that adults are taking on may influence your interpretations.

In making sense and coming to any conclusions about other adults, it is crucial to get yourself a reasonable 'sample' of behaviour. For example, the beginnings and ends of a day or of a session in an under-fives centre are not usually typical of the rest of the time — staff would be unhappy about being judged on what can be chaotic transition times. Yet I have had conversations with under-fives workers who have been judging parents' interest in their children on this very small sample of behaviour. A child may be playing up at going-home time and the parent losing patience, trying yet again to get outdoor clothes on an uncooperative small body — this is not necessarily typical of this child, the parent, and the time they spend together. Parents might just as unreasonably conclude that their children spend their day getting out of control, or being bored, so they go wild on leaving.

We are usually quick to point to the injustice of others coming to swift conclusions about us. We tend to be less sharp about our own unreasonable generalisations. As my daughter tells me when I am saying terrible things about fellow-drivers — 'They're just people, Mummy!'

Parents are interested in their children

Staff often point to low attendance by parents at particular activities arranged by the establishment as evidence that parents are not interested in their own children. This is not a reasonable conclusion. Parents may not attend parent-involvement activities for a number of reasons other than lack of interest in their children — they may have limited time free from other responsibilities; they may not share a first language with staff; they may lack sitters for evening meetings; the activities or meetings may not be about things which parents regard as high priorities.

In two books*, Barbara Tizard forcibly puts the view that parents can be involved with and intensely interested in their own children without necessarily sharing the same values and methods as under-fives staff. There are different routes to ensuring that children develop and learn, and there are other forums for play and learning in addition to the child-centred nature of under-fives establishments.

So, a high level of attendance by parents is not the only, nor necessarily the best, measure of the extent to which parents are interested in their own children. The same staff would most likely feel hurt and ready to defend themselves if a parent claimed that they (staff) were uninterested in that parent's child because the parent rarely saw the member of staff talking individually with the child. Again, it is a question of getting a reasonable and representative sample of behaviour on which to judge.

Parents are already involved with their children

Some reports written from the perspective of the under-fives establishment give the impression that getting parent involved in the children's life in the establishment is the only way to encourage them to become appropriately involved with their children. However, this is an inaccurate picture of children's lives. All parents are involved with their children in a way that directly affects those children's lives. For good or ill, parents are a formative influence on their children. Several research projects make the more specific point that many parents are positively involved with their children in ways that can directly encourage children's learning.

Staff working with young children often underestimate or simply have no knowledge of what parents undertake with their children at home. (See, for example, the projects described by Barbara Tizard and her team in the books mentioned below, or the work of Peter Blatchford and his team.†) This gap in their understanding is ironic when staff's own emphasis in interviews is often on how much parents underestimate what is done in under-fives centres; however, the staff's lack of awareness is not surprising given the very limited opportunities for conversation between staff and parents during the normal daily routine of under-fives centres.

*Barbara Tizard, Jo Mortimore, and Bebb Burchell *Involving parents in nursery and infant schools: a sourcebook for teachers*, published in 1981 by Grant McIntyre, and Barbara Tizard and Martin Hughes *Young children learning — talking and thinking at home and at school*, published by Fontana in 1984.
†Peter Blatchford, Sandra Battle, and Julia Mays, *The first transition, home to pre-school*, published by NFER—Nelson in 1982.

Being involved and being consulted — two different things

In their project with nursery schools mentioned above, Barbara Tizard, Jo Mortimore, and Bebb Burchell pointed out that wishing to be involved and wishing to be consulted about one's own children are two separate, although overlapping, areas. The team found little evidence that parents wanted to 'take over' the nursery schools in the project — a fear sometimes expressed by nursery staff or school heads. However, in interviews, about half of the parents said that they wanted to be asked for their opinions and suggestions about school matters. (The other half of the parents regarded what went on in the school as the teachers' business and best left to them.) Mothers who had not been involved in the nursery programmes were just as likely to say they wanted to be consulted as the 'highly involved' mothers.

So — parents may choose, for a range of reasons, not to become involved with an establishment that their children attend or, more specifically, not to become involved in the particular way that is on offer. They may, however, want very much to be consulted.

The perspectives of staff and parents should be different

It is sometimes said that parents see an under-fives centre in terms of the needs of their own child and that staff take a broader view. This is a reasonable thing to say except when the comment on the parents' perspective is expressed as a criticism — that parents take a 'myopic' view of under-fives services. This is a very one-sided attitude. Children need both adults who will champion them as individuals and adults who will look to the well-being of under-fives services. Both are necessary roles, neither need be exclusive, and both are equally legitimate. With an opportunity for conversation — seasoned with a respect for the other's position — staff and parents could see more through one another's eyes.

I think that staff who work with young children, particularly the under-fives, suffer from the burden that their professional status is less secure than in other careers, and this in itself can encourage a more restrictive sense of professionalism in self-defence. Under-fives workers, and parents responsible for their own young children, often suffer from the widespread and misplaced belief that time spent being responsible for young children is an easy option. The work and job status tend to be given a low value. It is particularly important that pre-school staff should value their own skills and experience. Confidence in what they have to offer is an essential basis for genuinely valuing and welcoming the contribution that individual parents can make.

It is the blend of the different and realistic perspectives of both staff and parents which builds the best environment in which children can grow and develop. The less each group understands the other, the more likely there is to be misunderstanding, confusion, and hostility, and the more difficult children will find their lives to be.

MAKING PARENT INVOLVEMENT WORK WELL – THE SKILLS

All activities which bring parents and staff together, however briefly, demand the skills appropriate to contact and communication between adults. As adults ourselves, we will to some extent be aware of these already. We tend, however, to be more aware of what it is like to be on the receiving end of poor people-skills — for example, we are usually quicker to spot someone who is not listening to us than to realise that we ourselves are failing to listen properly. The relationship between parents and staff is between adults; hence, the following discussion of skills is as relevant to parents as to staff. However, I believe that the onus is particularly on staff to build on the skills they already have and to make these more effective — they have a job to do!

ATTENDING TO OTHER PEOPLE

Learning to listen well

Some people are said to be 'good listeners' naturally. However, everyone can *learn* to be a good listener.

Firstly, you need to be aware of the barriers to listening effectively. You can tackle all of these, if you are motivated to do so. We do not listen well when:

- We want to hear a particular message (probably one that agrees with our own view) and we listen selectively for just that.
- We are too busy planning, rehearsing, or worrying about what we are going to say next.
- We are simply waiting for a pause to resume talking ourselves — we want our share of the conversation.
- We have little or no respect for the other adult — we mentally dismiss any value in what he or she is saying.
- We are uncomfortable (the chair hurts, or you have a headache).
- There are physical barriers between yourself and the other adult (a large table, or chairs at different heights).

Also, a particular feature of working with young children is

- You are trying to listen to another adult and still have responsibility for children, which leads to interruptions.

Active listening is hard work. Real listening means that you concentrate on what the other person is saying — both their words and how they say them. It means putting on one side your own views and what you want to say or ask — you are offering another adult the respect of your time and your attention. You can look at how the setting is influencing your ability to listen and how much you can rearrange — furniture, for example. A practical consideration for staff in under-fives centres is to have a strategy for dealing with interruptions when you are chatting with a parent in a room of children. You need to be adept at excusing yourself to deal briefly with children — 'Please excuse me a moment' — and then easing back into conversation with 'You were telling me about. . .'. However, if your listening is in the special context of offering counselling help to another adult, you should both be somewhere quiet where you are interrupted for nothing less than top-grade emergencies.

How you sit or stand in conversation with another adult can make a double contribution to listening — in helping you to listen better and in communicating to another person, in a way that is as loud as words, that he or she has your attention. It helps to be facing the other person squarely, so you can see him or her clearly and are not distracted by what else is going on around. It is encouraging to the other person if your posture looks open — not with firmly crossed arms or legs which give the impression of a barrier. It helps to lean slightly towards the other person, rather than being bolt upright, and certainly not leaning away. You can make eye contact with the other person in a way which is a regular and friendly gaze, but not an unblinking stare which usually makes people feel uncomfortable. Overall, you are aiming for a sitting or standing posture that looks and feels relaxed and attentive.

Our bodies talk too!

Researchers in this area have estimated that of the total message we receive from another adult in a face-to-face conversation, over 70% comes from non-verbal messages. Of the unspoken message, most comes from what we see in people's faces, and especially from their eyes. Whether we like it or not, we receive and act on these unspoken messages from other people, and, of course, others are receiving our own non-verbal communication. In face-to-face exchanges, we cannot stop ourselves from sending these messages but we *can* become aware and control them.

We need to be aware of our own body language. You can tune yourself in more, if you choose, by taking note of the internal messages of your body. You may feel yourself 'knotting up' inside as you approach a conversation with another adult. Unless you listen to what your body is saying and work to relax yourself, the tension will show and will inhibit your listening as well as giving a clipped tight edge to your talking. You will probably need someone else to alert you to your own non-verbal habits — for example, looking away from the other person when you are broaching a subject about which you feel angry, or coughing nervously when you are asked a question on which you are uncertain.

You can become helpfully aware of the messages you are sending by your facial expression, eyes, hands and gestures, and how you hold your body. It is equally important that you are fully aware of the conclusions you draw from the non-verbal communication of other people. Firstly, this can often help you to pin down the source of a 'gut' feeling about someone — sometimes it is not 'something she said', it is the non-verbal message. Secondly, some people are particularly influenced by, perhaps irritated by, certain gestures or facial expressions and it is useful to get these in perspective as your personal raw spot and not overgeneralise about the other adult. It is often helpful to look at photographs to highlight the richness of non-verbal communication, for example in a book such as Desmond Morris's *Manwatching* (published in 1977 by Jonathan Cape).

It is possible to become super-conscious of non-verbal communication when one is first made really aware of this channel for messages. With practice and a willingness to view 'body language' as interesting and helpful rather than alarming, this heightened awareness subsides to a more workable sensitivity to ourselves and others.

OUR SPOKEN LANGUAGE

Considering what we say and how we say it

Every profession has some shared 'professional' language, and the under-fives area is no exception. Taking account of this is not a matter of speaking slowly in words of one syllable, but rather of using words and phrases which are in general use. You might well realise that phrases like 'fine physical coordination' or 'social development' need concrete examples — 'how she manages to pour water' or 'how he plays with a group of children'. You might not realise the possible confusions in what seem like everyday phrases but are actually specialised — I have known parents new to under-fives centres be perplexed about what would happen in 'messy play' or not to share a view that children 'learn through play'.

You might like to 'listen in' to yourself and colleagues and pick out the shared 'under-fives language' and think how you could rephrase it. Start with phrases like 'We try to meet the needs of each individual child' or 'The morning is for free play' or 'It's not unusual for children to regress when a baby comes along.'

Giving and receiving feedback

The skills of giving feedback were discussed in chapter 5 in the particular context of sharing records and observations with parents. These skills are important in a broader context than conversations or written reports about children: constructively giving and receiving feedback is fundamental in effective communication between adults. There is no way you can ensure that nobody ever takes offence, any more than you can make sure that you yourself never feel threatened or anxious. There are, however, guide-lines which, if you make the effort to use them, will increase the chances that people on the receiving end of feedback will listen and learn rather than leap to their own defence. You will recognise the points below from the discussion in chapter 5. They are sufficiently important to be re-presented here in the context of adult communication.

- If you are expressing an opinion, then you can give it honestly, and tentatively, as a personal view, as 'I think that. . . .' or 'I feel that. . . .' The person on the receiving end may still feel the need to argue; however, you will have more chance of a conversation than if you go in heavy-footed with 'We all think that . . .' or 'It's obvious that. . . .'
- You can give feedback on your experience of what somebody has done or not done, and your feelings about this. However, this does not give you a basis for generalising about another adult's behaviour in other situations, nor to generalise from behaviour to personality. Consider whether *you* would feel differently on the receiving end of (a) or (b) which follow:

a) 'I didn't feel welcome when I was settling in my child because nobody said "Hello" to me.'
b) 'You staff are such an unfriendly bunch.'

- Nobody is a 100% expert, yet all of us have probably made pronouncements as if our views could not possibly be wrong. Other adults are likely to be more receptive to a suggestion they can turn over in their mind ('Have you considered . . .?', 'I was wondering if . . .') than to a statement which leaves no room for maneouvre ('If only you hadn't . . .', 'Well, of course, if you will insist on . . .').
- You may have experience to share, but this can be destructive if it is given as criticism. I am sure you can see the difference between saying, 'I've found that the children stay more absorbed in the story when I turn the book towards them', rather than saying bluntly 'That's the wrong way to read to a group of children.'
- We are quick to say that other adults (colleagues, family) make more effort to complain than to compliment. It is not possible to control directly the behaviour of another adult. It is, however, possible to

change our own behaviour and model the effort to praise, encourage, and support, putting at least as much energy into feedback on what has pleased us as on what has concerned or irritated us. A difficulty in increasing the compliments is that many adults find it hard to accept them graciously — they apologise or say something dismissive. Again, you can yourself model a welcoming reaction to compliments. For example, if someone says 'Thanks for listening to me yesterday' (positive feedback — a compliment), you can reply with 'You're welcome' rather than a self-deprecating 'That's all right — I don't suppose I was much help anyway' reply which also devalues the judgement of the other person.

If you are on the receiving end of feedback, it is possible to learn for the future. Feedback is not useful if we see it only as a source of regretful 'if only's'. If you want to learn, you can ask for feedback from others. When it comes, you need to listen carefully, and to check whether you have grasped what the other person is saying. You can turn over in your mind what has been said to you and compare it with what others may have said. If it makes sense to change how you behave, you can attempt small changes over time. It is, however, your choice as to what — if anything — you do in response to feedback.

DEALING WITH OTHER ADULTS WHO ARE ANGRY

Once again, there is no magical solution to dealing with the expression of anger from adults, but some approaches are better than others. I have found it useful to look at the following different aspects to this particular area of communication between adults.

1 Making some sense of how anger arises

The anger of another adult often feels like a personal attack. However, it is not helpful to see anger solely in this way. This is not excusing the behaviour, it is seeking a broader perspective.

Anger can be the tip of some very different icebergs. Sometimes another adult may be very angry — specifically with you. If parents, for example, do not have easy conversational access to those who are responsible for their children, then a resolvable issue can reach boiling point before parents grit their teeth to say 'Enough is enough!' The anger of some adults is a reflection of poor self-esteem; it is easier (not necessarily consciously) to keep having a go at other people than to take a cool look at yourself. For some adults, anger is a way of showing strength and individuality; for others, the anger is an effective way of keeping people at a distance. Sometimes, as unlikely as it seems, anger is a plea for help.

Sometimes, anger may be deflected on to you because you are available, unlike the true source of the frustration (for example the bus company, the housing department, this adult's family life). I am sure that everyone who is reading this book has at some time snapped at other people for this reason!

2 Knowing yourself — your own feelings and reactions

You need to get in touch with how you personally react to anger from another adult. Some people feel reasonably able to cope; others are very anxious. You need to know and be aware of your own reactions, to accept them but not to let them hinder you. Whether you like it or not, your body will react — when you feel under attack, your heart rate increases, your breathing is faster and more shallow, and you perspire. This is the 'fight or flight' reaction, which we share with the animal kingdom. If you see this positively, it can help — you say to yourself 'I'm ready.' If you see it negatively, it can sap your energy to deal with the immediate situation — 'On top of everything else, I've got sweaty palms!'

3 Preventing the incidence of anger — catching it 'early'

Some incidents of anger — not all — are avoidable. In my experience, the guide-lines on constructive feedback in communication make a great difference in encouraging conversation rather than argument. It is also possible by taking control of your own behaviour to prevent some incidents becoming worse. Guide-lines on this follow below.

4 Dealing with an angry adult

Many under-fives workers have skills for dealing with others' anger — they apply these skills in handling children. The skills are not so very different in communication with adults. A key point is to stay calm. If you answer anger with anger then an incident will quickly worsen, leaving your control. You need to show the other adult that you recognise the strong feelings and are listening — 'I can see you're very angry — please tell me what's up.' You do not have to feel that the anger is justified; you are simply accepting that it is felt. You need to realise that whatever you say to the other adult will be filtered through the strong feelings.

So, keep what you say simple and to the point. If there is a quick solution, because you are responsible in some way, do something. If apologies are due, then do make them without lots of self-justification. However, it is not appropriate to apologise solely as a means of self-defence.

It is helpful to allow the other adult to talk, while you show that you are listening. (Remember the points about active listening on pages 209—10.) When adults are angry, they are not responsive to logical arguments or to reasoning. Neither will they be responsive to questions — especially 'Why?' questions, which will probably fuel an angry self-justification starting with 'Because . . .!'

You can decide whether or not you take control of an incident in this way in your personal life — if you choose to have a row at the bus-stop, that is your own business. However, in professional life, more is appropriately expected of us in patience, self-restraint, and understanding the perspective of adults. In this sense, working does limit us to an 'acceptable' range of behaviour.

However, I do not think that holding a job should doom you to becoming a verbal, or physical, punchbag. It is appropriate to set limits, and these can be communicated assertively and not aggressively.* By spoken word and assertive body language you can take control — 'I can see you're angry. I'm willing to listen. I'm not ready to stand here and have you swear at me' or 'I believe your shouting is upsetting the children. I'll talk to you in the corridor, not here.' There may be times when you need to walk away or firmly accompany another adult out of the room.

The skills of good communication and assertion should enable most readers to handle and defuse incidents. However, some under-fives workers have jobs which bring them into contact with adults under extreme stress. These adults may have methods of coping with life which involve a very aggressive approach or an alcohol or drug dependence which makes their behaviour very unpredictable. Under these circumstances, the workers must know how to summon help quickly (from colleagues or from protection services such as the police) if an incident is moving beyond their coping skills and is becoming dangerous to children present.

5 Dealing with 'tomorrow'

In your job, many emotion-charged incidents (of anger or extreme distress) will have a 'tomorrow'. Someone needs to ensure that the relationship is re-established. It is not helpful to pretend that an angry incident never happened: it did, and relations need to be taken on from 'Things seemed to get out of hand on Tuesday. I'd like to talk it over with

---

*The difference between assertion and aggression can seem difficult to grasp initially. I would recommend two books to help in this: Anne Dickson's *A woman in your own right — assertiveness and you*, published in 1982 by Quartet Books, and *Assertiveness at work* by Ken and Kate Back, published in 1982 by McGraw-Hill.

you, if you're willing.' The answer may be 'No', but at least an effort has been made. Quite often the angry person is upset, embarrassed, and finding it difficult to apologise. 'Tomorrow' is not the time to get angry yourself; it can be the time for reasoning and explaining — for starting again.

6 Learning about yourself

You cannot directly control the behaviour of others. However, if you are prepared to try a different approach to dealing with the anger of others, you may be pleasantly surprised by your ability to cope with incidents which previously you dreaded or which quickly became shouting matches.

HELPING OTHER ADULTS WITH THEIR PROBLEMS

This is the area which some under-fives workers think — and perhaps fear — is what is meant by parent involvement. If you work in an establishment where the parents of the children have complex and long-term problems in their lives, then the prospect of helping can be daunting. In this case, learning the skills of counselling will be necessary for some under-fives workers. They are complex skills and they need properly supervised practice for people to become confident in being able to give effective counselling.

Counselling is not advice-giving; it is not telling people what to do (and then getting irritated because they do the opposite); it is not persuading people to see their difficulties from the perspective that makes sense to you. Genuine helping through the counselling process is about aiding other adults to understand their difficulties in ways that enable them to tackle their problems.*

For some under-fives workers, the responsibilities of their job with children will never allow time for more than brief conversations with other adults. However, even short conversations can be more helpful to an adult with a difficulty if the following guide-lines are followed. I would stress, however, that these guide-lines are *not* do-it-yourself counselling skills.

---

*For a sound overview of different kinds of counselling and the counselling process, try Stephen Murgatroyd's *Counselling and helping*, jointly published in 1985 by the British Psychological Society and Methuen.

Do avoid giving quick solutions

When other adults come to you with a problem, it is very tempting to deal with it by offering your ideas for what they could do as soon as they have given you a brief outline of the problem. Quite often, they are pressing you to give them a quick answer. Falling in with this is risky on several counts:

- You haven't had time really to understand the problem as the other person sees it. The danger is that you will make sense of the problem by assuming that it is just like something you have experienced, or 'just like Mrs Brown's problem with her child', and that what worked on those occasions will work now. This may not be the case at all.
- By slotting this problem under a label which is general, you are effectively saying to this individual, 'Your problem isn't that important — I've seen it all before.' This does not show respect for that individual.
- Because you are putting yourself in the role of problem-expert (and the other adult is perhaps pushing you hard in this direction too), you run the risk of taking the responsibility for the problem. If your quick solution works, the other adult has not learned that he or she can cope, because the suggestion was yours, not an idea reached jointly. If the solution fails, it will be your fault.

Do listen to what is being said

However hard the other adult is pushing you to 'Tell me what to do!', it is crucial to spend some time encouraging the other person to talk about the problem so that you can understand it from his or her point of view. This also says to the other adult 'I take your problem seriously. I am giving you some time.'

Everything said earlier about active listening applies here. You will be talking as well, of course, but what you say needs to encourage the other adult to talk. It is not helpful to cross-question people. It is a matter of ensuring that you understand what the other person is saying — 'If I've got it right, you feel that . . .' — rather than imposing your view — 'You clearly have a problem with. . . .'

Do talk about any suggestions

A single 'I suggest that you . . .' is not generally helpful — you need to talk around several possibilities with a person who is discussing a problem with you. It is helpful to explore what has already been tried by the other person — that is not necessarily a reason for throwing out the idea. The experience of 'failure' will mean that the other adult is unlikely to try again unless you talk through properly what is likely to make the idea work.

You need to talk about what may help or hinder 'success' in any ideas; however, it must be left to the other person to decide on a course of action. It is his or her problem and he or she has the right to decide what to do, including following none of the suggestions you have discussed. You may not like it, but this is the other person's right.

Do respect confidentiality

Even if they do not specifically ask you, most people expect that discussions they have with another adult about problems will remain confidential. This should be taken seriously and made explicit. If you judge that you need to ask someone else's advice about the problem, then this should be cleared with the adult experiencing the difficulty.

Respect for confidentiality may present you with a dilemma. Suppose that a parent starts to talk about something that you know you must pass on — for example, that they are hitting their child who is already on the at-risk register. The parent says 'This is just between you and me'. You have two choices, each with consequences:

i) Suppose you think to yourself 'I'll let him [or her] carry on. It may stop the conversation if I refuse to keep this secret.' The consequence of this is that you are being dishonest and abusing the other person's trust. If this person discovers that you have broken confidence, he or she is unlikely to trust you ever again and this may generalise to relations with other 'professionals'.

ii) The other choice is to be straight and say 'If you tell me more about . . ., then I have to tell my head of establishment [or senior worker etc.]. It's up to you whether you want to go on.' The consequence of this is that the other adult can make an informed choice about whether to stop, carry on, or return to you having thought the matter over. Whatever the decision — and people sometimes choose to carry on under these circumstances, he or she has experienced your honesty in a difficult dilemma.

Do be realistic about what is possible

It is possible to be helpful to another adult even when you do not have the time for lengthy conversations. However, you need to maintain a realistic view of your limits in such conversations. It is not responsible to encourage other adults to divulge their difficulties if you have neither the time nor the skills to help them tackle the problems. It is placing an unrealistic burden on yourself if you feel that you should be able, in brief conversations, to unravel complex adult problems. Set your expectations carefully.

Do remember that this is not your problem

Many people work on the principle of 'A problem shared is a problem halved'. Unfortunately, without a grasp of the skills of helping, adults can feel that listening to the difficulties of others has meant rather that a problem shared is two people weighed down with the same problem. Being truly helpful to another adult requires a tricky balance between caring enough to offer the time and effort while maintaining a detachment so that you do not take responsibility or feel overwhelmed by the problems experienced by the other person. You may be able to help other adults identify possible ways out of a difficulty, but only they can solve the problems in the end, and they will solve them in a way that suits them best — not you. As indeed you would tackle your own problems!

Some concluding remarks

There are two themes running through this 'people' chapter.

The first theme is the recommendation that adults look, at least sometimes, through the eyes of others — that we attempt to understand and respect the different perspectives of other adults to whom we relate. We do not have to agree with others' views, but communication between adults can be considerably improved if we all have some grasp of how life looks and feels from where another individual is standing.

The second theme is the encouragement to be willing to look at ourselves — our personal package of strengths and weaknesses — and to be ready to learn and so change. To do this, adults have to take responsibility for their own behaviour and for the consequences of that behaviour. If you view the world in terms of 'They ought to make the friendly moves' or 'She makes everybody feel small', then you are handing over control to others. Other people are responsible for their behaviour; you are responsible for how you experience it, and only you have direct access to your feelings. You can choose to view the world in terms of 'She should stop behaving that way and then I would stop feeling small.' Alternatively, you can choose to explore, in yourself, how that person's behaviour stirs up particular feelings in you and how you might deal with it. You can choose to leave the impetus for friendly moves with the other adult ('He's staff. It's his place. He should say "Hello" first' or 'She's a parent and a visitor, it's good manners for her to say "Hello" first.') Alternatively, you can change your behaviour. This in turn will often affect how you feel (at the time and before and after an event) and can influence how other people behave towards you.

None of this is easy. Who said relationships between adults are always easy? Parents are people; staff are people; and, although the relationship is of a particular kind, we are in deep trouble if we forget that we share an adult status and it is our skills in dealing with fellow-adults that need to be sharpened, not some specialised set for dealing with a different species.

16
WORKING WITH YOUNG CHILDREN — SOME FINAL THOUGHTS

When writing the final chapter of a book, it is very tempting to try to reiterate at length the major themes and ideas of that book. I am not convinced that this is useful to readers. I have therefore taken the approach of trying to state briefly what for me are the most important aspects to working with children. I do not feel it is possible to place them in any particular order of importance — they are simply the thoughts that I feel can most usefully influence adults' attitudes and behaviour in their work with young children.

There is great value in being willing to take children as individuals. This means making a genuine effort to respond to a child's feelings, reactions, and problems as one individual to another.

Just as children are individuals, so are adults. It is unrealistic, and unhelpful, for adults to ignore their own feelings or discount their own behaviour as ingredients in a situation with children.

Along with accepting and exploring what we as adults bring to our time with children, there is a need to be flexible in approach, open to ideas from others (although not uncritically accepting of just any idea), and willing to continue to learn. The best basic training is still not going to provide all the possible skills, knowledge, and insight to face any situation with children.

Along with other needs, children need the respect of adult attention so that they will learn to attend well in return. Children deserve this attention and they will learn from adults' willingness to listen to them seriously and to give time to them.

Another side to the willingness to attend to children is a valuing of what can be learned from observation of children. This is part also of the adult attitude that you do not have all the information at your fingertips.

An interest in and a willingness to plan some aspects of adult time with children is part of an openness to thinking long-term as well as short-term. This may be planning special time with a child to help her development, or it may be a willingness to plan and persevere with a particular approach to a problem. This may look like more work in the short term, but it can pay handsome dividends in terms of the child's progress and adult satisfaction.

It is a great asset to be willing to see matters sometimes from the child's point of view — in terms of her feelings, experience, and particular level of understanding. This often needs honesty from adults to admit that their feelings are colouring their perspective and that there are other ways of seeing events.

There is a need to accept that, for all the differences between children and adults, there are still many parallels in feelings and needs. Sometimes adults need to be willing to look for an appropriate example or memory from their own life. Sometimes they have to accept that small children nevertheless have strong feelings, are sensitive to subtle messages, and can be affected in similar ways to adults — for instance, in how anxiety can seriously hinder the chance to learn.

Adults do need to consider possible reasons which might underlie a child's delay, problem, or way of behaving. No matter how many of the 'Why?'s are only shrewd guesses, they can be helpful in deciding on the best place to start special work with a child. An adult can still help progress or change when the underlying 'Why?' is unclear or is completely out of that adult's control.

Adults can be active participants in children's progress without turning into interfering and controlling adults. This is because being an active participant does not always mean doing — sometimes it means watching and encouraging children in their own efforts towards independence and self-discipline. Mainly, it means believing that we as adults can make a difference to how children develop.

Part of actively helping and working with young children is the willingness to put aside some planning and thinking time, so that adult reactions and involvement are not solely on a day-by-day or moment-by-moment basis.

Adults do need to count on the positive support of other adults. In nurseries, pre-school centres, or playgroups, this means more than being able to assume that everyone will carry a fair share of the workload. It means that adults have the opportunity to talk with colleagues so that they can work consistently with children and towards similar goals. When there are children in a group who are particularly difficult to handle or who need a lot of help in their development, the support needs to take the form of both sympathetic back-up and time to discuss possible approaches in some detail.

Childhood should be fun. ▶

Children come equipped with parents. Adults who work with other people's children share their responsibility for the children on a strictly temporary basis. It is possible to work in partnership for the benefit of the children, and for the likely benefit of the adults as well. This means that adults need to be prepared to view children and their time with children at least sometimes through the eyes of another adult who has a different role with those children. It needs a willingness to respect fellow-adults and to learn from them.

As adults, we have much to learn and keep learning about children. The move towards parents and staff from under-fives centres working more closely together has highlighted that we also have a great deal to learn about ourselves and our relationships with other adults.

Time spent with children is not all sweetness and light. Even the more cooperative children and resilient adults have their off days. However, a very reasonable goal is that adults should have pleasure in their time with young children. If adults rarely enjoy the experience, children will probably not enjoy the time either.

In a book which discusses many types of problem and focuses on efforts to create a really positive environment for children, there is a risk that an overall impression of hard grind, continual striving, and unrelieved intenseness in work with children will result. I very much hope that this is not the impression left by this book. It makes a great deal of difference to children if adults are prepared to think seriously about what they are offering to children and to make efforts to deal with difficulties in a way which sometimes asks much of them as adults. However, at the end of the day, I would wish that adults have enjoyed themselves with children and that the children have enjoyed themselves too. Childhood ends so rapidly. Children deserve laughter and they deserve fun. It is not impossible for the adults who care for them to have the laughter and the pleasure as well.

INDEX

225